The Munros in Winter

Victory pose on Sgurr Eilde Mor (*A. Thomson*)

THE MUNROS
IN WINTER

277 summits in 83 days

MARTIN MORAN

Foreword by Hamish Brown

DAVID & CHARLES
Newton Abbot   London   North Pomfret (Vt)

British Library Cataloguing in Publication Data

Moran, Martin
  The Munros in winter.
  1. Walking – Scotland – Highlands
  2. Highlands (Scotland) – Description
  and travel
  I. Title
  796.5'22   DA880.H6

  ISBN 0-7153-8836-3

First published 1986
Second impression 1986

© Martin Moran 1986

All rights reserved. No part of this
publication may be reproduced, stored
in a retrieval system, or transmitted,
in any form or by any means, electronic,
mechanical, photocopying, recording or
otherwise, without the prior permission
of David & Charles Publishers plc

Typeset by Typesetters (Birmingham) Limited
Smethwick, West Midlands
and printed in Great Britain
by Butler & Tanner Limited, Frome and London
for David & Charles Publishers plc
Brunel House   Newton Abbot   Devon

Published in the United States of America
by David & Charles Inc
North Pomfret   Vermont 05053   USA

CONTENTS

ACKNOWLEDGEMENTS

Before and during the trip I am especially indebted to Steve Bonnist and Intermediate Technology who took the risk and gave us the chance to help their cause; Thomson McLintock & Co for being the most understanding, tolerant and supportive employers to a wayward accountant; my parents for maintaining our communications with the outside world and accepting the massive phone bills that resulted; and to Alan Thomson for his interest, company and excellent reporting.

For the provision of clothing, boots and rucsacs, I thank Berghaus of Newcastle upon Tyne; for willing service and generous discount, Nevisport of Fort William; and for help and advice with Nordic ski equipment, Tim Walker and Karrimor International Ltd.

To all those who joined me on the hill during the winter, I am grateful for your companionship, selfless support and the boost which you gave to my morale.

In the preparation of the book I wish to thank the following for their contributions, information and advice: Hamish Brown, Stuart Cathcart, Mr E. Cross of the Nature Conservancy Council, Chris Eatough of the Mountaineering Council of Scotland, Pete Simpson, Martin Stone (also back jacket photograph) and Simon Stewart.

The Scottish Mountaineering Club had kindly given permission to use slides and plates from their collection, and my thanks are due to Derek Pyper the Slide Custodian for his help in selection.

For the wealth of information used in compiling Appendix V I am indebted to the following: Roger Boswell, Hamish Brown, Chris Dodd, Colin Donnelly, Mel Edwards, Andy Hyslop, George Keeping, Robin Morris, Kathy Murgatroyd, Fred Rogerson, Pete Simpson and Tim Walker.

My thanks are due to the Meteorological Office for permission to use their data in Appendix IV. I owe special appreciation to Marjory Roy of the Meteorological Office, Edinburgh for her help in compilation, checking and review of the information, and likewise to Dr Jim Barton (of Heriot-Watt University), Bob Barton (of Glenmore Lodge) and David Rhodes (of Newcastle Royal GS) for their contribution.

And finally I wish to record my deepest gratitude and appreciation to Joy who not only underpinned the success of the venture, but also typed, retyped and checked the manuscript for the book with an unending care and patience; I know I am lucky.

FOREWORD

Completing the Munros is a challenge. It was a challenge for the Rev A. E. Robertson who first achieved this goal in 1901; it was a challenge for the next Munroist, the Rev A. R. G. Burn in 1923, and it has been a challenge to many hundreds since.

The list of Munroists, beginning with two reverend gentlemen, was itself a start to the long accumulation of statistics and records that have followed. The first lady, Mrs Hurst, entered the list in 1947 (also a husband and wife combination). There have been father and son records, people have gone solo, or in different seasons; Philip Tranter did them a second time and led to a row of multiple tallies. The ages of the oldest and youngest have changed steadily; even dogs have topped all the magic summits.

The game of Munro-bagging should have died with the maps going metric, which rendered obsolete the historic height of 3,000ft, but just enough people had completed the list, or were working on it, to ensure the game went merrily on. The number has doubled since and stood at 381 by the end of 1984. It was natural enough to go off and do them all in a continuous 'Walk' as I did in 1974. That jaunt has been repeated since, by Kathy Murgatroyd and George Keeping, who even added the English and Welsh 'Threes'. My mountain walk took 112 days of largely unspectacular and unhurried progress. Speed was far from mind and I resented being given the 'fastest-ever' label. For this reason, if no other, I am grateful to Martin Moran's contribution to our crazy game. He, for his sins, is now the fastest-ever Munroist!

In some ways that too is incidental. It was the *winter* aspect which was the new challenge that Martin set off to tilt at – a real Don Quixote effort compared to my Sancho Panza one. Scottish winters can be fickle and, far from having endless snow which would have been a joy, Martin had to cope with every variety of nastiness except midges. I was lucky to join him for one day of glorious perfection on skis, but even that entailed cruel living in our frozen motor caravans. The winter challenge is a mountaineering feat, not just a walking one, but then Martin is a lean, fit, well-equipped Don Quixote. It only took 83 days! I think he gave his wife Joy who acted as support sufficient grounds for a divorce. It was a not unadventurous escapade.

I am delighted that their adventures have been set down. Our escapist's literature has been given a lively addition. Suddenly, after a

7

decade with only *Hamish's Mountain Walk* for the armchair Munroist, there has been a flurry of books about the Munros. This one is different for here is the story of one man's accepted challenge. It gladdens my heart in these mean, grey days to see a young man putting feet to his rainbow dreams. Readers had best beware though: Munroitis is also a disease, a highly contagious one, which can be caught through the printed page. You have been warned.

Hamish M. Brown

MAP SYMBOLS AND
CONVERSION TABLES

Key to Map Symbols

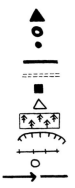

Overnight stopping point/terminus
Munro summit
Munro top or lower mountain summit
Metalled road with public access
Private road or unmetalled motor track
Habitation
Mountain bothy or refuge
Forest area
Major cliff or corrie edge
Railway
Rail station
Line of route

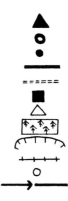

Height and Distance Conversions
(see also Appendix I)

1.6093km	=	1.0000 mile
1km	=	0.6214 mile
1m	=	3.2808 ft
300m	= 984.2	"
600m	= 1968.5	"
900m	= 2952.7	"
1200m	= 3937.0	"
914.4m	= 3000.0	"

Temperatures

These are all given in degrees Celsius (°C)
$0°C = 32°$ Fahrenheit
and for each increment or decrease therefrom $1°C = \frac{9}{5}°F$

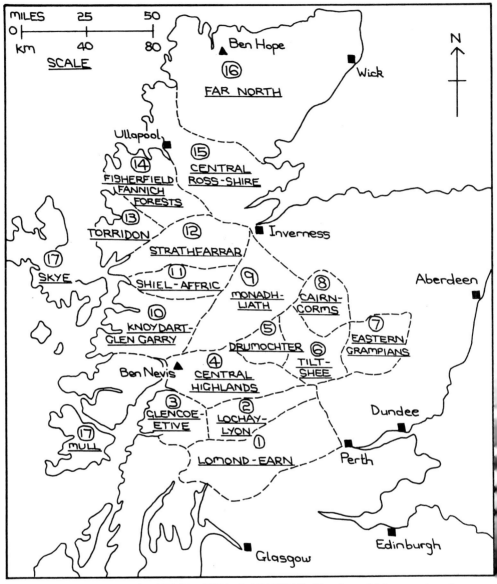

MUNRO'S TABLES: GEOGRAPHICAL SECTIONS (Number of Munros given in brackets)

1 LOMOND – EARN (20)
2 LOCHAY – LYON (25)
3 GLENCOE – ETIVE (23)
4 CENTRAL HIGHLANDS (35)
5 DRUMOCHTER (7)
6 TILT – SHEE (15)
7 EASTERN GRAMPIANS (14)
8 CAIRNGORMS (17)
9 MONADH – LIATH (9)
10 KNOYDART – GLEN GARRY (26)
11 SHIEL – AFFRIC (21)
12 STRATHFARRAR (15)
13 TORRIDON (7)
14 FISHERFIELD – FANNICHS (19)
15 CENTRAL ROSS-SHIRE (7)
16 FAR NORTH (4)
17 SKYE – MULL (13)

1

THE WINTER CHALLENGE

The Scottish Highlands have an aura that is unequalled anywhere within the small confines of the British Isles. Where else is there a natural domain of such infinite scale and unspoilt magnificence that one feels dwarfed and lost in its midst?

Think of any other upland tract – Dartmoor, Snowdonia, the Lakes; each one is touched and pressured, struggling for space, and even ravaged in places. The human hand is always in the view, and however lovely in certain parts or finer detail, Nature has surely lost her total freedom there in modern times. But up in the North you can still stand atop a lonely 'ben' and see no end or blemish to the expanse of mountain, loch and ocean that is spread out at your feet. The wilderness scene mocks our ego, and puts us in our proper place within the scheme of things, yet it also consoles and uplifts the spirit. And for the mountaineer, the array of peaks, which every Highland view includes, is an irresistible call to arms.

If the words ring true to those who trek and climb through the moist and misted months of Scotland's summer then they bear much stronger tone in the depths of the winter season. The numbers are fast growing of those who know the mountains to be at their finest when swathed in snow and battered by the year's worst storms, and no longer is one regarded as madly eccentric to take a winter climbing or skiing holiday in the Highlands.

The peaks may be relatively tiny in stature, but neither in shape, variety nor heart-stirring beauty do they yield much to any mountains in the world; and in winter their ferocious and unpredictable weather is renowned. They are indeed a forcing ground of technique and experience, and generations of British mountaineers have cut their teeth on Scottish ice before progressing to the greater ranges. But it is perhaps unfair to treat the Highlands merely as a stepping-stone to bigger things. Have they not sufficient challenge of their own to meet the highest ambition?

This train of thought attracted me to the idea of a prolonged winter expedition in the Highlands which would explore their great potential for adventure; a single challenge involving every type of winter mountaineering skill from Nordic skiing to steep ice-climbing, and giving complete commitment to meet the hills in all their moods, both fair and foul.

The exploit would necessarily be contrived in its design and rules; yet without a code of ethics and a personalised objective is there *real* adventure left anywhere these days? The age of pure exploration is long past, and it is the style of achievement which now counts for all, whether it is yachting single-handed or climbing Everest without oxygen. To do it in Britain without expense and fuss would also help to prove the lie that modern adventure is the slave of commercial interests. But above all a trip was sought that would fulfil a longheld passion for the Highlands and, despite its trials and dangers, would be a thorough enjoyment to undertake.

And of course the solution was obvious – it had to be the Munros.

When Sir Hugh Munro, in 1891, surveyed and tabulated the Scottish mountains exceeding 3,000ft in height he would little have imagined that he was instigating a challenge and a tradition that ninety years later has achieved the status of a cult. What was probably for him a purely personal indulgence, is now a lifetime ambition for many thousands of keen hill-goers.

His original Tables gave 283 such separate peaks, a total now trimmed by resurvey and reappraisal to 277 in the latest 1984 edition. At the end of 1984, 381 climbers were known to have achieved the ascent of all, and there are countless others making determined progress towards their completion.

Notwithstanding the many fine summits below 3,000ft in elevation, and leaving aside the Hebridean islands, a Munroist can reasonably claim to have encompassed the greater length and breadth of the Highlands in his travels; so the apparently senseless mania of Munro-bagging does have a 'real' purpose which on its achievement ensures an intimate and extensive knowledge of the country. The lure of the unclimbed Munro takes the walker far beyond his usual haunts.

The 'Winter Munros' story properly begins in the summer of 1974 when Hamish Brown made the first non-stop traverse of them all in a continuous walk of 112 days. His feat is known to have been emulated twice, but of a winter grand-slam attempt nothing was heard. Understandably so, for whilst the traverse in summer is essentially a marathon walk with just a little rock-climbing on the Cuillin of Skye, in winter it is transformed to a mountaineering proposition of high order. And so, as one man's endeavour merely points out the things left undone, the winter gauntlet was thrown down, and I eagerly took it up.

Having set the objective some ground rules were required. First and foremost was the problem of timing. What, or to be more precise *when,* is 'winter' in the mountains? The tops can bear a complete snow cover in any month from October to May, yet in a lean year can be almost bare in the middle of January. If a deep coating of snow and ice was prerequisite to my every ascent, it could take several years to finish.

So the strict calendar season from 21 December to 20 March was selected as holding the greatest probability of winter conditions. This would follow the practice in the Alps where the calendar limits are applied rigidly to all claims of winter ascents. More excitingly, though, these limits thrust upon me a ninety-day target, which when divided into the 277 Munros determined a schedule that made my heartbeat race. Three summits per day – now that looked interesting! It would make a tough test of endurance at any time of year, but was it remotely possible through the dark days and snows of winter?

One thing was certain at the outset – the target was unattainable on a continuous journey, and would necessitate the major tactical concession of using motor transport between the peaks. Not only would this save the 500 miles of valley walking and cycling by which Hamish linked his mountains (imagine pedalling into a Force 10 gale on a late December night!) but would also give the crucial flexibility to choose whichever summits suited the prevailing conditions. The joy of continuity was sacrificed but the spice of adventure maintained, for even with motor support the scheme looked marginal.

Winter weather data for the Highlands make a fascinating study, but one which leaves the intending climber with few illusions about the challenge ahead.

The notion that the winter brings less rainfall than the other seasons is something of a myth. Records for both the west and east sides of the country show that the months from December to March take slightly more than their one-third share of the annual total, and of course much of the winter precipitation comes as snow. Nor in winter are the high tops any clearer of cloud. The nineteenth-century observatory readings for the summit of Ben Nevis gave a 75 per cent average frequency of hill fog between November and March.

Summit air temperatures, as would be expected, are depressed throughout the winter. On average, 6°C should be deducted from the sea-level readings to give the temperature at 3,000ft. On the summit of Cairn Gorm, 1,000ft higher, the *mean* air temperature in the four-month winter periods between 1979–82 was −3.4°C.

But it is winter winds that are most to be feared by the mountaineer. A compass will see you through the fog, and a good set of clothing can keep both the cold and snow at bay, but against the wind there is no answer. It slows the pace, saps the strength and sucks away the body heat – a triple threat in a single foe. Not only are natural windspeeds 50 per cent higher at 3,000ft than at sea level, but also the mountain topography has a compressing and channelling effect which markedly accelerates the flow. Just how many gales might be faced on the tops in those ninety days? The question was crucial to the whole venture.

The data for Cairn Gorm summit for 1980–1 gave an expectancy of 53 days with gales (ie, winds above 40mph) out of the winter's 90. The figure looked intolerable, and a more kindly interpretation was anxiously sought. After all, a day *with* a gale doesn't mean twenty-four hours non-stop, or in itself makes all progress impossible. By making reasonable modifications the conclusion emerged that 32 days could be expected where progress was severely impeded (ie, winds between 40 and 60mph) and 10 where a climber would be stormbound (ie, greater than 60mph).

So those 277 peaks would have to be climbed in 80 days rather than 90, of which only 48 might allow full-scale expeditions. At least the storms would give some periods of rest!

October 1980: Sheffield
Having handed in my notice and abandoned an accountancy career a week previously, the preparations for the winter attempt had passed the point of no return. Even my wife, Joy, had with difficulty resigned herself to spending three months down here alone, keeping up her job and maintaining some semblance of security in our lives. And two months of hard running on our local hills and moors had built an enviable stamina and resilience to carry me through the coming struggles.

As usual the final light of a gloomy autumn evening saw me out training, pounding up a wooded clough towards the gritstone edges. With a lung-bursting effort I clambered to its top and turned to view the twinkling city lights behind. All was going well – the Munros dream was taking shape, its start just six weeks away. But at the beginning of the descent, without warning a shooting pain locked my knee-joint solid. Something was radically wrong. I tried to ignore it and went on, but ten more paces brought me staggering to a halt. It was four miles to limp back home, a slow and bitter walk.

Five days later I sat on the specialist's couch, and my worst expectations were realised as he delivered his solemn judgement:

'There's a piece of bone broken off your kneecap. If it isn't removed you will damage the joint, so you'll have to give up whatever it is you're planning to do . . .'

The anguish I felt when leaving that consulting room will forever haunt my memory. There I was, my spirit crushed, feeling an abject failure, out of work and without a future; so many people – companions, supporters and a local charity for whom I hoped to raise funds – to disappoint, and then facing the ignominy of asking for my job back. To my great gratitude I was re-engaged and the planned day of departure saw me back at a desk, pushing a pencil over ledger sheets once more, my escape hatch to the mountains firmly shut, perhaps for ever.

Yet this dream and challenge, so intently nurtured and pursued, was not to be forgotten. The knee recovered its strength from the operation. I worked and saved hard, climbed continuously and travelled afar. Self-confidence was slowly restored, experience broadened and four years later life was sufficiently organised to try a second time.

October 1984

Joy had noticed me creeping off upstairs of an evening for the last few months, and in her curiosity would come up to find me poring over Scottish maps, and scribbling notes of routes, distances and heights. She knew the truth without a word being spoken. The Munros game was on again!

But when the subject was broached and discussed, we made a firm pact to do it together. The lonely solo attempt planned in 1980 was perhaps ill-considered and very likely would have failed through lack of dependable help; for if there was one trump-card to play against the odds of wind and storm, then it was to have Joy with me, as companion, pacer, driver and provisioner. Most crucially, though, we would have each other for constant emotional support throughout the stresses of the journey. It would be an interesting test of marital harmony.

Joy was by no means overawed by the prospect. Her pedigree as a cycle tourer and marathon walker was considerable. Together we had walked the Pennine Way in winter, trekked over the deserted Norwegian plateaux in autumn, and now had just returned from an expedition in the Indian Himalayas. In fact she was so taken by the idea that she had already arranged the sale of our beloved terraced home even before my final decision to go was made. This was wisely deferred to the latest date possible for I wished no repeat of the cruel rebuff of 1980. First the strength of my creaking knee-joints needed conclusive proof, and they were subjected to a summer's mountain guiding in the Alps, followed by four weeks bowed under enormous loads on a Garwhal glacier, before a public commitment was chanced.

This left us just six short weeks from design to launch. Transport and accommodation en route were our prime concerns, and were together solved by thumbing through the 'yellow pages' to the Motor Caravan Hire section.

Old home and new – Sheffield, December 1984

'We don't usually get a lot of winter rentals. Will you be taking it far?' queried the owner of a white coach-built Ford transit which stood washed and polished in his drive.

'No, no, just up to Scotland to do a bit of hill-walking.'

'Oh well, that's all right then, but did I hear you right – it is three and a half months you want it . . .?'

We left him doubtful of our sanity but glad of the business all the same. The van was nearly new, fully insulated and with every imaginable fitment. All our hopes resided in its efficiency and reliability.

The trip was costed at £2,500, a figure which could at least be doubled if three month's loss of earnings was taken into account. And yet, retaining the style of simplicity and independence in which the venture was conceived, we sought no financial assistance from commercial sponsors. Berghaus served us proudly with their enthusiastic provision of boots, clothing and rucksacs of the highest quality.

16

Their gear would never have a better testing. But that apart, we bore our own expenses.

However we saw the expedition as an excellent vehicle to publicise and sponsor a worthwhile charity. Two visits to the Himalayas had opened my eyes to the hopeless poverty and environmental destruction with which India and so many Third World countries are beset. The work of Intermediate Technology in providing new tools and methods to help regenerate and improve rural societies in these countries was already known to us through the incredible 2,000-mile run, over the foothills and passes of the Himalayas, which the Crane brothers had undertaken on its behalf in 1983.

We liked IT's preventive approach to famine. The adage comes to mind: 'If you *give* a man a fish you'll feed him for a day; if you teach him *how* to fish you'll feed him for life.'

It sounded perfect common sense, but would they risk taking on another crazy exploit to promote their cause? We wrote in hope, and were quickly accepted. Within a month the 'Summits for Survival' appeal was mounted, and a flourish of publicity arranged for our departure on 21 December.

But before enthusiasm ran away with reason, the results of those months of route-planning had to be assessed.

The required total of eighty day routes was drafted, giving the most efficient means of ascending every group of Munros. They varied from short return trips to climb the many isolated summits like Schiehallion and Ben Lomond, to extended traverses of the great multi-peaked ridges such as the Fannichs or the Mamores, and 25-mile Nordic ski-tours in the Grampians. To cover the remote areas such as Knoydart or Ben Alder Forest, around sixteen nights would have to be spent in camp, bivouac or, more likely, bothy shelters. The variety was intended. Each itinerary could hopefully be matched to the fluctuating weather – easy hills in stormy periods and the big traverses on clear days and moonlit nights.

The showpiece of the whole winter would be the Black Cuillin Ridge on the Isle of Skye, much the most difficult set of Munros in summer, and in winter conditions a major snow- and ice-climbing expedition, which has only been achieved in full by a handful of parties.

The allowance of ten rest or stormbound days could be extended by combining some of the shorter climbs, but only with difficulty given that the eighty planned routes themselves produced a taxing daily average of 1675m (5,500ft) of ascent and 13 miles to cover all 277 summits.

Despite the van, our flexibility of movement was not unlimited and a logical progression had to be imposed to link the seventeen areas into which the Munro's Tables are divided. We chose to begin in the Southern Highlands where the better road network would give quick access to the peaks in the dark days of late December and early January. Then on into the central regions of Glencoe, Lochaber and Ben Alder; and as soon as the heavy snows arrived, we would take to skis on the rounded eastern hills. This would leave the final month from mid-February onwards to tackle the more difficult and remote peaks of the Western Highlands and the north, Skye included, where the two or three extra daylight hours could be of vital assistance.

The final details confirmed the initial inspiration. The Winter Munros looked at once a gruelling and rewarding challenge, and possessed the vital ingredient of uncertainty with which every adventure should commence.

2

THE STORMTOSSED START

21–25 December:
Ben Lomond – Arrochar – Ben Lui – Black Mount

The rain belted down onto Glasgow's streets, bouncing off the tarmac and sluicing into torrents along the gutters. The washed stone pavements gleamed brightly in reflection of the beams of passing vehicles as this urban flash-flood reached full flow. Overhead, twin lines of sturdy tenements formed a dark and glowering canopy to the drive along the Great Western Road. It was just the sort of night for seeking a warm fire and cheery company; yet we were bound far elsewhere, pitching ourselves into the wild blackness beyond the city limits.

Right turn at Anniesland Cross, a quick stop for petrol and then out towards Drymen. The neon threads of the city thinned, faltered and finally disappeared. Woodland and hedgerows now fringed the way; Balmaha's rows of buildings slipped silently past and the shores of Loch Lomond appeared on our left. Seven twisting miles further and we drew up at the empty parking lots by Rowardennan. In less than an hour of steady driving the transition was complete. We had entered the Highlands.

At last alone and unhitched from worldly cares, we were all but embarked on the reality of the voyage. But on top of excitement there was a tension induced by the elemental hostility of our welcome in the hills. Supper was sparse and brief, and my sleep was light. I suppose I tossed and turned in sympathy with the storm outside. Day one's diary recalled:

> Heavy rainbursts drumming on the van roof, an incessant wind howling through the trees, and the crash of wavelets on the nearby loch shore all combined with my apprehension at starting to ensure a sleepless night.

At 7.35am in the dim light preceding dawn Joy and I began the climb to Ben Lomond. There were no fanfares, not even the click of a pressman's camera. Yesterday's brief fame on radio and television seemed far removed. Yet the absence of a public send-off was not in the least demoralising, for the expedition was envisaged from its inception as a solitary commitment, so this was the right way to begin.

The slopes of Lomond were washed and freshened by the overnight storm. Scattered residual showers drew moving curtains across the distant view, but they kept a respectful distance and we were spared a drenching. With new snow above half-height, a translucent mist clinging to the final ridge, and the summit artefacts bristling with ice hoar, the mountain bore a wintry hue, which seemed proper for the opening day of the season.

A touch of stage-fright was perhaps understandable on these momentous first steps. Had we pulled the rug from under our feet? For there we were, homeless, jobless and with a large hole in our savings account. But all lingering doubts and apprehensions were quickly suffused by a delicious sense of freedom as soon as the heights were gained. Such a euphoric feeling of release is always present on any excursion into the hills, however modest, but now, with an extended three-month sojourn stretching ahead, it was many times magnified. And of course there was a surge of relief just in reaching the starting line, for the bitterness of the failure in 1980 had by no means faded with time. Exactly a fortnight ago I had finished a last temporary stint of accountancy work, eight hours pinned down by computer prints and audit files, while Joy had supervised the removal of our furniture into a storage warehouse. Returning from work, suit and tie were cast aside, and we had squeezed into our new four-wheeled home – outcasts of our own choosing.

Emerging from the cloud on the descent we saw the rooftops of flats and factories in Dumbarton glistening in low-angled sunlight and throwing the wooded fringes and island studs of the lower loch into deep-textured contrast. Down there in the city people were pursuing the daily round, many working, others celebrating the coming Christmas break; but few able to envisage the magical world which we had entered only a few miles away. That sight confirmed the divorce from normality.

Sadly, the new-laid sheet of snow was unable to hide the unsightly scars of the track to the summit. This is one of Scotland's most frequently trodden paths, a proliferation of deep muddy ruts spreading into oozing swamps in all the hollows where countless pairs of feet have tried to skirt the slough, little realising that such avoiding manoeuvres merely fuel the galloping erosion process. The broad highway seemed a ridiculous over-provision for the needs of two lone winter wanderers. Ben Lomond, as the most southerly Munro, is certainly the most vulnerable to the unintended impact of mass usage, and it echoes the widespread human erosion which threatens to despoil the English Lake District. That our most popular hills are simply being 'loved to death' is beyond question.

The urgently needed restoration and long-term preservation of both the Ben and the delightful environs of Loch Lomondside are happily two of the central objects of an integrated tourist development plan currently being formulated for the area. The result may be a managed landscape that is distasteful to lovers of untrammelled wilderness. Yet without forceful conservation measures our scenic inheritance could become a degraded wasteland, no longer capable of inspiring the elation with which we were imbued on this first morning.

But however pleasing and uplifting was the ascent of Lomond, the knowledge that a second mountain lay on day one's menu did not escape my note, nor Joy's:

> Chatting away about this and that, the descent passed easily, another happy outing together on the hills so it seemed – at least until we reached the van and I realised that our efforts today were far from over. No chance to rest, but a long tortuous drive to Glen Fyne ahead. Already the air had turned warmer and it was beginning to rain . . .

Beinn Bhuidhe's rugged crest rises to 948m above the head of Loch Fyne, another isolated Munro, comfortably overtopping neighbouring hills and an obvious peak to combine with Lomond to complete a respectable day's work. Though Beinn Bhuidhe is only 20 miles further from Glasgow the ratio of visitors between the two must be in excess of a hundred times in the latter's favour. The imbalance is wholly unjust, for whilst Ben Lomond displays the greater poise and elegance of position, its rejected competitor is a real rough diamond and perhaps the more worthy mountain.

It transformed the airy sublimity of the morning into a gutsy struggle that bore a closer affinity with our long-term expectations. From the lower glen the subsidiary ridge of Beinn Chas had first to be crossed, itself a tough climb in long grass and heather clumps. Beyond lies 2 miles of indecisive knoll and hollow terrain before the craggy upper ramparts of the mountain are reached.

Though 1.30pm was too late to be starting it was the best we could manage, having driven the 40 miles from Rowardennan without delay and lunched en route. The rain was now entrenched for the afternoon. We dug our heels in too, but up on the snow-covered plateau were helpless to defy a tide of fatigue. Our legs lagged far behind the unyielding momentum of my watch, and the repeated rescheduling of our progress indicated an unplanned benightment on the summit.

In a gloomy dusk we tackled the final rocky slopes, bearing direct for the highest point up into dense cloud. I kicked steps in the deep slush and coaxed Joy upwards with genuine concern, for the exposure was sufficient to signal danger. As we emerged on top at 4.10, a strong sou'wester blowing volleys of soft hail pellets knocked us into a state of total disorientation. For a minute we groped about unsteadily until the crowning trigonometrical column was spotted. A foul night was gathering up here, no place for man or beast, and we promptly turned tail hoping to slither as far as possible down the mountain before total darkness forced a switch to torchbeams.

We carved a direct descent to Inverchorachan in the upper glen, happy to tramp the 2 miles of road back to our van at Merk Cottage so long as the hill was escaped quickly. But short cuts rarely give a smooth passage, and so it was that the map's gentle burn enlivened into a deep gorge when met on the ground. The 1:50000 First Series map for the area is merely a metric reprint of the old one-inch sheet, and lacks the precise detail of the new Second Series survey, which is not due for completion until 1990. Confusion and bewilderment over the plethora of map scales and contour intervals used in the current Ordnance Survey lists were to beset my route-finding throughout the winter.

So with a frustrating reclimb and detour, and a forty-minute road bash, our first day was done – 2 Munros, 17 miles and 1965m (6,450ft) of climbing. It had left the protagonists of the drama sore-footed, leaden-limbed and profoundly downhearted. The future looked appalling – a ninety-day treadmill due for summary resumption at the stroke of 6am tomorrow. My appetite for the 'delicious freedom' of the venture had somehow vanished, and the 'euphoric release' which I was applauding but a few hours previously now hung round my neck like a Derbyshire millstone!

A long sound sleep proved the best medication for these arid thoughts, compensating for my restless night at the foot of Ben Lomond, rekindling a weary body and revitalising the digestion, as was self-evident at a hearty 7am breakfast. Stewed prunes, muesli and two rounds of toast and honey: this morning menu was to become an unvarying ritual throughout the trip, but one that never palled in the slightest.

We were nestled in the bottom of Glen Croe, a snaking corridor linking Lochs Long and Fyne, and carrying the A83 on its interminable and thankless journey in search of Campbeltown down in the Kintyre peninsula. The glen lies in the midst of the jumbled hills of Arrochar, a cluster of rocky knuckles which provides Glasgow's closest high-level climbing grounds. These Arrochar 'Alps', as they are affectionately called, contain four Munros. Up until 1974 the total was five but Beinn an Lochain, standing above Rest and be Thankful at the head of the Croe, has suffered an ignominious demotion, a startling 20m being lopped off its altitude between successive editions of the Tables, the result of resurveying rather than subsidence. Now it stands as a proud 'Corbett' at 901m.

It is unfortunate that the district's most striking summit – the crooked beak of The Cobbler – also fails to surface from the 3,000ft waterline, but I was still left with a fine foursome, all of them Bens: Narnain, Ime, Vane and Vorlich. They give a big climbing day with 2250m (7,400ft) crammed into a 12-mile itinerary. A pity then about the weather forecast – a deep depression in the Atlantic and a warm front tracking in from the south-west.

We climbed up the Croe Burn onto Bealach a' Mhaim, an unusual three-sided col. Such a configuration is notoriously confusing in mist, and sure enough we were 50m up on The Cobbler before I checked the compass for Narnain! Joy stayed with me for the first pair, then dropped down from Ime to take the van around to Inveruglas by Loch Lomond where my finish was planned, an arrangement that was often repeated in the coming months – risky maybe, but because of our utter interdependence we tended to feel closer when working apart than together.

As I pushed on through the fog and drizzle over the shaggy summit of Ben Vane, the windspeeds remained modest and the air warm. Thankfully they were no worse, for again my pace slipped alarmingly behind the desired time schedule, and no quantity of willpower or chocolate bars served to raise it. The second day of any expedition is often the toughest. Without warning a physical barrier is met which can only be overcome by brutal persistence in the face of considerable torture. Once the hurdle is cleared stamina and rhythm are usually picked up which see the rest of the journey completed in relative comfort.

But of course this was no ordinary journey. How do you prepare for three months of unceasing effort – a fanatical 'Messner-like' olympiad*, or a determined aversion to all exercise in the 'Whillans' style? My own solution was a reasonable compromise. There was no point in setting off at a perfect peak of fitness which could not be sustained; indeed, my frantic training regime in 1980 had led only to injury and disaster. Better to start mentally fresh for the task and with plenty of reserves to draw from en route. So the final month had oddly been spent weight-training in a gym to put some bulk on the muscles, with no more than two short hill runs a week. Don Whillans had other ideas of where the extra weight should be carried but the intention was the same! And in these early stages a steady pace was essential to adjust to the new demands without risking a sudden exhaustion that could be fatal in the damp chill of a winter night.

Well after 2pm I crossed the dam on Loch Sloy and squared up to the mighty 600m flank of Ben Vorlich. My slower speed was deliberate on this unremitting slog, and the top was not gained until

---

*Reinhold Messner claimed to run 1,000m uphill in 35 minutes when training for his remarkable Himalayan climbs.

nigh on 4pm. The ascent was reversed to get back to the dam road. Initially skirting the summit cliffs, then plunging down in carefree style, I was brought to an abrupt halt by the scarps and clefts of ancient landslips on the lower slopes. By barely a glimmer of residual light I tip-toed through this ankle-breaking terrain, then weaved around a field of giant fallen blocks to gain the tarmac.

The immediate vicinity of Loch Sloy and the Coiregrogain valley below it has been scenically abandoned to the needs of hydro-electric power production. Pipelines, road and pylons link the loch to the generating station at Inveruglas. Half-way down I passed out of the wet darkness into the piercing glare of a floodlit power plant. Eerily deserted, grimly defended by barbed wire, and emitting a constant low-pitched hum, it looked like something out of the 'Gulag Archipelago', and sent me hurrying towards the dimmer but more welcoming lights of the van.

Easter 1905: a rope of four wool-clad pioneers with lengthy alpenstocks cutting and chopping up a sweeping slope of névé snow; a final cornice juts far over their heads, the summit cairn is perched tantalisingly just beyond, and the white-streaked caps of unknown hills float in the smoky distance. The caption reads simply 'Beinn Laoigh, Summit', and the photographer is Rev A. E. Robertson, the first-ever Munroist. I can almost smell the historic atmosphere of this fine print, slightly faded and tinged with age, a priceless remnant from a classic era of mountain exploration (*see page 26*).

It lies hidden like a jewel in the 1949 Scottish Mountaineering Club guide to the Southern Highlands, which I bought all of eighteen years ago for the handsome sum of twenty-one shillings and still possess with pleasure. What a scene to fire a romantic attraction to the hills and what better an incentive to make the climb to Lui's twin-topped peak. It is sad that the modern editions of the district guides no longer use these magnificent old stills. Though highly professional, the newer publications miss the epochal quality of their predecessors.

But 23 December 1984 was decidedly *not* the day to realise those youthful stirrings for what is arguably Scotland's most splendid mountain south of Rannoch. We tackled Ben Lui and its three Munro satellites in abominable conditions. The Atlantic depression had only deepened during the night sending a strengthening gale whistling through Glen Lochy like the Oban–Glasgow express.

Superlatives are not required to colour the account of our traverse; my clipped diary notes tell the whole grim truth:

> At dawn the Lui group bore a heavy shroud of mist. Tattered shreds of cloud raced overhead in clearer skies. Fording the River Lochy posed the first difficulty. Then came the tricky negotiation of the sprouting new

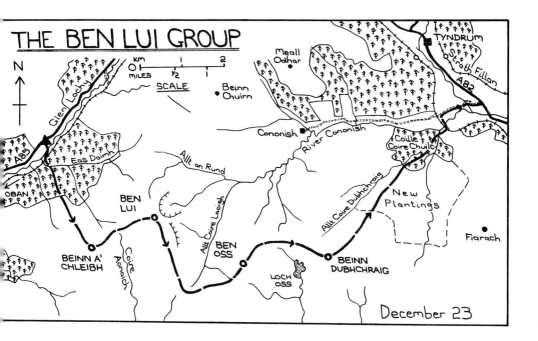

THE BEN LUI GROUP

plantings on the side of Beinn a' Chleibh. We climbed into a real howler on the summit. Today the rain lashed down without pause and an amazing thaw was visibly clearing the remaining snow . . .

Descending Lui we found a large stone giving dry shelter for a brief lunch. The rain simply blew horizontally overhead. We were wind-assisted up Ben Oss, and nearly blown off our feet crossing the following bealach onto Beinn Dubhchraig . . .

To our dismay heavy rain restarted as we wound our way through new plantations towards Tyndrum . . . bad route-finding in fading light among the ancient pines of Coille Coire Chuilc forced us to ford a rushing stream which proved waist-deep. Drenched, and in ill-temper, we made the road at 5pm.

That washed-out feeling must be familiar to every regular hill-goer, but let me remind you! Your nylon leggings sag to the knees, sloshing audibly at every pace. Numb white knuckles are clenched and curled into the shelter of cagoule sleeves. A warm puddle slops about in your boots, and icy raindrops somehow penetrate your goretex armoury to trickle down the neck and back. And if like me you are a wearer of spectacles, the vision becomes so steamed and spattered that you can't even see the clammy mists outside. Then you stop, and the wet chill attacks, reducing you to a shivering wreck in half an hour.

We stood by the roadside with merely six miles to hitch-hike back to our van. In our waif-like state, and with Christmas just two days hence, there was every reason to expect generous charity from some knight of the road, but after a dozen cars had flashed past sending

only plumes of spray in our direction my mood had changed to outright indignation. We started to walk.

Finally a delivery van halted, its driver an exiled Yorkshireman. Oh yes, he was a mountaineer, just twenty Munros left to climb he proudly declared. We brightened considerably:

'Oh, really,' said Joy, 'well we are trying to do them all this winter – perhaps you might have read about it.'

His response was flattening: 'Impossible – you haven't a chance; it's taken me ten year and more.'

My hackles rose at the derision in his voice, and Joy was glad to bundle me out at our destination before a full-scale argument erupted. After seven years living in his home county I should have known better. The man was only colloquially expressing his very real admiration of our project! Looking back, he was treated roughly in my thoughts.

While Joy displayed an admirable equanimity all evening, she was forced to bear the brunt of my continuing annoyance:

> Once inside the van a major drying operation was commenced, the first big test for our gas radiator. Through all the aromas of our cooking dinner, Martin remained fractious. After eating, we drove the narrow road to Bridge of Orchy and when I swerved to avoid a ditch he loudly berated my driving capabilities. I seethed but stayed silent. At around 11pm he was calming down enough to get some sleep, and making final preparations for the next day, when his camera's rewind mechanism jammed solid. For an hour he vainly fumbled with it, driving himself rapidly towards distraction before sheepishly appealing for me to go into Fort William tomorrow to get a repair or a replacement. Though it was my role to shoulder some of Martin's cares, there were times when I felt no more than an ill-used 'skivvy'!

On Christmas Eve the process of pecking at the Southern Highlands cake continued with an excursion north to the Black Mount hills. Such disjointed progress could never be as satisfying as a smooth continuous sweep, but the tactic was premeditated to accommodate the expected early fluxes of weather and fitness.

In view of the execrable weather we felt drawn to take the soft option of a trip to Mull and its lone Munro. However, in all good conscience it was too early in the expedition to be thinking of a semi-rest day. Valiant battle must be maintained on the mainland peaks, and Mull kept dangling carrot-like as a future reward for the present trials. After all, the Lui group, at 12½ miles and 1615m (5,300ft), had been a modest outing, notwithstanding the tempest, and it established

(left) 'Beinn Laoigh, Summit', Easter 1905 (*A. E. Robertson/SMC Collection*)

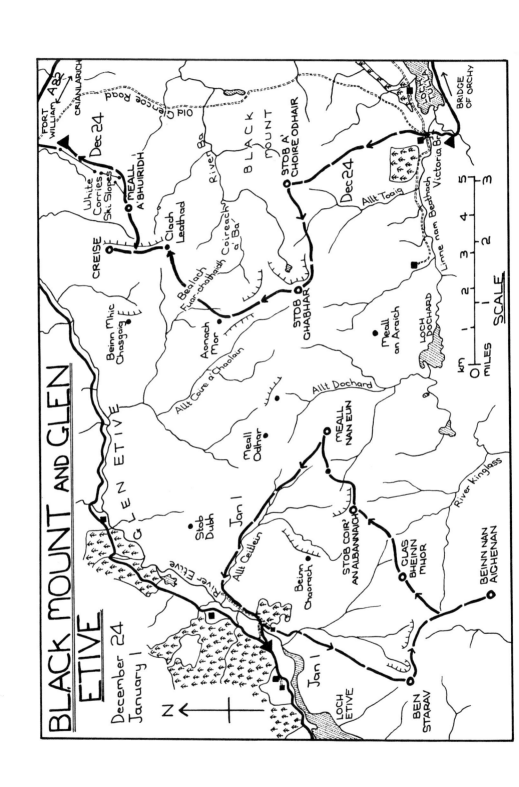

the vital cumulative target of at least three Munros per day which I was loathe to lose again so quickly.

Black Mount, more precisely retitled 'the Coire Ba range' in the new Tables, occupies the northern end of the wild tangle of hills rolling from the rim of Rannoch Moor over to Lòch Etive. The range forms a majestic tableau at several stages on the wide arc of the Glencoe road, especially the prospect of Stob Ghabhar viewed over Loch Tulla, and the frame of Meall a' Bhuiridh and Creise from the Kingshouse Hotel.

With the first flutter of ecstasy since Ben Lomond I sprang out of bed when Joy reported a star-filled sky at 6.30am, and at the back of 8am left Victoria Bridge, briskly in step with a dawn of distilled beauty. Deer were at play on the moors approaching Stob a' Choire Odhair and the summits lay lightly coated with overnight snow. The breezy cold front that completed the cyclone's passage had brought us firmly back into winter's grip.

Gentle snow showers confused perceptions on the following tops. Stob Ghabhar is a great and complex mountain, radiating an array of long ridge spokes, and harbouring a fine cliffed coire to the north-east, which carves the summit into a graceful edge that is a joy to tread. But tracking out on its northern spoke of Aonach Mor I was foxed not only by the shifting visibility, but also by another topographic dispute with the map, which here shows a broad level sward nearly a mile in length. Two tiring scrambles over rocky knolls, each near to 40m in height, put me in serious doubt of my whereabouts, and only a lucky clearance in the clouds enabled me to find the connecting ridge to Clach Leathad. Because the relief of the range is aligned transversely to its main watershed, the linking ridges are indistinct and often hard to locate in mist.

Here a late lunch was taken and Christmas cake forced down with an unwilling appetite. My prediction that the fitness hurdle would be successfully scaled on the second day was proving amiss, for here on the fourth I was still dragging a complaining body around the hills. The Bealach Fuar-chathaidh is a good spot for lonely exaltations, a deep pass lost in the heart of the range, yet commanding an expansive view across the Rannoch Moor where the distant lines of the Glencoe roads, both New and Old, lend impressive scale to the scene.

There was a blast of wind back on the tops. The eastern edge of the Clach Leathad–Creise ridge was rapidly cornicing. After detouring to the summit I was relieved to find a wooden post, stolen from the nearby ski-slopes, marking the point of departure for the final stage of the day to Meall a' Bhuiridh, which although an outlier of the group is in fact its highest top at 1,108m. In theory I view such indicators as infringements of liberty, valuing the freedom to make my own errors in the hills; but when they are met on ground in tricky conditions complaints are rarely heard.

The White Corries pistes were silent and stony, still awaiting the big snowfall that would herald the start of the new ski season. It was heartening to be clear of the tops before dark and doubly delighting when Joy produced the camera on my return, restored to operation in a trice by skilled hands in Fort William's photography shop. Last night's frenzied worry over the device now seemed ridiculous. In any case with only two out of fourteen Munro summits so far having given a hint of a view it was hardly fulfilling an essential function! Yet there could be no discontent over the Black Mount day. The peaks had given an absorbing encounter, with winter walking of the highest class that would hopefully be resumed when the southern half of the massif was tackled from Glen Etive at a later date.

The jangle of the morning's alarm brought the usual muted response. Joy's arm stretched from under our duvet quilt to flick the radio into life. A flood of pealing church bells resounded forth, and we remembered it was Christmas Day. The already familiar patter of rain on the metallic roof of the van struck a discordant accompaniment to these happy notes.

It was really a hopeless move to have driven down to the base of Ben Cruachan in full knowledge of a diabolical forecast. Yet another trough was in passage – only this one was 'occluded', which strictly means a fusion of cold and warm frontal systems but, to speak more plainly, spells a profusion of snow and rain.

A selection of carols sung in the villages around our Sheffield homeland followed the bells, and tugged at our heartstrings, awakening a longing vision of the brown windswept moors of the upper Derwent and our forsaken gritstone house.

We waited uneasily until mid-morning, allowing the day ahead to contract to crisis point, while the rain outside maintained its tempo. If the airy crest of Cruachan was a forlorn hope, then the only possible alternative was Ben More by Crianlarich (see map on page 36), on the twin counts of its bulky simplicity and immediate access, for you cannot take two steps off the main road in Glen Dochart without steering onto the 1000m staircase to its summit.

As we drove round, the sky cleared briefly, and we hurried off upwards, determined to salvage the day. Rhythm established on the long grassy slopes was not to be ruffled by the renewed rain, nor its transition to snow higher up. We were on top inside ninety minutes in time for a quick festive lunch of soup and biscuits.

Roads, villages and hills, all were deserted. Never would we feel so isolated. *Everybody* must be enjoying home celebrations on this symbolic day. For years past we had always sought refuge in the mountains at Christmas, thankful to escape the ballyhoo and indulgence, but this year for the first time we had a sneaking envy of comfort and conformity. Turning my palms up to the swirling storm was a gesture of despair and a silent prayer for our rapid reincarnation into a bright new world of azure skies and sunglazed snow peaks.

Joy excused herself from further duty and sped off down while I made my bid for Stob Binnein, Ben More's Siamese twin. Together the pair form the most distinctive peaks in any Southern Highland panorama, exceeded only by Ben Lawers in height and by Schiehallion in symmetrical form. It is a remarkable testimony to the channelling effect of the terrain on air movement that the gale was nigh on intolerable on the connecting bealach, whilst I could amble peacefully in still air on the succeeding summit.

Any day that is rescued from the dead, however minor its achievement, gives the spirits a great fillip, and all was rosy that evening. We even partook of a little merriment ourselves, rousing both our families and Steve Bonnist, Intermediate Technology's press officer, from their post-prandial slumbers with telephone greetings and an epic saga of sixteen storm-whipped mountain tops. Then over our tête-à-tête at dinner we heard glad tidings from the weatherman, and as we settled down for the night at Bridge of Orchy saw the thermometer make a satisfying plunge towards zero.

A break in the weather's grip would see off my first great mental challenge of the winter, and it was a reasonable reflection on this Christmas night that 'a job well begun is half-done'.

3

FIRST-FOOTS IN ARGYLL

26 December–1 January:
The Orchy and Crianlarich Hills – Ben Cruachan – Mull – Appin and Etive

The Bridge of Orchy hills at 16 miles would give our longest day so far. They are a compact group of five Munros formed in the likeness of a clenched fist. The outer four knuckles command the southern defences of Rannoch Moor and provide an effective shield to the fifth and lowest, Beinn Mhanach, which is stuck like a sore thumb in the lonely hinterland of upper Glen Lyon. But for the necessity of an awkward detour to Mhanach the range offers a satisfying, well-linked traverse, and the idea of taking on this minor *tour de force* rustled up an eager anticipation, which was amply repaid by the conditions:

> On a calm frosty Boxing Day morning we felt borne up onto the Orchy skyline on nothing more than the floating gossamers of mist which rose from the glens and diffused in vapour above the summits. In less sublime conditions the slog up the runnelled slopes of Ben Dorain would have been a toil on a par with yesterday's approach to Ben More!

We emerged on the ridge half a mile to the north of the top, and made a detour to the final prong. At this early hour the mists were still billowing from below, and tricked us into thinking a prominent cairned eminence to be the summit. Already turning to retrace our steps, a cursory check on the large scale 1:25000 map, which had been propitiously brought along, indicated a separate but higher knoll some way further south, which we were now bound to visit.

This in fact was the closest I was to come to missing the top of a Munro. It was of course the essence of the game to touch the true summit of each, and this necessity haunted me into the labour of combing guides, books and maps for any sundry details that would assist their location in bad visibility, especially on the 200 not previously visited. Imagine the agony of subsequently discovering that a top had been by-passed by a few paces. That knowledge would have torn my conscience to shreds until the situation was rectified by reclimbing the mountain on another day. In such event an oversight

(right) Martin Moran on A'Chralaig above Loch Cluanie (*M. Stone*)

like that so nearly committed on Ben Dorain could mean the forfeit of my ninety-day target.

Coming over Beinn an Dothaidh the tops finally shook off their veils of fog, briefly revealing the dome of Ben Nevis in lordly dominance of the Lochaber horizon before we tacked off into the outback towards Beinn Mhanach. Whilst the Christmas snow had largely drifted off the ridges, the flanks and hollows were the prime targets for its deposition, making this next stage a fagging plod. The heavy labour involved in crossing drifted snow makes it easy to overestimate vastly one's rate of progress. Even at a push we barely made one and a half miles per hour on this section.

By the time we resurfaced on the Orchy crest at Beinn a'Chreachain the hills were already cradled in evening's sweet embrace. Mellow lighting and lengthening shadows coupled with the awesome stillness to create a scene of unruffled dignity. Even the lochans on the Moor mirrored water-colours of the encircling mountains. As we stood transfixed by Chreachain's monolithic cairn, watching the sun drop past the horn peaks of Cruachan, we were seeing the whole winter in a new shining light:

> The stormtossed struggles so far on the trip faded into insignificance. For just one perfect day like this each week I vowed I would suffer hell and high water on the other six!

Though happy to linger here, there was a fifth Munro to cross before darkness, and all speed was made to Beinn Achaladair in the final flickers of sunset. The snow's reflection gave just sufficient illumination for us to negotiate the steep descent to the valley. With a dark mile along the West Highland rail line and a short hitch-hike we were back at Bridge of Orchy in the nick of time for the five-to-six forecast – and a good one it was too. Christmas 1984 was certainly coming late for us both.

To be granted a second consecutive day of icy splendour was something of an overload to our limited sensory expectations, used as we were to the traditional fickleness of the Scottish weather. Fullest advantage had to be taken of this good fortune, and another tough traverse was attempted, the five Crianlarich Munros, a 13-miler with 1980m (6,500ft) of climbing.

Down at Benmore farm, our thermometer had plummetted to −8°C by dawn, confirming the first deep frost of the winter. Colder heavier air from the upper atmosphere had drained into the valleys overnight and condensed into a blanket of freezing fog. Up in the Benmore Glen

(*left*) Descending Ben Lomond on the first morning (see Chapter 2)

35

this shroud was pierced at 250m. Above the air was dry and already sunwarmed. Such a sharp temperature inversion is typical in winter whenever stable air at high pressure descends over Scotland. Minimum temperatures are always recorded in the glen bottoms as a result of this cold air subsidence, Braemar holding the record in modern times with a chilly −27.2°C on 9 January 1982. By comparison the minimum observed on Cairn Gorm summit at 1,245m was only −15.3°C in February 1979.

These Crianlarich hills are a rugged set, much in the Arrochar mould, but without the unbroken exposures of rock that would interest the climber. Though somewhat dwarfed by nearby Ben More to the east, the culminating point of Cruach Ardrain being 130m lower, they form fine tramping country, and were one of the few groups of Munros which we had traversed previously, on a December camping trip two years ago:

> Joy's company was, as on our last visit, a great pleasure and a positive boost to my pace, for thus far she was showing an equal if not greater fitness than myself. But the last icy stack of Cruach Ardrain as we approached from Stob Garbh looked too intimidating for her, and I strongly counselled that she contour the summit to meet me on the following bealach before Beinn Tulaichean.

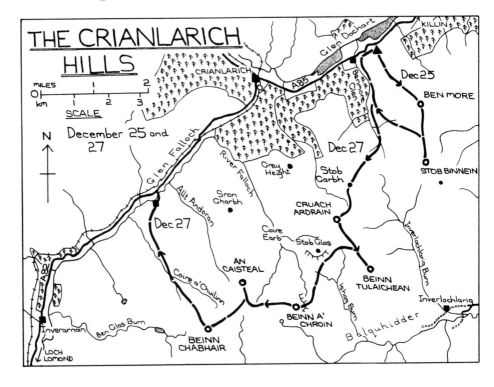

These situations have usually descended into argument and rancour between us. Joy has a self-confessed paranoia in steep or loose places in the mountains. Once gripped by panic, she is impervious to all persuasion, and has never overcome the fear despite her many years of experience. Fortunately, on this occasion I saw the danger approaching long before she got stranded half-way up the 40-degree ice slope:

> Such foresight on my part was quite unusual for I am normally pig-headed and obstinate, trying to coax then drag her up against her will until a flood of tears enforces a retreat. Why this intolerance, when I love her so dearly? Often my personal ambition to reach our target overrides care and good reason, and on other occasions it is an exasperating inability to appreciate that what is simple for myself can be beyond Joy's capabilities. Yet this is never felt when I am guiding or instructing others, and I guess there are some areas where illogically even the closest of spouses cannot co-operate, and remain with daggers drawn

We were rejoined in harmony for the easy dog-leg to Tulaichean, and then, traversing beneath the crags of Stob Glas towards Beinn a'Chroin, were stopped in our tracks by a remarkable sight – another human being, the first person encountered on the hills during this whole first week. He was a shepherd up from Balquhidder, looking over his beasts while the weather allowed. He met our wondering gazes with merely a perfunctory greeting. After bumping into two walkers only twenty minutes later, grumbles could be heard about the hills getting too crowded these days!

Just two nights of hard frost had stilled the copious stocks of surface water and the abundance of rivulets into so many sheets and cataracts of ice. It was comforting to have true winter conditions at last, for after all this venture was designed to be a 'show on ice'! But sadly the waves of alto-stratus cloud already spreading in from the south-west portended the return of warmer air, and those devitalising winds. Even as the clouds appeared on the far horizon the bite was removed from the air, but we were safe from a storm for many hours yet.

All that remained today was the now familiar race against time over our last two summits, An Caisteal and Beinn Chabhair. The strain of a second hard day was telling in leg muscles that made painful protest at the start of each climb. But our fitness was now gaining ascendancy in our battle with darkness. Descending to Glen Falloch by Coire a'Chuilinn we were on the tarmac of the A82 soon after 5pm.

Immediately noticeable was the greater volume of cars on the road. The great New Year exodus to the hills had begun. This was most opportune, for we had 6 miles to hitch-hike or otherwise walk, and promptly obtained two lifts back to the van, both from walkers. One of the drivers was en route to Kintail, and a three-day trek to 'bag' the remote An Socach above Glen Affric. This unassuming summit would be our host's 200th Munro or thereabouts, and had been unaccountably left unclimbed when he had traversed the neighbouring peaks, so that now a minor expedition had to be mounted for this sole objective. His approach seemed grossly inefficient compared to my own attempt at a non-stop 'grand slam'; yet his own 'desultory campaign' was probably giving an immense pleasure spread over many years that my inflexible regimen would not allow. To enjoy the quest, whatever the style one chooses, is more important than the ultimate achievement. My tactics were decided because I love an intensive commitment in pursuit of my mountaineering goals, whilst others prefer a leisured journey towards them*. It's all a matter of personal taste, and thankfully, such is the freedom of the hills that they will accommodate either approach.

In dismal imitation of the previous day's freezing fog, dawn on 28 December provided us with a moist and muggy mist, the change noted by a 12°C climb on the mercury. We were back beneath Ben Cruachan, to which today I was a lone suitor, for Joy had to make a trip to Oban to replenish our dwindling stocks of food and fuel.

This was not a morning for gleeful inspiration, especially given the sea-level starting altitude which presented a full 1100m climb to the crowning peak. Whilst in the Southern and Western Highlands we often yearned for a spell in the Grampians where the roads can usually contrive at least 300m of initial assistance. From the Visitor Centre beneath the Falls of Cruachan a muddy path fights up through the woods on the west bank of the burn:

> Beginning the ascent fully clothed, I was so wretchedly soaked in sweat by the reservoir dam at half-height that I rashly stripped down to a vest. Swopping the sopping mist for a thicker belt of cloud I aimed for the subsidiary ridge of Meall Cuanail, the usual means of access to Cruachan's 2-mile summit crest. But instead of a well-graded track, snow-covered crags were encountered where a slip could have been disastrous. This route-finding mishap made me irascible and even more careless.
>
> Failing to heed the frost and the chilling breeze above 3,000ft I stumbled up to the top in a dangerously underdressed state – fingers numb and teeth chattering.
>
> 'Get a grip, Martin!' I murmured beneath my breath, then fumbled with poppers and buttons for aching minutes until I was a fair replica of Nanook of the North. A brisk march eastwards down the crest forced the blood back into circulation, and my stiff staggering gait soon smoothed into its normal rhythm.

*No one more so than Fred Wiley who took fifty-seven years for his completion of the Munros between 1921 and 1978.

Such a trivial instance of personal negligence even in this undistinguished weather had taken me to the brink of exposure.

Momentarily a smudge of blue appeared in the clouded vault over my head, but it was obvious that the humid maritime influx was winning the battle of the airmasses. The joys of the Cruachan ridge sadly could only be sensed rather than indulged – yawning gully mouths and corniced curves on my left, an occasional flash of the reservoir down right and the hint of a sweeping knife-edge to Stob Diamh ahead. It was tempting in these conditions to feel short-changed by these grand mountains which had been sought for so long. Yet this could not be otherwise, for the multitude of worthy Munros on my itinerary far exceeded the number of clear days in any winter.

With the sacrifice of only 450m of height, Beinn a'Chochuill and Beinn Eunaich were conveniently added to the Cruachan pair – hills which intrigued me by their relative anonymity. There is a risk of their becoming further cloistered if the 2,100 acres of new forestry plantings proposed by the Dutch owners of the mountains are installed on the flanks. Given the wide swathe of trees already clothing the heights above Dalmally the local scenery would be a lot better off without any further encroachment. Neither summit yielded easily today:

> When I am low on energy and enthusiasm only my watch can provide the vital discipline. I would set a target time on each bealach then drop my head and go for the top – hardly an aesthetic way to treat the hills, but on this 'dreich' afternoon, which had now degenerated into a mournful drizzle, the only available tactic.

The descent of Eunaich was not the easy jog expected:

> Eyes straying from the compass, I lost the south ridge and dropped eastwards into a deepening cleft. A stream of invective was hurled at the enclosing walls, and I madly skated across the wet grass slopes above the ravine desperately seeking an escape corridor; but no, the gorge held me in its grip right to its end. A rowing rabble of dogs at Castles farm then guided the last mile to the road in darkness.

After such a harassing day my spirits badly needed the boost of a visit to Mull:

> Goodness, I am tired tonight! There is no doubt whatsoever – I want a day ticket to Mull; some small respite, a taste of softer pleasures, and even a little daytime comfort, dare I ask. Tomorrow will be a stolen holiday. The conscience is clear – thirty Munros in eight days is a progress scarcely imagined in my plans.

We spent the night by Oban's shore-front, ready and waiting for the morning ferry.

The Island of Mull is an unknown world to most mountaineers, usually being ignored and by-passed in harebrained dashes to more spectacular climbing grounds. But that is not to say that Mull has no potential for exploration. Impressive basalt and granite cliffs have been reported on its remote western peninsulas but as yet are untouched. 'The Wilderness' on the headland of Ardmeanach is 350m above the sea at its highest point.

The 7.45 ferry crossing to Craignure was therefore a voyage of discovery, but an unpromising rain sheeted down onto the boat decks. The crew ambled about in their yellow oilskins, while we took breakfast inside the van. 'Hardly the best holiday weather', I mused, remembering that Ben More had to be scaled during the next seven hours.

Mull must be a special place because we were enchanted by every mile of the drive round to Salen even though one could barely see beyond the treetops. There seemed a wooded softness in the central island which complemented the bleak headlands, surf-topped lochs and lonely crofts of the peninsulas to give a more wholesome landscape than can be sensed on others of the Hebrides. Skye for me is wild and grand, but too desolate to generate the warmest affection, whilst Mull seemed a place where one could put down roots and settle permamently.

Salen village and Gruline looked especially beautiful oases of repose, but to my horror Joy drove straight through them to the gale-battered shore of Loch na Keal where rise the long slopes of Ben More. While I sought a suitable excuse to delay our departure – a nice cup of tea and a look at the map maybe – she proceeded to don boots and waterproofs and then pack the sack.

'Are we going just yet?' I was querying the obvious.

'Well, why not – the sooner we're out the quicker we're back', came the retort. Joy had spotted my wavering will and was not going to let me off the hook.

But reluctance soon turned to vigour as we splashed up over An Gearna and onto the final screes of the north-west ridge. The circular shelter on the summit gave us respite from the blustering sou'wester and here we left the first of sixty-seven plastic-backed brochures which were to be deposited in selected Munro cairns throughout the winter, each containing the presumptuous request that they be returned to Intermediate Technology as proof of my visit, and hopefully accompanied by a 'small contribution to our appeal'.

Why sully the mountain tops with this sort of propaganda? The action brought a couple of letters from disgusted discoverers making this very challenge. Well, whatever my personal honesty, there was a need to give proof of at least some of the ascents, not so much to the

Joy about to plant the first appeal brochure on the top of Ben More, Mull

walking and climbing fraternity among which there is a tradition of trustworthy reporting that is rarely abused, but more for a sceptical media and a disbelieving public. One canny journalist was quick to see ripe potential for the perpetration of a gross fraud in this venture. His article read:

As a cynic weaned on professional sport in which cheating is par for the course, the thought occurred that the Morans could be staying in the warmth of their van playing Trivial Pursuits, and simply telling the world that Martin had done the Munros.

Already I was making painstaking notes of the summit details of each Munro, shape and size of cairn and so on, but that didn't evidence my ascent during this particular winter. Photography was planned as a less equivocal proof, but apart from the discomfort of taking shots of each summit cairn in obnoxious conditions such as today, the results were a series of blurred and misted mounds that even Hamish Brown would have a job to sort out. So instead of wasting camera film, the brochure idea emerged, though not without some misgivings, for I abhor litter on the hills as much as anyone.

Coming off Ben More, we followed a line of tall cairns down Coire nam Fuaran towards Dhiseig cottage. They indicate the mountain's

41

singular popularity with summer visitors, for it is substantially the island's highest summit, dominating a surrounding group of conical hills which are reminiscent of the Red Cuillin of Skye, and have a similar volcanic origin. However, whilst Mull is still largely covered by the basalt outpourings of active Tertiary volcanoes, on Skye these layers have been eroded to expose gabbros and granites formed by the cooling of intruded lavas which were thrust up *under* the surface at a later time.

Passing by the gushing waterfall on Abhainn Dhiseig it was hard to visualise our charity. Here we were, nearly flooded into submission trying to help people on the Saharan margins who haven't had a drop of rain for years and desperately need the windpumps and irrigation techniques that IT are designing for them. What a crazy and cruel world! Yet we could be consoled, knowing that our fund-raising efforts might enable the symbolic transfer of a small portion of Scotland's deluge to these arid lands.

The seashore was in full-blooded uproar on our return, a cacophony of crashing waves, booming wind and soughing grasses. Man's presence is a rude impertinence on these untamed western margins. Once tasted this raw brand of Hebridean scenery can make all else seem very tame and tailored. If only there were more Munros on the Islands!

After a delightfully recumbent afternoon we were back on the mainland by nightfall, parked in Glen Creran in the Appin peninsula. Our brief and wet sojourn on Mull seemed all but a dream already.

There were others besides ourselves afoot on the Creran hills in the murky clouded dawn of 30 December. Lights were aflame in the windows of Glenure Lodge, so a shooting party must have been preparing for a day's sport. Not wanting to get involved in any crossfire we thought it wise to be away quickly and over the hills, whilst a continuing wet outlook was further persuasion to an early spurt of energy.

Between Glen Creran and Glencoe is a lonely outback containing three isolated and untracked Munros which rise above a moorland plinth where water is abundant yet the drainage sluggish and confused. Only the Forestry Commission's unquenchable lust for new plantings has borne any human inroads into this piece of wilderness.

Beinn Sgulaird was the first objective with a straight 900m climb to its summit complex of knolls and crags. Despite thick mist my routefinding brought us direct to the highest cairn, where Joy left me to return to the van, happy to be clad in a jacket of bright red which would serve as a warning beacon to any trigger-happy stalkers.

The crossing to Beinn Fhionnlaidh typified the most soul-searching sections of my travels, being rather hard on effort and short on achievement. Compare the Cluanie Ridge of Glen Shiel for instance. In the same distance one can pocket four or even five Munros, so that the brain is fully occupied merely keeping check on the cumulative tally. Here, though, a more detached frame of mind was needed. How admirable the mental fortitude and tenacity of those lone marathon walkers who can pound unvarying miles day after day with nought but their own company and yet stay sane. Thinking of John Merrill's daily 25 miles round the coast of Britain, or George Keeping's 165-day summer trek over Britain's 3,000-footers, I was glad of my support 'team' who was never more than a couple of glens away.

Indeed, today was the first where a slight boredom was admitted. All that splendid powder of Boxing Day had been washed away leaving just a few dirty patches of what the skiing reports call 'spring snow', yet the winter season had barely begun. There was just a little dissatisfaction in what the Highlands were offering me. Had the forecast rain materialised I might have felt better served, but conditions stayed imperturbably dull and dispiriting. But before I succumbed to this dejected mood, the terrain with typical caprice produced a surprise which jerked me back to life. Fhionnlaidh's northern spur abuts in a craggy nose above the Bealach Caol Creran:

> I tried to outsmart this on the left, but was blindly enticed into a real 'cleft stick' – a waterworn rock chimney oozing green and greasy slime. Every downward step took me deeper into danger as its angle veered from steep to vertical, and a final chasm choked with fallen blocks would have rated 'Severe' even without the icy streams that first froze the fingers then trickled down to the armpits. Emerging onto the Bealach, I looked back up, and of course my route had chanced upon the most diabolical piece of the whole cliff! Yet the incident restored the adventure and zest which for me is the essence of climbing.

Sgor na h-Ulaidh, evocatively named 'the peak of the treasure', opened my route to a snowless Glencoe. On the edge of its northern cliff a rent in the clouds framed the sweeping sides of Gleann na Muidhe:

> The scene seemed a symbolic gateway to a grander mountain domain, well earned after this day of misted exile. With renewed excitement I broke into a jog all the way down to the valley.

New Year's Eve was a dashing day – vigorous activity on our part such that one would have thought we were doing some early 'first footing', and to match it a bracing north-east wind which seemed to be swinging the weather out of its wet cycle. We rose in Glen Etive having planned to tidy up the southern half of the Black Mount range, but blustery morning squalls sent us over to Ballachulish in search of an easier option, namely the Beinn a' Bheithir group, a lofty set of ridges towering above the mouth of Loch Leven and culminating in an elegant pair of Munros, Sgorr Dhonuill and Sgorr Dhearg.

Their summits can be sneakily accessed via forestry roads in Gleann a' Chaolais to within 200m of the intervening bealach. Putting a spring in our step we were round in under four hours, returning with lungs cleansed and our cheeks on fire. But our short-cut to the summits, however convenient, fails to capture the full glories of a complete circuit of the range, which is truly a 'ring of bright water' with great vistas down Loch Linnhe to the shimmering seas and the floating castles of Mull and Jura.

The whole afternoon was yet to unfold, and in our ventilated state the pick of the peaks of Glencoe lay within our compass. The Buachaille Etive Mor was Joy's choice, for she had often admired its cliffs and chasms from the safety of the main road. On the assurance that these savage ramparts are completely circumvented by the walker's route up Coire na Tulaich she needed no encouragement.

The 'Great Shepherd' is still perhaps the greatest climbing magnet in the Highlands whether ascended by the easy back-way, or one of some two hundred routes on the north-east faces. In winter the scope ranges from the beginner's course of Curved Ridge to the grade VI technicalities of Guerdon Grooves on the Slime Wall, a very hard mixed climb put up in 1984 by Dave Cuthbertson and Arthur Paul. But, apart from variety, perhaps the mountain's special attraction is that a successful ascent places one on the finest of summits, a rare experience on the mainland peaks.

After a dry scramble up the lower cleft of the Coire, we met a runnel of frozen snow barring the exit. Happily a line of old bucket steps had been carved in the exposed centre, to provide Joy with a feasible passage. Though slow and tremulous, her caution was infinitely preferable to the 'devil-may-care' attitude of the many who 'glissade' this slope. To the skilled snow-climber, glissading is the technique of skiing down on one's heels using the ice-axe shaft as both brake and rudder, but to the majority simply means sliding down on the back-side at an immodest speed. Many have lost control here and hurtled into the rocks at the bottom. Accidents might be understandable on the vertical snow and ice courses of the north face, but are less excusable on the tourist's descent. In repeated cases, the victims of glissading accidents have worn crampons and simply been somer-saulted out of their tracks.

Sadly, swirling cumulus cloudbanks denied us the airy summit views, but one could sense an encouraging dryness in the wind which

(*right*) Pioneers on the Crowberry Tower of the Buachaille Etive Mor (*SMC Collection*)

at times produced unsettling gusts. Yet its force was feeble compared to the gales witnessed 60 miles away in the eastern Grampians on the same day, which reduced several Hogmanay revellers to crawling on the plateaux above Glen Clova, and this was before the festivities had even begun!

Other parties were also out on the Buachaille, kindling their thirsts for the evening's celebrations, full of cheery bonhomie and salutations. As one of Scotland's most popular winter mountains, it can become overcrowded later in the season when a good cover of ice has developed. Classic climbs like Crowberry Gully, where Bill Murray and his friends made their bold and lonely forays in the thirties, may now see half-a-dozen parties kicking and whacking their way up on a mid-February day, with as many dissuaded by the falling ice and equipment. Guided groups of which I have been a leader on several occasions are perhaps the main contributors to this thronging of the routes. We instructors often can detract from the enjoyment of individual climbers by our presence en masse in the hills.

The waning of 1984 saw us tucked away back in the depths of Glen Etive, fast asleep long before twelve. Not for us the all-night carousing and dancing by which millions of Scots were welcoming the New Year. Our monastic routine would admit no disturbance, and in any case the clearing skies and a bright half moon were enough to warm our spirits.

The northern arm of Ben Starav (see map on page 28) had long appealed as one of the most direct and continuous ways to the top of any of Scotland's major mountains, and so indeed it proved a 1,050m stairway to heaven, taking a carpet of dry springy heather succeeded by a rocky crest without pause or ponder all the way to the summit cairn. The mountain is a grandly positioned guardian to the head of Loch Etive, radiating a beautifully proportioned ridge structure which today was flecked by the remaining snow patches into dramatic relief. We could have envisaged no finer start to 1985.

The northerly wind on top was bitter and sapping, a mite stronger than yesterday, and extracting every ounce of our available energy, for not only did it retard and deflect us from our course, but it also exerted a severe cooling effect. Technically 'wind-chill' is the process of accelerated evaporation of the body's surface moisture, caused by the continual motion of dry air on the skin. The effect initially increases with velocity to a maximum of $-20°C$ at a wind of 30mph. Its impact reduces the sensed temperature to Arctic levels, and prolonged exposure can dangerously deplete one's heat reserves.

So we were in dire need of our hot drinks and sustenance after the long detour to Beinn nan Aighenan, the day's second Munro. Regaining the main ridge at Glas Bheinn Mhor we pushed on north-eastwards to unravel the heartland of the range. The necessary pace was forthcoming but we were both suffering from stiffening joints. Joy showed a quite unwarranted self-disparagement when she later noted that her knees felt like 'rusty hinges on an old tea-chest!' With the concern that the remaining life of my own battered kneecaps was strictly limited, it was comforting to know that Joy was complaining of the same ailment.

The broad backside of Stob Coir'an Albannaich was a perfect incline of wind-hardened névé snow, giving no clue as to the impressive serried slabs of its northern downfall, which dropped sheer beneath a neat summit plinth. Flanking this drop by an eastwards detour we continued to the 'plum pudding' dome of Meall nan Eun. Beyond lay the twisting barricade of Stob Ghabhar and the northern chain – so this unassuming top wrapped up the Black Mount Munros.

The day's five peaks had pushed us up 2450m (8,000ft) of ascent yet it was now only 2.45pm, and there was plenty of daylight for a leisured amble down the Allt Ceitlein during which my eyes made a more detailed assay of Albannaich's cliffs and ravines. They unfolded sufficient winter climbing potential to amply repay a future visit.

As we turned into the main glen the day's tranquillity was abruptly shattered by the drone of a helicopter. Sure enough its winking light could be spotted hovering just above Starav's summit. The idea of the Glencoe rescue team doing a training exercise on New Year's Day was quite preposterous, so this must be a real accident. The helicopter made several sorties, then dropped and landed by the head of the loch, no doubt to unload the victim. No more than a minute later an ambulance pursued by a stream of cars roared past us on the road, creating the nearest to a traffic jam we had seen since leaving Glasgow. We later learnt that the climber had broken his ankle in a fall on the bouldery final slopes. His rescue had arrived at an opportune moment for the sunset glow was fast fading from the western sky as he was picked up.

Stretching out and sipping tea, it was now the time for a progress appraisal. A change of direction was needed, for our piecemeal campaign had completed the Etive, Orchy and Crianlarich hills – a total of 42 Munros just twelve days into the expedition. Already I had notched up 22,860m (75,000ft) of climbing and walked 150 miles, and if fitness was not exactly burgeoning forth, then the aches and strains most certainly were! Our plan was now to go back south to cover the rolling tops of Breadalbane, a three-hour drive to Glen Lyon before we could rest our weary heads. Only with sadness did we leave the lovely Etive, already thinking with regret of those roads and glens of Argyll that our journey would not traverse again.

4

THE SOUTHERN SWEEP

2–7 January:
Carn Mairg – Ben Lawers – Glens Lyon and Lochay –
Schiehallion – Ben Vorlich

If a long drive in the black of night to an unfamiliar destination is tortuous, trying and even unnerving, then it pays fair compensation when one wakes at dawn to a new enticing world which is unveiled with a swish of the curtain. We had parked incognito on the roadside at Invervar, a hamlet in the middle reaches of Glen Lyon, barely able to decipher the treetops in the murky darkness of our arrival. So with eager eyes the bright scene of morning was absorbed.

Immediately a sylvan beauty was sensed in the tree-clothed strath that is lacking in the unkempt roughs of the western glens we had just departed. Neat copses in squares and strips sheltered solid well-kept farms and manses. Oceans of dead bracken spread up onto the higher grazings, and of wild mountain summits little could be seen. The impression was of a 'parkland', created and preserved by Man in his more tender guise.

We were reminded of The Cheviots, the local hills of our youth. Indeed, the topography hereabouts links this district more closely to the rolling Border counties than the rugged Highlands. A conglomeration of mica-schists, granulites, schistose grits and countless other metamorphosed bands form the hills, which are quite considerable in both girth and height. But forgetting the geological jargon and its infinite shades of classification, all these rocks have the common property that they wear well with age, stoutly resisting the march of time, and slowly rounding off into broad swells and pleasing convexity. They show few wrinkles or ragged edges, and have even survived the ravages of the Ice Ages with barely a scratch.

The Carn Mairg group – our first itinerary in the area – exemplified the scenery, four Munros and a handful of 'tops' all around the 1000m mark, criss-crossed by sheepwalks and derelict fenceposts. They were a fast, simple round on this frost-hardened morning, and a welcome break after the rigours of Etive. The wind had slackened to an endurable tempo, and here lay a dusting of new snow which was absent further west. The Tilt and Shee hills to our north were also freshly whitened, bearing the delicate brushmark of passing cloudbanks which breezed in from the North Sea.

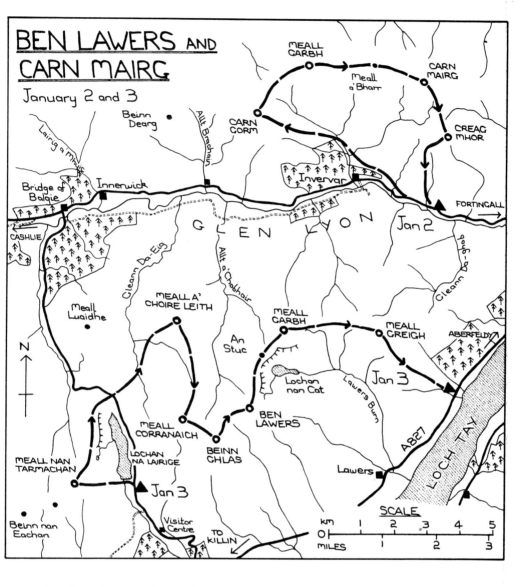

BEN LAWERS AND CARN MAIRG

January 2 and 3

My first ailment of the trip was manifested today by the penetrating cold; not frostbite, nor even frostnip, but a distressing case of chilblains, a condition usually symptomatic of old age and a weak heart, and hardly flattering to an ardent mountaineer supposedly engaged in a heroic exploit. But lanky individuals like myself tend to have poor blood circulation and are therefore prone to such afflictions. Like frostbite you feel nothing when the icy wind is doing its damage. The exquisite pain comes later. That afternoon, with the van radiator belting out a scorching heat, my hands responded by itching and tingling relentlessly for an hour, while purple blisters of chapped skin

49

swelled and cracked. My feet remained unscathed. They were perhaps working too hard to ever think about complaining! But however carefully my fingers were protected with gloves or mittens, this session of mild torture was often repeated in forthcoming evenings.

At 6pm we met Simon Stewart, the first of several supporters who had been arranged to join us at various stages through the winter. Having settled comfortably into a hermit-like lifestyle the idea of company was quite unsettling, especially in this case as we had not met Simon before. His acquaintance was arranged solely on the recommendation that he was a dedicated hill-man, and in the knowledge that he was only seventeen years old. An infusion of youthful energy would do us both a power of good, but there was a worrying doubt whether his experience and stamina would be sufficiently developed to cope with prolonged winter exertion. His father passed him into our care at the Bridge of Lochay Hotel by Killin – a long-haired gangling character, his beanstalk build not dissimilar to my own.

Any doubts over Simon's mountaineering pedigree were dispelled as soon as the ice was broken. After laconically dispensing the initial formalities, he opened up into some extended monologues which centred on three topics only – mountains, climbing and especially Munros! It was hard to believe that he was just eleven summits away from finishing not only the separate Munros but also the 240 additional subsidiary 'Tops' and, for completeness, all the 'deleted' Tops which have been relegated from older volumes of the Tables.

'Just to make sure in case any are resurrected in future editions', was Simon's rationale for this unprecedented mania.

My estimation of him was rising so fast that it was me who was left feeling like the young upstart, weakly clinging to a pathetic tally of eighty Munros before this winter's effort. We drove up to Lochan na Lairige for the night, high in the folded flanks of the Lawers group; at once a team knitted by a mutual respect, and looking to a common objective – the remaining sixteen Munros of the Breadalbane district, for which a maximum of five days was allowed. Simon's already intimate knowledge of the area would help greatly, for coming from Dundee these are some of his nearest hills.

Tomorrow's traverse of the seven Ben Lawers summits would be an ambitious opening gambit to this plan. Fifteen miles and 2,250m

(*right, above*) Ben More and Stob Binnein from the summit cairn of Cruach Ardrain, with the Ben Lawers group framed in the distance (see Chapter 3); (*below*) Joy and Simon Stewart mounting the final slope of Ben Challum looking north-west to Beinn Dorain and Glen Orchy

(7,400ft) of climbing would see us over the highest ground in the Southern Highlands, which is just 5m short of 4,000ft at the Ben itself. Simon promised me a fine, open, high-level walk, with a few surprises along the way.

Coping with three in the van at 6am in the morning promised to be a battle against anarchy, but Simon was effectively stunned to inaction by the proffer of a cup of tea up in his narrow bunk over the driving cab. You could read his thoughts – such unwonted decadence was totally beyond his own hard experience in the hills. He slept fully clothed, without a sleeping bag, presumably in a despairing attempt to simulate the open bivouac he so desired. While he drank, Joy and I self-consciously packed away our pillows and feather-down quilt and got breakfast started.

To be out on the icy road at 7am was a tribute to our powers of communal forbearance. Meall nan Tarmachan was the quickest Munro yet, merely an hour's climb from the lochan dam. Tarmachan at 1,043m crowns the eastern end of a four-peaked ridge which, if followed in full, would provide good winter sport. Of the other three tops Beinn nan Eachan looks sufficiently substantial to deserve a full Munro rating, but unaccountably it was ignored by Sir Hugh and has not since been elevated. His classifications never pretended to be anything other than subjective in basis, and though spared an extra effort it was aesthetically displeasing only to touch the edge of such an attractive group. It seemed that the real kernel of their challenge was being avoided.

This want of fulfilment had already been sensed on the Buachaille Etive Mor where of its trident of tops only the northernmost bears the full Munro stamp. One can while away a few stormbound hours devising a list of suitable candidates ripe for promotion, but as the preface to the current Tables comments: 'if effect were to be given to all the changes proposed the Tables would no longer be "Munros"'. And there are many who are downright indignant that the guardians of the Tables should assume the divine right to make any alterations whatsoever, except on the grounds of resurvey.

However, the crux of our day lay across on the eastern side of the Lairige. Thither marched Simon and I, while Joy descended to the unenviable tasks of laundering and restocking. From the summit of the Lairige at 540m we made, in Simon's words, 'a blistering fifty-

(*left, above*) Martin and Joy leaving Meall Glas with the last Munro, Sgiath Chuil, and success on the Glen Lochay circuit in sight (*S. Stewart*); (*below*) Beinn Eibhinn summit with its western panorama over the Loch Treig hills and the Grey Corries (see Chapter 5)

Simon Stewart on the summit of Beinn Ghlas, Ben Lawers group

minute ascent' of Meall a'Choire Leith, the northerly outpost of the group. Any secret hope I fostered of 'burning off' the youngster on this section were emphatically dashed. The lad raced like a whippet!

The snowfields of Meall Corranaich were tackled more sedately, and debouched onto a slender summit crest that is barely hinted by the map contours. Hereon we were treated to an exhilarating ridge walk, sufficiently narrow and icy to merit our strapping on crampons for the final link from Beinn Ghlas to Lawers.

What a pleasure at last to have good reason for the crampons. Save for that treacherous runnel on the Buachaille, mine had so far served only as a fearsome decoration to the rucksac. Modern mountaineering opinion in Scotland recognises their obligatory use as the crucial hallmark of a true winter ascent. This is a complete reversal of pre-war tradition when nailed boots and alpenstocks sufficed for the most vertiginous passage, and crampons of any sort were ethically taboo. In that era many crampon-clad English climbers hastily left Ben Nevis with their ears burning from the wrath of some outraged doyen of Scottish climbing interests. How times change. Nowadays we all gleefully stamp about in our twelve-pointed foot-fangs even on the nursery slopes. But on testing ground they do ensure speed and safety, both of which were demanded on the crossing of An Stuc, a remarkably craggy top which took us from Lawers to Meall Garbh, the next Munro on the round. The Stuc and its south-east bastions above Lochan nan Cat are one of the few examples of glacial impact in the area, and the corrie formed a magnificent retrospect from Meall Greigh, the seventh and last of the day.

An hour ahead of schedule at 3.30 we met Joy by Loch Tayside. Our final descent was regaled with a mosaic of lush late autumn colours which was perfectly reflected in an unbroken loch surface, a scene which I later noted:

> . . . was impossible to grasp without long pause and meditation. I regret my impetuous haste earlier in the day, and now am disgruntled. In future I must never rush such perfect days.

No change was observed in Simon's demeanour that evening. The Munros repertoire flowed on unceasingly, except when his jaw dropped in silent disbelief as we took our daily bucket wash.

Above the Bavarian splendour of Meggernie Castle and its surrounding estate, Glen Lyon splits two ways into wilder upper reaches, each fork containing a barren, dammed loch. Three isolated and unsung Munros flank the upper glens, each involving a separate ascent from valley level and in no way the 'semi-rest day' by which Simon later classified the outings.

We started from Loch an Daimh on the northern fork with an unenthusiastic plod to Meall Buidhe – its unimaginative name, 'the yellow hillock', being often used to delineate the retiring moorland tracts of the Grampians. Its unresisted admittance of Land-Rover tracks to within a few yards of the summit further persuaded me to a derogatory impression, but rather than demeaning the qualities of the hill I felt greater disgust at the abuse which such tracks are perpetrating on our gentler heights. This was not an isolated reflection, but was raised with depressing regularity during my subsequent wanderings.

Conditions were misty and humid yet quite still, New Year's winds having faded without trace. This weather was as perplexing as it was pleasing, for early January usually sees the worst of winter's fury unleashed in great winds and blizzards. Taking the experience of early 1984 as a model had prepared me for Armageddon. Then we had spent New Year at Ullapool, and I vividly remember watching a factory fishing ship sheltered at the head of Loch Broom, pivoting on its anchor in endless circles throughout a two-day hurricane. Tempestuous conditions persisted without abatement to an unprecedented climax in the blizzard of 21 January in which five lives were claimed on the Northern Cairngorms. Thanks to a polar anticyclone settling over northern Europe, 1985 was producing less a battle for life than a fight against boredom. Only weak fronts trailing up the North Sea threatened to produce a whisper of dissent and no change was forecast.

Stuchd an Lochain bounding the south side of Loch an Daimh raised the day's interest a timely notch for it sports a precipitous northern corrie containing another Lochan nan Cat, which Simon told me is to be included in his list of 'the 100 finest campsites in the Highlands'. Peering into this mist-filled bowl we could see little of its qualifying merits, yet the depths exuded a mystery and charm which is absent on Scotland's countless Meall Buidhes.

With the addition of Joy who had driven round to meet us in the main upper glen at Cashlie we embarked as a threesome towards Meall Ghaordie, the third peak of the day, which fills the middle skyline between Lyon and Lochay and posed us an unvarying slope of 740m. Despite good company and the brief highlights of Stuchd an Lochain I could not shrug off the tedium of the day. Dismal, unchallenging weather, and this untroubled pace; an extra commitment was needed to bring the hills to life:

> Breaking decisively clear of Simon and Joy to avoid any suggestion of a race, I extracted a maximum physical effort and attacked Ghaordie with intensity, pounding feet and heart at full tilt up its bouldery slopes. Quite suddenly the lethargy lifted, and my perceptions were electrified. The scene whirled round my momentary glances – frost-furred heather, ice-caked rocks, a fleeing ptarmigan and the leaden expanse of Loch Lyon away behind. Wild and free I moved with the spirit of the hills, alone and lost in the immensity of Nature's empty theatre.

There can never be an excuse for finding any of this great country boring. The failure is surely of our own making. The climber must respond physically or else seek a little more closely, and far from being shortchanged by the mountains there are many times when we fail to do justice to them, and simply do not give enough of ourselves. Up in an hour, sitting warm and snug in the summit shelter, there was a deep pleasure in having created a valuable experience from the day. However, the others were somewhat perplexed by the sudden hurry, having suffered no comparable urge:

'What on earth got into you? Got a train to catch or something?' they laughed, and made me feel most self-conscious.

The next night's halt in Glen Lochay lay only a mile to our south yet we were bound by our transport to return down Creagan an-t Sluichd to Lyon. But, although tortuous, the daylight drive back to Bridge of Balgie and over the ice-smeared Lairige road enabled our fullest appreciation of one of Scotland's longest and most varied glens.

*

Our day in Glen Lochay aroused special excitement, for there was a chance of achieving the complete circuit of the upper glen, a scheme which was undreamt of in my original routeplans, and which if effected would save a full day on the ninety-day target. The prospect was rendered possible only by the still air and hard snow. Joy wrote:

> We left in the dark at 7am, our spirits hungrily awaiting the clear dawn views which would meet us on the tops; 9,000ft of ascent, five Munros and 21 miles awaited our steps.

The day's tops encompassed the 'Forest of Mamlorn', or King's Forest. It is hard to conceive that these hefty grassy bulwarks were clothed with trees within historical memory. No remnant can now be traced save on the vegetated cliffs where the odd withered rowan still ekes out a living, safe from the predations of sheep and deer.

Joy's prediction of summit views went sadly awry. First light found us lost in dense fog somewhere on the southern shank of Beinn Heasgarnich. Simon's canny route-finding took us to the highest point after many a bemusing undulation, but this mist already threatened to curtail our ambitions. Daylight's few hours would not accommodate complex navigation in addition to the exertions of the itinerary. Trooping down off the west ridge our hearts already were drooping in this knowledge, when as if by magic a great hole was torn in the vapours to reveal the white ramparts of Creag Mhor looking every inch an Alpine 'Nordwand' in its framed isolation. The day was saved, and we hurried on, weaving a satisfying line up those shadowed icy slopes to pop out into blazing sunshine just 10m from the cairn.

Hereon a pattern was established, with myself striding a little ahead lost in introspection. This unceasing effort and especially the thought of the hours, days and months to come required my total concentration, numbing any conversational capacity. Happy chatter and laughter floated forwards in lilting waves, so my silence was more than compensated for by the remainder of the team.

Ben Challum, the figurehead of the upper glen, was the next and most crucial object of the day, but first the transverse top of Cam Chreag had to be crossed, our attempts to contour it falling foul of countless streams of water ice. Then from the pass at the head of Allt Challum came a cruel 400m climb to the top. We were all starting to tire but it was gained on time at 1pm. A tiny wooden cross adorns the cairn, a delicate gesture unique on Scotland's high summits, and a miniature imitation of innumerable such crucifixes and statuettes which mark the peaks throughout the Italian Alps. Especially here, in this far-flung outpost of European civilisation, its discovery provoked a moment of quiet contemplation.

A biting cold enforced a swift resumption, despite the glorious views which the unrolling mists had bequeathed. A 600m drop before gaining the southern side of the watershed called for a stiff mental resistance. How tempting to quit the challenge and slink back down into the glen! Down the chilly snowfields of Challum's north-east spur, across the ice-clogged burn, then up the green and sunbaked south-west flank of Meall Glas. It was 3pm, and ninety minutes of light were left. That last enticing summit, Sgiath Chuil, could just be attained by sunset.

The southern pair are the lowest of the round and lack the class of Challum or Creag Mhor, but they are marvellous viewing stations for the empty quarters of Mamlorn as well as affording majestic prospects of the Lawers assembly and the massive Crianlarich silhouettes. But hardly had Joy and Simon touched the cairn of Meall Glas than they were motioned to continue. How surly and taciturn they must have thought me. Yet there could be no relaxing until that fifth top. Joy's hind view of me possessed a healthy irreverence:

> On the descent of Meall Glas, Martin was seized in an extra flurry of energy, and bolted off ahead like a deer that has scented Man in its nostrils. We followed some way behind, appreciating the frozen ground; none of the peat bogs that I remembered from our previous visit.

Stopping on the bealach, with only 300m to go in the evening gloaming, Simon ambled up in the rear, laid down his sack and ingenuously declared: 'Look, I'll go down and take your loads. You'll be much faster, and anyway I can make a meal for when you return.'

We were momentarily left speechless in the face of this selfless offer; but steadfastly refused to accept. This great day was a team effort to be completed by all. But underlying our refusal there was surely a slight fear of the disastrous recipe Simon might concoct out of our pile of pulses, vegetables and spices, for he had exhibited absolutely no culinary skill during his stay other than for boiling mountainous bowls of porage, whilst his only other dietary preference was for an endless stream of Mars Bars and fruit pastilles!

So with a full moon rising over Lawers, and a pink sunset fringing Ben Lui, we stood atop Sgiath Chuil – a very happy trio, but all on our last legs after much the hardest day of the trip so far. The round should be high on the list of objectives for the ambitious hill-walker. Endless peat groughs by the Lubchurran Burn laboured our final descent, and it was well after darkness when we wearily reached the valley road and tramped the last mile to the public roadend at Kenknock. At least we were assured of a delicious celebratory spaghetti expertly cooked under Joy's safe guidance.

*

The 1,083m cone of Schiehallion was now the only outstanding peak in the Breadalbane area. Its shapely pile has been one of the Scottish Tourist Board's greatest assets. With the foreground of Loch Tummel or Rannoch, here is all the romantic beauty of the Highlands captured in a single view, which though somewhat hackneyed nowadays is nevertheless an inspiring prospect. It is a mountain that people approach with the greatest of ardour yet rarely climb more than once, for its unrelieved scree and heather slopes have little intrinsic interest that would beckon a return visit.

The peak presented a relatively short interruption to a day of rest and recuperation, but the chance of a lie in bed was passed, our mental alarm clocks throwing us wide awake at the normal hour of 6am. At Killin it was lightly snowing. One of the North Sea fronts had breached the Highlands, and we were to be denied all impression of Schiehallion's famous symmetry by dense milky cloud.

By 11am we had roused sufficient energy to drive round by Fortingall to the Braes of Foss carpark and commence the climb. Here was a typical example of Forestry Commission 'recreational management' – neat parking lots, waymarked nature trails, and the marching columns of pines – all very attractive in isolation, but tedious in its proliferation throughout the British uplands. The scenic diversity, so prized and vaunted as an unmatched quality of our small islands, could easily be reduced to a dreary monotone.

Above the trees a maze of peaty tracks desecrated the lower slopes. Without a lofty summit to behold, our eyes inevitably focused on this pointless spoilation. Man's lust to wander at his individual will often frustrates the most worthy attempts at environmental control. Schiehallion is clearly a very popular hill, and it is sad that its distant inspiration is not fulfilled on detailed acquaintance. The paths coalesced on the long east shoulder, where a strong gale bent us over like the newly-planted saplings in the woods below. The ascent seemed untowardly hard, for we all carried mental hangovers from our exertions in Mamlorn, and were pleased to have the job done inside three hours.

Driving down to Crieff in the afternoon we touched the edge of the richer rural garden of the Central Lowlands. The lush grazings, fattening livestock, deciduous copses, mown lawns and scattered golf links all struck an unsettling contrast to the snowy heights just quitted. This would be our last contact with lowland scenery for some time, but its lazy Sunday atmosphere was no attraction for us to stay.

Simon's time with us was now over, and his parents were already waiting in the town centre to collect him, bursting with pride and affection while Simon shrunk in embarrassment. His dour persona is but a weak disguise to a boundless love of the mountains, a warmth of spirit and a lack of ego that is unusual in someone so young. A couple of months later we read with pleasure but no surprise of his completion of the Munros and Tops – Blaven on Skye was his final peak. Two months before his eighteenth birthday he thus became the youngest Munroist to have completed the peaks without adult support, three months ahead of Andrew Nisbet who had been the existing holder of this juvenile crown since 1972*. His company had been an inspiration, as well as a sometimes painful mirror to our adult affectations. So, feeling just a little bereft, we turned the wheel back into the hills, to Glen Lednock above Comrie. Our Breadalbane plot had borne full fruit, and only three summits remained of the southern sweep.

There was an unholy row on Ben Chonzie at 8am the next morning – a din of bickering voices which even woke the sheep and sent them scurrying off into the dank mist.

'You're just an elitist; always preaching to people', came Joy's yell from the rear.

'What's wrong with beliefs?' I roared back, and stalked onwards.

A minute later came the despairing female scream, 'Wait for me; if you don't stop, I'll . . .!'

Some faintly tendentious remark I had forwarded about the environmental dangers of new ski development had goaded Joy into stubborn defence, for she loves downhill skiing and views it as a wonderful family pastime. And as our tempers frayed we swopped a crescendo of insults, until I was reminded of Robert Louis Stevenson's perceptive observation that: 'to live out of doors with the woman a man loves is a fellowship more quiet even than solitude.'

Chonzie was but a passive spectator to this display of marital discord. The clouded tussocky climb up from Invergeldie held no great appeal, but the hill carries an aura of timeless peace, which should have been respected. It is the only Munro in the upland country between Loch Tay and Strathearn, a barren plateau of rough grazings, which is dissected by glens of great charm, and crossed by a series of old droving paths.

Our fracas quickly subsided once we were back within earshot of the farm, but it had given immediate relief. Freed from the confines of etiquette in Simon's company, we could blow some steam off the conflicting pressures and strains which each of us felt. Soon we were laughing again, and the contest was quickly forgotten under the urgencies of the moment, for I was due back at Comrie by 10am to

---

*Simon Dale at fourteen years is the all-time youngest, if Hamish Brown's dogs can be excluded from the count! However, his climbs, which were completed in 1982, were done under parental supervision.

give a live telephone interview for a Tyneside radio station. After more than a fortnight this was the first reminder that we were embarked on a public enterprise.

With only minutes to spare we found a vacant call-box . . .

'Tell us, Martin; what's it like up there in the frozen North?' asked the interviewer.

Looking out of the sun-glinted kiosk panes at the Monday morning scene in Comrie – delivery vans unloading, housewives shopping and old ladies gossiping – I could easily have shattered his vision of the snow-bound wastes, but cheekily chose to foster the deception.

'Pretty rough', I replied, as a ten-ton lorry rumbled by. 'We've got severe conditions here – fresh snow, a biting cold wind and deep frost!'

'Thank you and good luck, *Mr Munro!*' he concluded.

After that little farce it was a pleasure to get back to the tangible world and tackle the broad bulk of Ben Vorlich, starting from Ardvorlich on the south side of Loch Earn. With its craggy partner, Stuc a'Chroin, Vorlich is the first rugged mountain outline to arrest the eyes on the approach from Stirling to Callander, the pair forming a north-east continuation of the Trossachs country.

However, Joy was profoundly depressed by yet another 'heads down' climb:

> Glen Vorlich was so beautiful that I wanted to tarry awhile and meditate on the splendour that the mountains offer. But no; each Munro seemed to be a target to be conquered in the fastest time possible. Martin's intensive mood is getting on top of me, but I guess he knows that his goal requires total concentration. It was a relief for me to turn back from Vorlich's summit whilst Martin made for Stuc a'Chroin. As the tenseness unwound on a leisurely descent, my animosity towards him disappeared and I felt my spirits uplifted; so it was a smiling Joy and a hot drink that greeted his return at 3pm.

By contrast I viewed the climb as:

> a great romp – hard, dry, direct and airy with the summit trig visible all the way – no false tops on Vorlich!

Stuc a'Chroin then provided an icy and intricate scramble through its north-eastern ramparts. Morning mists had cleared but valley fog still clothed the broad Forth valley. Only the rocky neck of Stirling pierced the blanket. And lo and behold, down to the south-west there were the razor-edges of Arran's peaks poking up in the gap of the Clyde. Central Scotland was mapped at my feet and resting easy under a docile mass of rippled cloud. With a neat contour under Vorlich and a heathery descent of Coire Buidhe I was soon trotting back to Ardvorlich. Sections One and Two of the Tables were now complete, and we could joyously turn a page and sense real progress.

5

INTO WILDER DOMAINS

8–13 January:
Glencoe – Glenfinnan – Ben Alder Forest

The Buachaille Etive Beag resembles an upturned clipper's keel, sandwiched between and truncated by the Lairig Eilde and Lairig Gartain – a mountain shunned by the majority in favour of Glencoe's more famous peaks. Yet transported to the English Lakes or Snowdonia, it would be idolised as an upthrust of unparalleled grandeur. Such are the quality and extent of the Highlands that even great peaks are often forgotten.

Lacking a convenient connecting ridge to any other summit, the Beag had to be tacked awkwardly onto the Bidean nam Bian to effect my morning's scheme of completing the southern side of the glen. The Aonach Eagach would follow after lunch. Vaulting ambition was galloping ahead of my good reason. Not content to have compressed my schedule by one full day in Glen Lochay, I now greedily aimed to devour another.

With cocksure enthusiasm I marched off at 6.40am into the moon-shadowed depths of Lairig Eilde, and immediately lost the track. Instinctive navigation struck a diagonal line up towards Stob Dubh, the mountain's southern and higher top, but my intuition served me ill. Ice-filled gullies tumbled down the flanks, barring progress and enforcing a series of slippery detours to gain the miniature coire that is cradled under the summit shoulder. Up here, the fines of the screes weirdly crunched and collapsed under my step. A perplexed examination revealed dense spillikins of ice needles raising the pebbles several inches into suspension – the remarkable result of prolonged frost expansion of the ground moisture.

As I hoisted myself onto the lofty summit perch an equally strange and macabre view met my gaze. Rising dawn dyed the boiling mass of westward cloud a lurid mauve. The Bidean formed a sheet-white shroud beneath, whilst a bright full moon above kept guard over this witch's brew of colour, which surely heralded a calamitous storm.

However, only a wet cloak of mist transpired, and it enveloped the climb to Bidean without a single breath of breeze. The spidery tentacles of Glencoe's crowning peak give some of Britain's best ridge-walking. The route over Stob Coire Sgreamhach passed the rocky

prow of the Sron na Lairig – a first-rate winter scramble in itself –
then encircled the clefted head-wall of the fabled Lost Valley before
ending abruptly on Bidean's tiny top. But today the climb took the
wind out of my sails:

> Due back in the glen by 11am I was forced to hurry, but the sticky
> humidity slowly suffocated my energy and stifled the composed determina-
> tion with which I had set out. I slumped down on the summit lathered in
> sweat, salopettes torn, and both toes of my gaiters unstuck and flopping
> uselessly off the boots.

With a mask of overnight powder snow obscuring the iced track the
descent served only to weaken my resolve. First, a narrow nape of
rocks lured me off-route leftwards until I was teetering on the brink of
the Diamond Buttress. Later, dropping off the north-east ridge into
the Lost Valley, a hidden ice patch upended me with such violence
that my head ricocheted perilously close to its brick-like surface. And
finally, the mass of jumbled boulders which blocks the mouth of the
valley triggered many a bone-jarring slither.

Half-an-hour late, wet and enfeebled I reached the van. Alan
Thomson was already waiting. Alan is a freelance journalist, resident
in Glencoe for ten years, a climber of considerable experience and a
member of the local rescue squad. Naturally he was taking a close
interest in my travels. His chirpy chatter over coffee cheered my
spirits, but he professed a cautious scepticism about my chances of
success.

'Things are going well for you now, Martin', he would say. 'But it's
certain to come in the next two weeks. In last year's storms the rescue
lads spent three days just digging cars out of the road in the glen,
never mind tackling the mountains!'

Perhaps he saw a ripe potential looming for an epic melodrama
with me as the missing victim and Joy as his 'femme fatale'!

The mist and drizzle precluded our planned photographic session
on the Aonach Eagach that afternoon. Its postponement offered me
the desired excuse to terminate the day. Bidean had effectively
squashed all zest. We drove on to Fort William, and new intriguing
mountain domains opened on all sides. But first the mundane task of
laundering had to be attended to. Caol's 'washerama' must surely be
Scotland's slowest, and delayed our exploits by nearly two hours,
sufficient time to shrink my salopettes to an alarming tightness.

A fifteen-minute drive whisked us away from the looping streets,
drab housing and smoking mill of Corpach and into a fiery mountain
sunset at Kinlocheil, a transition of worlds that was barely compre-
hensible in its immediacy. We were treating ourselves to a brief
preview of the West Highland challenges that were to be our succour

in the months to come, although the three Munros to the north of Glenfinnan posed such an arduous tour that one would wonder whether we were seeking reward or penance. I would be glad of my afternoon's rest come tomorrow night.

Gulvain it seems is *not* Scotland's best-loved mountain. Even the Gaelic forefathers must have turned up their noses, for its likely derivation 'Gaor Bheinn' means 'hill of filth or faeces'. My district guide drily notes it as 'a somewhat uninteresting mountain', whilst Hamish Brown failed to offer a single word of flattery as his account of his 1974 walk passed this way. My friend Chris Dodd was more to the point. He climbed the hill on a six-day round of twenty-four of the Section 10 Munros in 1983 and libelled it thus: 'The slopes are endless; definitely the most depressing mountain in this area.'

Yet no hill should be damned before being sampled, and indeed we paid it eager court, for here and northwards to Glen Shiel lay a grandiose mountain realm, which we were penetrating for our first time.

Black ice flowed in streams of treacle down the track from Wauchan, making the night approach up Gleann Fionnlighe a trial of patience and nerves. Passing the farm buildings gave us a second waking, as if the 5.30 alarm hadn't been enough:

> Glancing beyond my torchbeam I was suddenly confronted by a ghoulish white wraith, its two eyes gleaming like gemstones. I started back in panic, fully convinced that I was encountering some sort of spectre. Only when I dared a second look did I discern a docile farm horse turning and trotting off.

The dawn which found us toiling up Gulvain's south ridge came as a greater relief than usual after this apparition. Frigid still air, the bone-like ground and a distant haze today gave the mountains an especially empty and soul-less tinge, to which the twin-topped summit ridge formed an airy viewing platform.

Endless waves of jagged ridges stretched to our north, frozen like skeletons in a prehistoric museum. Most prominent was the long Glen Garry spine which could be traced westward from Gairich over its contorted vertebrae to the culminating horn of Sgurr na Ciche. In a one-day traverse this was schemed as my route of entry to the Knoydart peaks beyond, but now, beholding the prospect in its awesome reality, my paper plans promptly crumpled.

After an icy descent hot coffee and sandwiches were well in order to console our spirits. Our route now manoeuvred a northern circuit of the two Streaps which could aptly be renamed 'the steeps' for they are undoubtedly the finest hills in the locality and sadly miss the Munro mark by only 5m. In recompense for their avoidance we faced a tough watershed crossing from Gleann Camgharaidh to Gleann a'Chaorainn, both deeply incised valleys twisting tortuously towards Loch Arkaig. In this outback we were forcibly reminded of the increased commitment of winter travel west of the Great Glen. The security of the Mallaig road here lay fully 8 miles through an untracked pass to our south.

Mounting the crest of Sgurr Thuilm brought the return of reassuring views – the Glenfinnan rail viaduct and the Jacobite monument standing guard to the head of Loch Shiel. Without further detour we could hold the main ridge to our third Munro, Sgurr nan Coireachan, but quite suddenly the going became rugged and broken, rock slabs and dykes outcropping at awkward transverse angles to slow the pace by half – another foretaste of the 'rough bounds' of Knoydart.

The long wedge of Loch Morar stretching out to the sun-dappled sands of Arisaig afforded a majestic view from Coireachan's top. The loch plunges to a maximum depth of 310m, yet is barred access to the sea by a slender neck of solid land at its outlet. What gouging processes could have formed such a trench? At least a 1300m thickness of overlying ice was estimated at the height of glaciation; but why the overdeepening at this particular point? Even the expert glaciologists are still hard pressed to produce a convincing account of fjord origin.

We quickly turned our steps down the side of Sgurr a'Choire Riabhaich as another cold night gathered; but, as is my wont, I would several times pause to peek down slanting gully shafts. How deep, how steep; the lure of the unknown mapping my future life! At the price of a few miles walk-in there is a wealth of winter pioneering still awaited in these hidden corries; nothing on the scale of Nevis, granted, but huge scope for private and more personal experience far from the 'madding' crowds.

A perfectly drained and graded stalker's path cushioned the final drop to the valley at Corryhully, yet was obviously disused. We soon encountered the reason – a brand new forestry road carving a swathing scar into the heart of the hills. Shocked? Oh yes. Outraged? Without doubt . . . yet we still used it to speed our final miles.

The main road was black and deserted. A long wait or a longer walk back to Kinlocheil? We were obliged to wait under the firm orders of our buckling legs. Ten silent minutes ensued, and then a lonely shaft of light broke the western darkness. As the engine droned closer our hearts raced in hope. The blinding beams swung round the last bend. We had brief seconds to make our case, and some grovelling tactics were employed. With theatrical bows and expansive sweeps of our outstretched arms the lorry was implored to an immediate halt.

In magnification of our 20-mile trek the driver was completing a 200-mile nightmare of ice-bound single tracks, his weekly delivery run round the scattered hamlets of Moidart, Sunart and Morven. These little-known mountain tracts to our south form the largest area in the Highlands without a Munro, yet possess sixteen separate peaks above 2,500ft, a rich harvest for the 'Corbett' collector. We tumbled out and back into our van a little after 6pm. Fresh clothes, a wash and a hurried meal and we were driving again, down through Spean Bridge onto the Loch Laggan road. Tomorrow was almost upon us before we could catch a breath of reflection on the events of today. Only the dull throb of fatigue in our legs left a lingering memory of the Glenfinnan heights. And old Gulvain? Well, it's not such a bad mountain after all.

Fersit, 8am – a string of silent cottages spanning the River Treig. It is deep in the raw middle of January; seventy Munros are climbed but a hell of a lot more remain to do, and a colourless dawn reveals the many dim shapes of untrodden peaks. Inside our cocoon of warmth I am slumped forward, arms propped against the breakfast table, bloated, befuddled and hungover. A second potato scone dripping with margarine is unwillingly forced down with a swill of tea. Eight hours of sleep has done little more than scratch the eyelids, and a well of fatigue remains untapped.

Four days' supplies are now to be packed and then shouldered for our first extended bothy trip of the winter through the Ben Alder Forest, the heart of the Central Highlands. Trust the weather, and take our chance though it could so easily snow today. Excited anticipation is absent. Only an instinctive dread preys on my soul that exhaustion is lurking just round the corner. After three weeks of preliminary sparring the pace has stepped up. My real Munros battle is started at last:

> We noticed a covering of fresh snow which yesterday's western hills had escaped and which was thick enough at lower levels to reveal countless imprints of the overnight couches of red deer. The 30lb loads spared us no effort breaking trail onto Stob Coire Sgriodain, and our 10½-mile route to Loch Ossian quite innocently took on an epic quality.

The day's three Munros – Sgriodain, Chno Dearg and Beinn na Lap – form the turning point of 'Ramsay's Round', one of the most taxing mountain tours in the Highlands. Extending a one-day circuit of Glen Nevis originally devised by Philip Tranter in 1964, Charlie Ramsay's jaunt takes in not only the Mamores and Ben Nevis–Grey Corries ridges, but adds the Loch Treig group of hills to give a total of 24 Munros, 58 miles and 8530m (28,000ft) of ascent. The attempt was made over 8–9 July 1978. Charlie crossed these Loch Treig hills in the

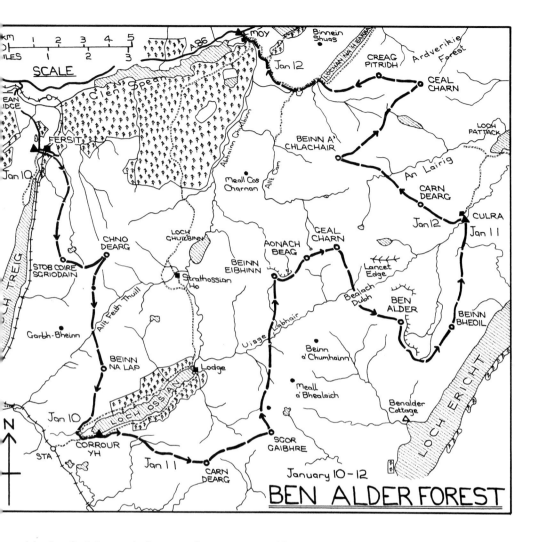

BEN ALDER FOREST

black of night and then made some appalling route-finding errors in mist on the Grey Corries, before flying down Ben Nevis in 30 minutes to arrive at the Youth Hostel starting point just 2 minutes inside the target time of 24 hours. There have been few takers for repeats even among that rare and crazy breed of fell-runners, and Charlie's record still stands. This is the greatest number of Munros that has ever been climbed in a continuous one-day effort.

Knowledge of such a magnificent achievement severely dented our pride as we struggled to complete even the easiest quarter of the round:

We shared the lead over Chno Dearg, then ploughed down into the deep defile of Allt Feith Thuill which isolates Beinn na Lap and presented a major potential impasse. A bar of fudge was requisitioned from tomor-

67

row's rations and divided two ways to avail the 400m climb to the last summit. Slowly and stoically we made the long haul. Had there been a wind to disturb this sullen afternoon it would have bowled us over and back down, so weak did we feel. The sight of Loch Ossian's wooded shores was gratefully received from the summit tumulus, our focus immediately homing onto the tiny Youth Hostel building perched on a headland on the opposite bank, for there lay our promised sanctuary for the night.

One hour later at 4.30pm we were 'knocking' at the front door. The hostel is staffed only during the summer months but we had been assured by the Scottish YHA that it is left unlocked in the winter. Rattling and wrenching at the handle brought not an inch of response:

> I was already reviewing the habitability of the surrounding woodstores and hutches, and composing an enraged letter to the authorities when a soft grinding and a delighted shout came from the rear. Joy had found an entry, and we could escape the repellent gloom without for a wood-panelled interior.

Then to compound our woes the stove refused to work at more than a pitiful hiss. Cartridge and burner were of different makes and refused to marry. Mid-way through our protracted cooking operatings another couple arrived, kindled a roaring wood fire in minutes, then nipped out for a dip in the loch. What vigour and energy! Where on earth was ours? After stealing a seat by their fire for an hour, and plundering some leftover food from the kitchen we slunk off to bed, profoundly concerned how we would cope with Ben Alder itself tomorrow. That cold was getting right to our bones.

Strath Ossian with its loch, lodges, plantings and railway halt is a happy oasis of shelter in a cirque of bare hills. To leave its harbour in the black of night was not easy, especially in the grim recollection of the tragedy of 1951. Five climbers were overtaken by a snowstorm as they attempted to reach Ben Alder Cottage by Loch Ericht from an overnight bivouac at Ossian, almost on the exact line of today's planned route. One by one, four of them yielded to exposure. The fifth member of the party, a girl, survived.

As we traversed Carn Dèarg and Sgor Gaibhre, the two Munros to the south of the loch, any dismal thoughts were dispelled by a sudden clearance of the sky. A light east breeze rolled back the blanket of leaden clouds and a golden dawn flooded the horizons. Blizzards forgotten, this was going to be a marvellous day:

> Immediately my senses perked up, and abandoned reserves of strength returned unannounced. Purgatory changed to enlightenment as an audacious change of plan emerged. Today's route was originally conceived to continue direct over Ben Alder to Culra Bothy, leaving the Aonach Beag

group to the north of the Bealach Dubh for another full day. Now, if from Sgor Gaibhre I crossed the Uisge Labhair and took in the three main Munros on Aonach Beag I could then return across the bealach to capture Alder tonight and make a whole day's saving – a scheme so obvious, yet never considered until that flaming orb rose in the east. Who says that we aren't all sun-worshippers at heart?

Only with Joy's assistance could this possibility be realised. Having dropped the 450m to Uisge Labhair we rearranged the loads, and as I departed for Beinn Eibhinn burdened by little more than a camera and waterproofs, Joy tottered off towards the Bealach Dubh, and thence the bothy, dwarfed by a lop-sided sack crammed to over-flowing with our overnight kits. No wonder she failed to share my sudden inspiration:

> The snow was deep and powdery and within a mile the track petered out leaving me to settle my own route to the top of the pass. The load was doubly cumbersome on the boulder-strewn climb and I resorted to counting my steps to keep up any momentum. I occasionally looked up to see Martin strolling across his next Munro, having a great time no doubt! However my own thoughts centred on reaching the welcome of the bothy . . . a hot cup of tea and a fire . . .

The Bealach Dubh is an important natural thoroughfare linking the Spey Valley to Ossian and then Glen Nevis, and cuts an impressive slice through the centre of the Alder plateau. Surprising then that it has no well-defined walker's path. Stalking tracks abound but none traverses the bealach, for here is a boundary between estates and the tracks of each pursue independent courses up into their respective deer retreats.

The 30-mile trek from Dalwhinnie through to Glen Nevis is one of the Highlands' grandest, crosses no public road, yet is well supplied with bothy shelters en route. It forms the central section of the 'Scottish 4,000ft Munros' tour, often being done during the night to link the daytime ascents of the four main Cairngorms and the Lochaber quartet.

Once reached, the Aonach Beag peaks gave a narrow and exhilarating ridge-walk, their summit snows burnished to a hard windcrust in contrast to the valley powder. Beinn Eibhinn's English appellation, 'the delightful hill', was no.misnomer on this sparkling day. After crossing Joy's staggering line of prints on the bealach a dogged effort took me onto Alder's broad summit where one encounters a perfect piece of Cairngorm-style plateau terrain.

Ben Alder attained, the day was won, leaving me the sunset hour to wearily wander over Beinn Bheoil stopping frequently with the excuse of making identity checks on the surrounding ranges. The sight of the

Breadalbane massifs across the southern end of Ericht jogged my memory to the happy days so recently spent there, whilst the nearby view across the parallel spurs of Alder, Aonach Beag and Beinn a'Chlachair was quite perplexing in its longitudinal regularity.

Even from the top of Bheoil's northern spur a welcoming light was espied in the bothy window, hastening me towards its comfort. Joy had suffered similar delusions a few hours previously:

> Culra at last appeared – but there was no sign of life; no smoke from the chimney. I crept into its dark and musty inside cell. There was no fresh stack of dry branches and peats, only a few green lumps of soaking bogwood. Oh well, I thought, I may as well have that cup of tea. I grasped the blackened kettle to fetch some water only to scream at the sight of a drowned mouse floating inside. Utterly dejected I settled into my sleeping bag for a long wait . . .

Just before 6pm I plunged across the burn and cheerily hailed at the bothy door. To my dismay a scene of Dickensian misery met my gaze within. Rivulets of damp streamed down the walls, a pile of rotten wet wood was belching smoke in the fireplace and huddled beside a single flickering candle was Joy, wrapped in her sleeping bag, only a pallid face and weary eyes poking out, and trying to coax a flame from that damned stove of ours. She looked for all the world like Little Dorrit sitting at her sewing in Bleeding Hearts Yard. Culra is *not* one of Scotland's most luxurious mountain haunts.

By dint of holding the gas canister in an inverted position and shaking it vigorously every ten seconds a big spaghetti was prepared and wolfed down. Then we retreated to the sleeping benches, lying close for warmth, and very quickly dropped into deep dreams.

During our slumber, late into the night, a lone walker had arrived and as he enjoyed a lie-in we secretly commandeered his stove to ensure a quick hot brew before setting out into a hard frost – an underhand action which roused pangs of guilt.

The sight from the doorway of Alder's scalloped flanks, with the pointed Lancet Edge to its right confirmed the real joys of mountain bothying. It held me in awe for a full minute despite the urge to get my numbed toes and fingers moving. For Joy's part, she was visibly brightening in the realisation that my extra stint yesterday meant that a second night in this 'black hole' was obviated. Only the final summit of the Aonach Beag chain, Carn Dearg, needed to be crossed and we were left with the three Munros of the Ardverikie Forest, and a walk out to Moy Lodge, our original schedule for a fourth day.

Crossing An Lairig from Carn Dearg we climbed Beinn a'Chlachair by its steep east spur, a fine mixture of easy rock and ice work which to my delight Joy found truly pleasurable. Up on its frosted summit against the sweeping backdrop of Creag Meagaidh's many corries a quite ridiculous scenario was enacted – husband and wife penning a shopping list with gloved fingers before splitting company:

'Please don't forget a newspaper, and I'll meet you at 3.30', I called as she disappeared towards the distant Laggan road with a hitch-hike to Fersit and a mad dash to Spean Bridge in prospect. Fetching the messages back home in Sheffield was never like this!

The Ardverikie district contains an extensive and imposing range of hills which would have been well suited for skiing had there been an unbroken snow cover. Instead, the route to Geal Charn was a tough plod. Where the snow was deeply drifted it strangely formed a bottomless pit of sugary granules quite without cohesion. The puzzle of 'how?' occupied my attention for several minutes. Perhaps this was a 'depth hoar' formed when persistently low air temperatures create a steep heat gradient through the snow layers. It was, however, plainly obvious that a new fall of snow on top of this unstable mass would produce an unlimited avalanche potential.

Creag Pitridh was the last Munro of the group, merely a craggy eminence on Geal Charn's north-west shoulder and which by universal agreement is an unworthy member of the Tables. Despite the map's indication the summit is too abashed even to sport a cairn, one of only four Munros on which no man-made marker was found in the vicinity of the top.

The walk back to Moy Lodge was untowardly chilling. Once again exhaustion seemed to be catching up on me. But with an uncanny telepathic timing, just as I crossed the bridge onto the main road Joy trundled along in the van, her remarkable speed saving me a frozen wait. In the back was a hoard of fresh groceries which ensured our self-sufficiency for a few days more.

Smooth unquestioning teamwork had seen us through Ben Alder Forest a day ahead of time and without a hitch or pitfall. But Joy's demand that night was: 'When are you going to take a complete rest day? You'll drive yourself into the ground if you're not careful.'

'How can I, as long as the weather stays like this?' I moaned.

The sustained bout of anticyclonic conditions was beginning to produce its own particular stress, namely a morbid fear of when the storms would arrive. In their absence I was risking a physical rundown by ploughing on so relentlessly.

How keenly I had looked forward to straddling the ridgetops of Glencoe in their full winter garb, and how disappointing that my brief days in the glen coincided with the only hiccups in this marvellous weather spell. My rearranged assignment with Alan Thomson on the Aonach Eagach was plagued by the passing of another weak front from the North Sea producing a light snowfall and shifting clouds – conditions which were 'atmospheric' rather than 'photogenic':

> Alan arrived an hour late with the lovely excuse that he thought we would want a long lie-in after our three days on Alder. I darkly suspected a heavy night at the Ballachulish bar! Nevertheless Joy and I were quickly organised for a series of shots in and around the van, and then I set off with him at a fair trot up Am Bodach which is the gateway to the 2 miles of pinnacles and knife-edges that constitute Scotland's most renowned mainland ridge. With a Munro at either end, I was committed to completing its whole.

After a lengthy sequence of pictures on this first peak Alan returned to the road full of hope for the results, leaving me to continue alone, rather disoriented and off my guard. Such prolonged halts on the tops made me impatient and unsettled, especially the repeated stilted poses poised on the brink of the southern chasm which were enough to induce a mild attack of vertigo.

The instant one embarks onward from Am Bodach on the winter traverse true climbing terrain is encountered – an icy chimney, then the 'hogs-back' of The Chancellor which leads onto Meall Dearg, the first Munro, at 951m. Conditions on the ridge can vary enormously. Verglas on the rocks would be the least desirable. Today there was a light layer of fresh loose snow, and though the rocks beneath seemed dry, crampons were strapped on just in case there was any hidden ice. The main aid to route-finding hereabouts is indeed the scratchmarks on the rocks caused by scrattling crampon points.

An innumerable series of pinnacles links Meall Dearg to Sgurr nam Fiannaidh, the higher Munro at the western end. Over or round them? Always a vexing question on a 'gendarmed' crest, and one must be prepared to proceed by patient trial and error, never loath to retreat from blind alleys. Today the process was frustrating to me:

> An experience I should have enjoyed was rather marred by the bad visibility and a jaded mood. Intermittently a window in the mist would open the excitingly precipitous drop to the green floor of the glen, but otherwise I wandered nonchalantly along, head in the clouds, and lacking the precise edge of control that I usually demand of myself when climbing unroped.

Near the end, I passed two lads who were tortuously picking their way along in a series of roped pitches and abseils. Solo climbing is

Looking along the Aonach Eagach ridge from Am Bodach (*A. Thomson*)

certainly faster but should be entertained only by the highly experienced. Better a late finish or even a benightment than a sorry rescue. The Aonach Eagach is a notorious venue for extended epics on account of its inescapability, and bobbing headlamps are often witnessed up on its crest long after darkness during the winter months.

Instead of the direct knee-grinding descent down the right side of the Clachaig Gully, a more subtle line using Fiannaidh's little south-eastern coire gave me a softer landing back on the Glencoe road. The invitation for tea, snacks and, most cherished of all desires, a hot bath, from Alan and his wife Ann was eagerly accepted. Already Alan had the contact sheets from today's films hanging up to dry, displaying an admirable professionalism that made me take proper regard of his solemn auguries of the pending storms.

Yet the forecast remained dry with the easterly airflow still dominant, and my thoughts were irresistibly drawn back to the west, to Glen Garry and Knoydart. Out towards the seaboard there would be minimal hindrance from the drifts which had proved so troublesome on Alder, and the Grampians and Cairngorms could be conveniently left until a heavier snowfall established better scope for skiing. To steal the Knoydart pack while conditions held would so strengthen my hand that three or four stormbound days could be withstood with indifference. But I also knew that these wild hills, of all Scotland's Munros, would not forgive an indiscretion.

We pulled up from a two and a half hour drive at the concrete bastions of Loch Quoich dam. The time for a change of mind had passed. I was committed to go, and nervously wrote:

> Is this a rash move? Twenty miles, 9,000ft tomorrow and the roughest yet, heading alone for a bothy in the middle of nowhere, nine or ten miles from a roadhead, and inevitably arriving in pitch darkness. I fear I'm going to be running on empty. The prospect is alternately mouth-watering and spine-chilling!

6

ROUGH BOUNDS PASSAGE

14–18 January:
Glen Garry – Knoydart – Loch Lochy hills – Loch Quoich group

The 1964 SMC Western Highlands Guide proclaimed that the ridge from Sgurr Mor to Sgurr na Ciche 'must be counted amongst the finest in the country. Not only is it narrow enough in places to provide a genuine mountaineering atmosphere, in hard winter conditions it demands care.' To this we were obliged to add its detached eastern outlier Gairich, 'the hill of roaring', its name a resonant clarion-call to hasten our approach on a dull and oppressive Monday morning, which could otherwise have easily killed the spirit. Up the long east ridge with a stalking path to help until the final rocky neck of the mountain, and out onto the snow-sheathed top – it is a long climb but well repaid by the sight of Loch Quoich slowly unfurling to its farthest reach.

We parted reluctantly. Joy retraced the route down to the dam, and took up a lonely watch for the day, which offered an ample opportunity to inform anxious parents of our movements:

> From Gairich Martin has carried on into Knoydart on his biggest day yet. He is aiming for a bothy tonight, while I wait here by the foot of the loch in case he has to retreat. Tomorrow, on the assumption that he has pushed on to another bothy over his next two Munros, I will drive 15 miles to the head of the sea-loch and hike in 8 miles with extra supplies to meet him when he arrives. Then, weather permitting, we will do the last peak together on the third day, return to the bothy and walk back to the van. I *hope* this gives you some idea of what we are up to!!

How reassuring it is to see your plans in writing. And I hardly think our families would have been much the wiser even had Joy interposed the missing placenames. Sourlies, Meall Buidhe, Luinne Bheinn, Kinloch Hourn, Barrisdale and Ladhar Bheinn is an obscure mouthful to inflict on most lowland Scots never mind my Tyneside brood.

For myself, I swallowed the anguish of the 550m drop from Gairich and marched stoically up onto Sgurr an Fhuarain where the high road to Knoydart truly begins, and where sadly today the mists chose to draw their veil. My pace was steady not frantic, and twice delayed for

On the rodeo crest of Garbh Chioch Mhor with 'the great wall of Knoydart' stretching westwards

nourishment – well judged, gauging from the smooth promenade over Sgurr Mor, Sgurr Beag and An Eag, to quite the mountain by nightfall. But then came Sgurr nan Coireachan, and a rude change of terrain. Simple ridge-trotting with warmly-pocketed hands switched to a melée of contorted outcrops destroying all directional awareness and enforcing many a scrambling detour. As I paused by the iron-speared final cairn the parting clouds briefly revealed the way ahead to Garbh Chioch Mhor. Commencing on the next bealach a black stone wall etched a snaking caterpillar up and over a host of slabs, dykes and towers to be lost finally in the haze somewhere about the summit.

Yet if the distant view was slightly daunting, in no way did it suggest the horrors of actually riding the crest, for it proved to be a real mountaineering rodeo. How a wall could be constructed in such a place confounds me yet. And to what purpose? But it exists as a lasting statue to hard skilled labour and the days when the whims of the landowners could be cheaply indulged, and as a firm companion to over an hour of torment:

My time slipped, slid and then raced away. The drifted snow-banks to either side drove me to the despair of hopping along the top of the wall at many stages. At 4pm I staggered down onto the asylum of the Feadan na Ciche col, the toughest mountain of the trip finally vanquished, though not without a tooth and nail fight.

76

And still the day's crowning peak, the terminal cone of Sgurr na Ciche, remained to climb. Leaving my sack by the wall but taking my headtorch lest night should fall I panted off up. A broad ramp slanting up to the left outwitted the rocky crest and in thirty-four breathless minutes I was back on the col, stealing only the shortest of stops on the top to peer into the clouded recesses of the Knoydart peninsula.

A joyous relief to have the ridge done welled up but was firmly brooked before it overflowed. Celebrations must wait until the tiny house of Sourlies, 900m below, was safely found.

Oh, for a full moon! The last light saw me down the boulder-choked cleft below the col but then all was blackness, without even a star to guide the descent. Steely sheets of ice underlay the bog-grass tussocks lower in the corrie. I would twist and turn around them until encircled, then attempt to skate an escape to the next dry island. From an especially bruising crash I stayed down on my back, flattened and for one painful minute wholly defeated. But as my breathing subsided the awesome silence of this West Highland night embraced my thoughts, softly whispering: 'Why despair? What matter another hour to the hut? Isn't this the land of your dreams? Calm down and keep your faith. It will soon be over!'

Such simple penetrating advice brought me back to my feet, and to a rational and hopeful renewal of effort. And indeed the misery was quickly ended. Tracking left out of the Allt Coire na Ciche and dropping between bare rock slabs, the Glen Dessarry path was met half-way down its serpentine descent from Mam na Cloich Airde. Twenty minutes later my torchlight picked out the squat shape of the bothy. My thoughts were still brimming with self-pity. Imagine then the shock of hearing merry voices babbling from within the walls, breaking the spell of solitude.

'My goodness, there must be some diehards around to want to come here on a January mid-week', I thought. The two inmates must have thought likewise, for they were no climbing vagabonds. Far from it; my night companions were married bank managers investing a precious week of their annual leave to seek a short adventure in the hills. 'Last winter we found the Cairngorms a bit crowded, so thought we'd try somewhere more remote' was their reasoning. Adding my chartered accountancy qualification onto their pile the three of us could have set up a finance bureau on the spot. So the day concluded with timely conviviality. One is never alone in one's madness!

Geographically, Knoydart is not entered until the River Carnach at the head of Loch Nevis is crossed. The aura of magic evoked by the name owes much to its difficulty of access. The occasional ferry from Mallaig to Inverie, a chartered boat from Arnisdale, or the treks from

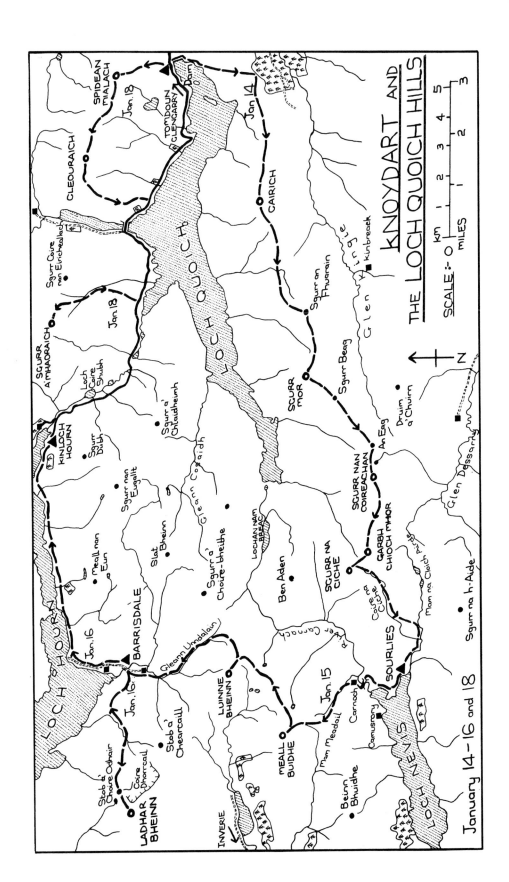

KNOYDART AND THE LOCH QUOICH HILLS

SCALE:-

km 0 1 2 3 4 5

MILES 0 1 2 3

N

January 14–16 and 18

LOCH QUOICH

LOCH HOURN

LOCH NEVIS

SPIDEAN MIALACH
Jan. 18
TOMDOUN CLENGARRY
Jan. 14
CLEOURAICH
GAIRICH
Glen Kingie
Kinbreack
Sgurr Coire nan Eiricheallach
Sgurr a'Mhaoraich
Jan. 18
Loch Coire Shubh
Sgurr Dubh
Sgurr an Fhuarain
Sgurr Beag
SCURR MOR
An Eas
Druim a'Chuirn
Glen Dessary
SCURR NAN COIREACHAN
KINLOCH HOURN
Sgurr a'Chaoidheinh
Gleann Cosaidh
Sgurr nan Eugallt
Sgurr a'Choire-bheithe
GARBH CHIOCH MHOR
Sgurr na h-Aide
Meall nan Eun
Slat Bheinn
Lochan nam Breac
Ben Aden
SCURR NA CICHE
Coire na Ciche
Mam na Cloich' Airde
BARRISDALE
Jan. 16
Jan. 16
Gleann Unndalain
River Carnach
SOURLIES
Stob a'Chearcaill
LUINNE BHEINN
Jan. 15
Carnach
Mam Meadail
Camusrory
Stob a'Choire Odhair
Coire Dhorrcail
MEALL BUIDHE
Beinn Bhuidhe
LADHAR BHEINN
INVERIE

Kinloch Hourn and Dessarry: none is easy, and the overland entries are often plagued by heavy rains. A rain-gauge at the head of Loch Quoich recorded 44in of rainfall in January 1916. What price my chances had I chosen that year for my Munros venture? With the acres of bare rock exposed on the slopes, the direct run-off can approach 95 per cent in heavy storms, swelling dancing burns into raging torrents which can be impassable for many miles upstream.

The Carnach mudflats are especially prone to swamping due to the tidal damming of the sea-loch, and the Sourlies bothy book recounts a host of aquatic epics either in reaching or quitting the peninsula. A new bridge over the river at Carnoch has partly allayed the challenge (or the danger, depending on your viewpoint) of the approach in recent years. Today the idea of being flooded seemed laughable, but sea-level frosts and winter droughts are quite exceptional here by the coast. And although we still shivered a little by the seaboard, the thermal effect of the Gulf Stream was keeping these western margins the warmest part of Europe in a spell that broke new records of frigidity on the Continent.

The seashore ambience burst refreshingly forth onto my senses as I left the hut in a clear dawn. The smell of salt air, and the cry of gulls – here was another of Knoydart's attractions, the incomparable grandeur and variety of maritime mountains. Ciche's tapering cone sailed gracefully above the Carnach glen with the Garbh Chioch Mhor peeping sheepishly from behind. My appreciation of the pair was much improved in retrospect.

But the day's two Munros demanded the fullest attention, and such idle reflections were soon forgotten. On Mam Meadail an easterly wind sprang to life, and a ten-minute halt was required to struggle into 'long-johns'. The decision of whether to don extra underwear at the outset of the day is one which confounds the winter mountaineer. If the prejudgement of conditions is made wrongly (and it usually is) one suffers either heat exhaustion or frostbite, until forced to strip naked and reclothe, which is no picnic on an exiguous ledge or in a bitter gale.

> Ominous cloudbanks appeared with the breeze. Was this the approaching blizzard? Meall Buidhe was a straight and simple haul from the Mam, but gave me sufficient excuse for an early lunch break. My last chocolate and biscuits disappeared with distressingly little effect. From here to Barrisdale there would be no more fuel.

And beyond the twisted 2-mile ridge to Luinne Bheinn lay a sore trial of conscience in the guise of a potential Munro. The OS were up to their tricks again, raising Sgurr a' Choire-bheithe, the peak on the opposite side of Gleann Unndalain, from 913 to 914m in their new

1:25000 edition. This gave it a one in ten chance of being above 3,000ft which is 914.4m to the nearest point. The guardians of the Tables had written off for clarification but received the brusque reply that the OS no longer dealt in decimals, so the matter is left to be clarified by amateur surveyors. My initial intention had been to 'knock it off' just to be sure, but now a host of reasons were found for its exclusion. Strictly one qualifies as a Munroist by completing all summits currently listed in the Tables. More pressingly, at that moment there was a big enough problem getting my carcass over Luinne Bheinn. The logic was indisputable. Original intent was quietly and gratefully ditched.

At least the snow clouds in the east broke rank and removed the fear of a storm, but I had little energy to spare on reaching the triple-topped summit of Luinne Bheinn, and sat down for a good rest and an early matinee of breathtaking views down to Barrisdale Bay and over to Ladhar Bheinn. It was a privilege to be there, the only spectator to Britain's finest and wildest land out of all her 50 million inhabitants.

A daylight descent was pure luxury after the happenings of the previous night. My worry now was not in reaching the bothy at Barrisdale, but how to replenish my famished and depleted resources to cope with Ladhar Bheinn on the morrow. To my eternal debt Joy was there to provide the solution:

> Parking by the tiny jetty at Kinloch Hourn I shouldered a big load of fresh food, fuel and clothing, and embarked on the mule track which wended an undulating route above the lochside. As the loch broadened from its innermost arm, wonderful romantic views opened up, and the two-hour trek was a delight throughout. The last mile lay along by the seaweed and driftwood at the water's edge as I turned into Barrisdale Bay, passing a deserted lodge and disturbing a group of stags who were grazing around the bothy buildings.
>
> As usual I entered with fear and trepidation, shouting 'hello' at the door and feeling stupid when I found it empty. A quick tour of inspection revealed ample potential to make this place 'home' for the night. There was a well-appointed kitchen, a coal heap and bedrooms with fireplaces, plus a 'conscience box' for contributions. I gladly dropped some money in the tin and set about kindling a roaring fire.
>
> Soup was already on the simmer when I spied Martin wandering down from the hills. He arrived looking chilled and dead-beat, his eyes glazed and hat askew, and promptly dived inside . . .

Soup was succeeded by tea, fresh cheese omelette, carrots, garlic potatoes, then creamed rice and fresh fruit. The fire crackled gaily throughout this three-hour feast, our legs stretched in front and bare toes toasting with the heat, while tension unwound and spirits soared. This was the perfect convalescence for the careworn climber.

The bothy is open to use by the public, thanks to the courtesy of the estate keeper. One stupid act of vandalism could ruin this bond of trust and it is to be sincerely hoped that every future habitué respects its wonderful facilities. But the fear of abuse is not unwarranted. Knoydart is certainly becoming popular in the summer months, for which the bothy register evidenced a constant stream of visitors, including a recent foray by Hamish Brown who had arrived by canoe from Arnisdale and then ticked off *all* three Munros on the peninsula in a single day, a feat which would have far eluded me in my present state.

With growing notoriety, the awareness of its unique and unspoilt scenic value has raised the district to the forefront of environmental concern. When the Knoydart Estate was offered for sale in 1982 the Ministry of Defence expressed a close interest in purchasing the area for military training purposes, which would effectively bar all other visitors and curb any further development of its crofting community or indigenous industries. The idea provoked an outcry from conservationists, but early the next year the scheme was quietly shelved without any clear explanation.

However, the main conservation bodies, the Knoydart Foundation and the National Trust, were themselves unable to formulate a co-ordinated plan for its purchase, and the estate eventually fell to a private bid from two Surrey property speculators. The initial ideas of this partnership for holiday homes and camps in the area caused no less suspicion and horror. However, their detailed proposals for 'time-sharing' ownership of parcels of land are in fact couched within close environmental constraints, so for the moment the protection lobbies are breathing easy, and it is certain that exploitative schemes, which might have proceeded unchecked twenty years ago when Knoydart was an untrodden backwater, will never again be countenanced.

As we snuggled down on the floorboards that night there was no sound save for the spitting of the waning fire and the scuttle of the resident mice.

What makes a truly 'great' mountain climb, an ascent that leaves one glowing with an unforgettable excitement? That of Ladhar Bheinn from Barrisdale possesses every required ingredient. There must first exist the mystique of the unknown and the unseen. From the bothy one discerns just enough of the mountain's subsidiary spurs and spires to attract yet not reveal. In particular the turret of Stob a' Chearcaill rears up its head in bold defiance as if to shield a wealth of hidden cliffs. Of course, the approach should quicken the interest as well as display a charm and beauty in its finer detail, and the winding stalker's track up into Coire Dhorrcail fulfils these demands admirably, relinquishing the seashore to be gradually absorbed into high mountain terrain.

Then, and most crucially, the revelation of the crowning peak and the climb to its summit need to be direct and stunning. As the savage array of cliffs and chasms at the head of the corrie meets the forward gaze at a sudden turn in the path the upwards urge becomes truly uncontainable. These mica-schist precipices reach in excess of 300m in vertical height, and in a hard winter have an impressive potential. However, the approach is long and conditions so prone to freakish change that only the patient and dedicated have staked a claim up there. In 1962 the irrepressible Aberdonian pioneer Tom Patey climbed the first significant routes which were not appreciably augmented until 1978 when the visits of Con Higgins, Andy Nisbet and friends raised the standards to grades IV and V.

The top lies on the right of the coire, and is airily gained over the knife-edge arête of Stob a' Choire Odhair. The icy and viciously gusty conditions which we met on the ridge were enough to deter Joy from continuing but provided me with an exhilarating finale. Muffled up in hood, balaclava and double mittens the blast could be faced with impunity, although the flutters of snowflakes racing past brought back an undercurrent of anxiety. And the summit itself? An elegant edge of snow is capped with three neat pikes to ice the cake.

Ladhar Bheinn well deserves such extended praise, but perhaps it commits a despicable sin to put this in print, tearing aside the cloak of

Ladhar Bheinn from across Barrisdale Bay on the trek out to Kinloch Hourn

secrecy which has kept the mountain inviolate. Given ten years we might see its demise under a plethora of cairns and signposts, erosion scars and scree runs. Along with praise the peak deserves respect, and one can only plead with all who go to leave no mark of passage.

By 1.30 we were back at the bothy, and after a hot drink bade goodbye to Barrisdale. Joy relived each step of the walk by Loch Hourn as my animated guide, proudly pointing out each new view and feature as the track unfolded. Yet there was relief in seeing the van on rounding its final turn. The enclosed trough of Kinloch Hourn would so easily have trapped us had the snows come, for the road escapes to Loch Quoich only by a tortuous climb of 200m. And it was doubly comforting to get down to the sheltered woods of Glen Garry where we halted that night, for Knoydart in winter leaves a lonely print in the memory.

Next morning there was smug satisfaction and celebration to see low cloud and a fine drizzle that was surely falling as snow not far above our parking height of 150m. We had beaten the weather, but only just, and several easier options were now at our disposal. Number one in Joy's mind was a rest day for me. My revival at Barrisdale was no more than a short pause in an overall physical decline and the mental strain was now so insistent that sleep was coming only with difficulty.

There was no personal precedent to guide a decision. Twenty-seven days without a break was far beyond my previous experience, but the exploits of others could possibly give some guidance. However much I had admired the Himalayan run of the Crane brothers, their initial tactics were primitive and almost fatal. Setting out in a mood of 'do or die' they piled on the agony for seventeen days of non-stop effort, until ground to exhaustion during a headlong dash from Everest Base Camp to Kathmandu. Demoralised, close to abandoning the attempt, and prey to illness, especially dysentery, they barely made any further advance for the next week, and only by calling upon remarkable powers of recovery were able to complete their triumph at a slightly more modest pace. Their salutary experience was not lost on the staff of Intermediate Technology, and Steve Bonnist often reminded me of the proverb 'slow and steady wins the race', for the 'Summits for Survival' appeal depended totally on my ultimate success.

However, in every accountant there is a tidy mind and an exasperating obsession to balance the books and rule off, so I could not have rested easy until the Garry and Quoich hills were complete. Joy knew when argument was pointless, but vehemently branded me as an incurable 'head banger', before acceding to my day's scheme – a short jaunt from Laggan Locks to the two Munros above Loch Lochy.

We stopped at Invergarry post office en route, eager to see whether Alan Thomson's photos had achieved due acclaim in the national press; but no, our faces did not grace that day's edition, and yesterday's had all been sold or returned. Yet the proprietor surveyed us with a penetrative stare that brought a happy sequel two days later. When we called again by chance for stamps and milk, his wife casually asked us: 'Wis it you in here asking for old newspapers during the week?' and on our confirmation promptly produced the desired cuttings from *The Scotsman* and *Press and Journal*.

'They don't miss a trick these Highlanders', whispered Joy. Yet what thoughtfulness to have sought out the copies on the slim possibility of our return. And of course her disclosure precipitated a lively and prolonged conversation. Once the reserve of the local people was breached, their warmth to us was unlimited.

The 'Lochy hills' are a compact chain of summits but lack the bare ferocity of the peaks further west, and only at two points, Meall na Teanga and Sron a'Choire Ghairbh, reach over 3,000ft. As always we approached by the quickest route possible, tramping along the roads of South Laggan Forest and up the track to Cam Bhealach from where the Munros are immediately accessible.

Indeed it was snowing steadily above 300m, and drifting on the higher slopes, but conditions were severe rather than atrocious, grade 4 on the 1 to 6 scale which I had devised to classify their daily fluctuations through the season. Grade 6 would denote a storm-force blizzard, when I would be best tucked up inside the van.

Our descent passed through a forest patch where industrious felling operations were in full swing. Diesel-powered winches and pulleys assisted the labour but Joy was quick to observe as we passed the drenched group of loggers: 'I only hope they're getting paid well working in conditions like this.'

Yet I wonder on their comments on a pair of volunteers like ourselves. 'Bloody crazy!' I should imagine.

The five-hour round was as much as could be managed today, and it was difficult for me to handle the various tasks during our subsequent visit to Fort William, especially a radio interview for the *Good Evening Scotland* programme, on which for once my weary grunts and groans were quite authentic.

Once familiar, 'the Fort' is a warm and friendly town, and does not deserve the verbal slanging to which it is regularly subjected by tourists who search for Disneyland perfection in their resort. The place makes no pretensions to beauty and it bustles with a life both seemly and unsavoury. Long-term unemployment and the abject resignation of its victims are to be seen as well as happy indulgence and thriving business. It cuts a vivid slice across the state of modern

Britain. The visit was especially welcome following our seclusion out west, but by 8pm we were back in our preferred haunt – the soft woods by Tomdoun.

At 1am I was wide-awake and ferretting about the van like a bothy mouse. A cup of hot chocolate and an hour's reading later I drifted reluctantly back to sleep.

'My body-clock has gone haywire, this will definitely be my last day', I declared over breakfast.

Only the three big hills on the north side of Loch Quoich separated me from that vital rest, but was I capable of making 1980m (6,500ft) and 13 miles in the day?

The weather was bright and breezy at Quoich dam, and bitter and blustery 760m higher on top of Spidean Mialach. The snowstorm had passed on without decisive impact, and still the dry easterlies blew, rushing through the col to Gleouraich at gale force and whisking plumes of powder snow high into the air. They rendered the buffeted crawl to the summit every bit as thrilling as the final steps to a Himalayan giant. Like a yacht caught in a storm I tacked between the southern ridges, trading drifted lee for blasted foreslope, then slid down the grasses to the road where Joy was stationed after a direct descent from the Spidean and a short drive with the van.

Split days on the hill brought a problem which centred squarely on the reclining lunch break. After soup and oatcakes and a couple of crumpets you feel so nicely attuned to the lunchtime radio that even *The Archers* make palatable listening, and the immediate attraction of Sgurr a' Mhaoraich, the third fine peak of the Quoich trilogy, quickly loses its appeal. But towards 2pm we took the van across the bridge which spans the loch's long northern inlet, and made tentative motions back towards the great outdoors. My morning elation evaporated, and feeling like a tin kettle boiled dry I immediately fell into Joy's footsteps, and trailed behind her all the way up Coire nan Eiricheallach and onto the top. It was definitely the time to cry 'enough'! Joy herself was amazed at my dismal abdication of the route-finding role.

Summit vistas, as so often in recent days, were obscured by a light cloud capping. We waited for fifteen minutes with camera shutter poised but not a chink of view emerged. I could tread most of these hills a second time yet see them as new.

Mhaoraich was one of many mountains in the district which bore the fleeing steps of Prince Charlie in the months after Culloden. He sneaked past a line of English sentries at Loch Coire Shubh and escaped to Glen Shiel by Coire Sgoireadail on the western slopes. The prince's game of cat and mouse with the Redcoats has written one of the most romantic episodes in the history of the Western Highlands, and establishes him as a mountaineer of considerable calibre, for he was forced to stay high and live rough for many weeks as he awaited tidings of ships to France.

Emotion rose close to the surface as we drove away from Quoich for the last time to a third night's stay at Tomdoun. Ninety-nine Munros was hardly the most desirable number on which to pause. They had occupied 29 days, a total of 375 miles and ascent of 53,030m (174,000ft). By compressing two days into one on Alder and in Lochay, and skipping a statutory rest day, I was fully three up on schedule. But above all this, there was a humble gratitude for my good fortune just to be there, right in the midst of the struggle.

7

BLIZZARD OVER KINTAIL

19–22 January:
The Cluanie Ridge and The Saddle – The Brothers and Sisters of Kintail

Moving north from Glen Garry the ever-rolling West Highland chain folds dramatically into Glen Shiel, and it is here that the Munros population reaches its greatest density, no less than twenty flanking the Road to the Isles as it snakes its famous path from the Cluanie watershed down the 8-mile glen to Loch Duich. And behind these immediate ridges lies a tempting host of more reclusive peaks.

This array of nearby summits makes the Cluanie Inn an incomparable centre for a mountain walking holiday for it is sited magnificently at their focal point; and the hotel returns the compliment of its location in full measure, exemplifying the traditional warmth and quality of the Highland coaching house, its panelled walls steeped in centuries of travelling history. It was by the inn that we drew up our modern-style coach towards the end of that precious day of rest that all too predictably had disappeared in a flash, and ironically flowered into one of the season's loveliest – tranquil, sunny and laden with dew. So rapid was its passage that I wondered how it could succeed in recouping the strength that was now required to traverse the southern side of the glen. Logically, our route was moving north until the long-awaited blizzards arrived, an event so far postponed that we might yet reach Ben Hope before turning to skis and the eastern hills.

The day proposed not only spanned the Cluanie Ridge but continued over Sgurr na Sgine to The Saddle, and so would complete one of Britain's longest high-level traverses, for this multi-peaked roller-coaster never falls below 650m throughout its 10-mile length. The Cluanie Ridge itself gives seven Munros and an oft walked edge of guileless simplicity quite in contrast to those tortuous crests of Glen Garry. Such a facile solution seems barely plausible to the westward traveller down in the glen who blinks at a kaleidoscope of mountain outlines which change at every turn of the wheel. Yet even with the labour of breaking through a virgin snow cover, the end-to-end crossing from Creag a' Mhaim to Creag nan Damh took us little more than four hours, and though airy never held a hint of danger save perhaps on the rocky descent from Aonach air Chrith, the highest of the chain at 1,021m.

But ploughing on towards The Saddle this wholesome entertainment darkens towards a late-night thriller. Just as the legs are feeling the strain, out crops Sgurr a' Bhac Chaolais, where the ghost of Garbh Chioch Mhor raises its ogreish head in an evil series of dips and bluffs. There is even an imitating wall, and to add insult to injury, at 885m this peak doesn't count.

In quick succession one hits the striated cliffs of Sgurr na Sgine which stand square athwart the ridge. With cheek and effrontery a line of fenceposts attempts a head-on assault on the 130m precipice. This tempted me into headstrong pursuit, when to have stopped to ponder a suitable diversion would have ensured an easier if extended passage. By this stage Joy had thankfully descended to the glen to collect our transport, no little relieved, for her eagle-eye had spotted this bold buttress from afar. Only when the angle rears to vertical does the fence desist its challenge, and it left me to 'enjoy' some grade II mixed climbing; 'mixed' in this instance being a gruesome combination of loose rock ribs, snow-filled grooves, heather tufts and sods of turf. Such an eccentric means of progression is perhaps unique to the Scottish winter ascent, and indeed defines an art of its own, which

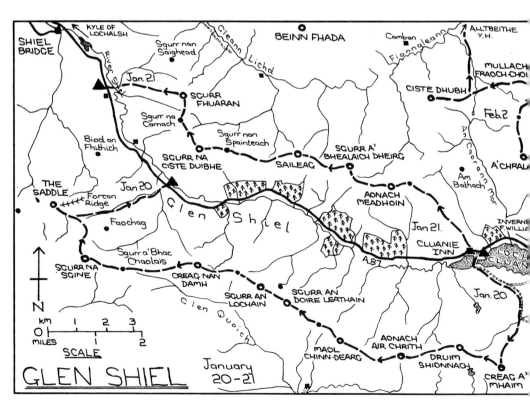

is addictive when sampled, but to the visiting stranger seems madness itself. But the use of the frozen clod should never be decried for it gives the perfect lodgement for the ice-axe pick when all else fails or falls away, and only with such aid did my attempt succeed.

The walker approaching from the west could be abruptly deterred by the downfall, for he will lack all impression of the terrain below, but by trusting to a detour down the southern ridge an impasse can be averted. Alternatively, the north-east ridge offers a reasonable passage of moderate scrambling.

Then finally comes The Saddle, the westernmost and finest peak of the range. Unlike the foregoing chain of summits, it possesses striking independence and is worthy of a thorough winter scrutiny. The horse-shoe traverse of the peak and subsidiaries gives a great day from Shiel Bridge, whilst for the climber there is the prickly Forcan Ridge where a predominance of solid rock over rotting vegetation can be guaranteed for those who would shudder at my route on Sgurr na Sgine. Just south of the Forcan arête are easier slopes which give a speedy passage to the top, and then by reversing steps to the Bealach Coire Mhalagain a direct but knee-shaking descent to Glen Shiel can be effected.

Nine Munros, the three-figure milestone duly attained and a measure of recovery conclusively proven; at 19 miles and 2800m (9,200ft) the South Shiel traverse is no mean winter's day. Surely now with the hundred up, the credibility of this venture was established beyond all doubt. These were rich laurels on which to pass the night back at Cluanie Inn but the weather portents motioned caution. A dark pall of cloud gathering in the east and the withering wind of late afternoon were menacing omens that could not be ignored.

'Here is the 6am shipping forecast for 24 hours to Tuesday. General synopsis: complex low, 974, Shannon, expected N. Ireland 963 midnight . . . Rockall, Malin: easterly backing northerly, 6 to gale 8, occasionally severe gale 9 . . .'

Take a deep breath and switch to the regional detail:

'. . .in Grampian and Highland snow will soon spread to all parts, and it will struggle to get above 1 or 2 degrees. Under a strengthening easterly gale conditions could be *difficult* in the mountains . . .'

Snuggle under the bed quilt and let it sink in. If he says 'difficult' it usually means 'desperate'. The moaning wind and gently creaking joints of the van were certainly not disputing his presage. Those days and weeks of tense expectation were finally over. After smothering the whole of southern Britain with frost and snow, the storms had found their way north to their true home and would doubtless strike with redoubled force.

But my first response was neither panic nor dismay. Instead, a lie in bed was savoured, stretching aching legs and taking a long draught of morning tea. Still wallowing groggily in the satisfaction of yesterday's marathon, I had little immediate urge to greet the rising tempest, and yet, how could I justify a second day of rest in three? Joy was non-committal, and sensibly left me to wrestle with my own conscience. It was a case of pitting zeal against sloth and seeing which side would win; but today the odds were surely loaded in favour of staying put. For more than an hour an air of unruffled calm was displayed, but then the inner qualms began to surface, niggling and eventually gnawing relentlessly at my inertia so as to compel a decision. That obligation could never be ducked however much I tried.

From Cluanie Inn there was the pick of any of the eleven Munros on the north side of the glen. They fall into two convenient sets of five, the Conbhairean–A'Chralaig group and the more famous Brothers and Sisters ridge, with the isolated Ciste Dhubh placed awkwardly in between to be tacked on to one or the other. I opted for fraternal friendship, having previously traversed the Brothers of Kintail, and additionally hoped that the east wind would blow me speedily along its westwards switchback. If I was coping with the storm, a continuation could be made over the Sisters to complete the day's schedule.

A quick look out into the opalescent light of morning dispelled any lingering doubts that I shouldn't be going at all. After all it wasn't actually snowing, at least not yet! Soon after 8am I left the van swopping civilised living for raw survival in a dozen paces. Such a sharp transition was hard to accept, and only by getting my head down for the initial 620m climb onto Aonach Meadhoin was I able to shut out the inevitable temptation to return to comfort. Joy was briefed to post the van at various points down Glen Shiel during the day to coincide with the alternative outcomes of retreat, escape or eventual victory.

Up on top I was warming to the day's challenge, when a strafing gust of wind caught me teetering cramponless on the icy arête of the Aonach. Total commitment and nothing less would suffice today. Following traces of the narrow track wherever visible I crossed onto Sgurr a'Bhealaich Dheirg, picking my way out along the rocky northern crest to gain its finely perched cairn. Recognition of familiar features recalled our recent summer traverse to mind – a warm breezy afternoon, the two of us trotting along the grassy summit crests with the green straths of Affric and Shiel sweeping away beneath, their twisting rivers shining like threads of silver in the sunlight; a day completed with a pot of tea at Cluanie Inn, rewarding our toils as it quenched our thirsts.

Now the snowfall began, hardly distinguishable in the milky cloud at first but soon noticeable in the rapid accumulation of surface drifts. Saileag completed the three Brothers; not a bad morning's work in a gathering storm. A stop was made on the following bealach to ponder the situation.

The road in Glen Shiel lay only 600m and half an hour below. Up here, sitting in a slight lee-hollow, the drifting snow half-buried me in the time it took to eat a bar of fudge and drain my flask. With the wind blowing hard and visibility dropping below 50m, conditions were quickly deteriorating even during those few minutes of rest. Meanwhile, Joy was stationed down on that road, and having a few adventures of her own:

> At 10.30 Martin had not returned, so I drove lower down the glen finding a lay-by sheltered by the plantings beneath his main escape route. The snow started soon after, and thickened by the minute. I settled myself to a variety of tasks but my glance was frequently drawn to the visibly worsening scene outside. Cars were still flashing past, apparently unconcerned that the road was already carpeted white, and it was just as I was thinking on their blind indifference to the snow that I saw an Escort leave its tracks fully 200m away and come hurtling towards the van, spinning from side to side. In a second I leapt outside and onto the embankment hoping to escape disaster, but only yards away it left the road, and somersaulted before coming to rest on the verge. A young male driver and two passengers emerged, stunned and shaken, so I ushered them into the van, proffering hot drinks to help them recover their senses. Surprisingly their car was drivable although battered, and they restarted their journey at rather more prudent speed. After that my attention was riveted to the road. Yet at the same time I wondered how on earth Martin was coping on the summits if things were as bad as this down here!

On a stormbound mountain decisions preferably should be made then followed through with clear conviction. The Five Sisters ridge now stretched ahead of me. Despite its popular name the climber will be perplexed to find that the ridge has six summits, but only two are Munros. Two of the extra tops have to be crossed to claim the pair. Then from the second and highest Munro, Sgurr Fhuaran, there lies a safe and direct descent to Shiel Bridge. If retreat was sounded now, the Sisters would occupy the better part of a later day, a worrying addition to the schedule. Believing myself to be physically fresh and having four hours of daylight to play with, I acted decisively and continued. But underlying these bare bones of logic was a strange curiosity to follow the progress of the storm, an intrigue to see how the drifts, cornices and wind flutings would be sculpted, to inspect the processes at work rather than returning only in fine weather when the snowscaping was complete.

But however convincing the decision it was with rather less than complete conviction that it was pursued. Once again I was strangled by my own ambition. The snow piled up with surprising rapidity. The undulations of Sgurr nan Spainteach, the first top, must give a delectable summer's ramble but now its crest was fluted into a razor-edged drift which was quite invisible in the prevailing maelstrom. Staggering and ploughing from side to side without any semblance of balance, I consumed a precious two hours and a vital slice of energy. The 'peak of the Spaniards' came near to cracking my will.

After this, the simple climb to Sgurr na Ciste Duibhe, the first Munro, was much appreciated but then came Sgurr na Carnach, the second unavoidable connecting top. Its 150m boulder-strewn slope posed a big pyschological obstacle, height gained with such strenuous flailing effort only to be sacrificed in full on the far side. Suddenly beset by an overwhelming fatigue, my progress wilted under the sensations of deadly chill and damp. Hypothermia was waiting to strike if I couldn't get over Fhuaran.

The final craggy slope was masked by a ½m layer of new powder. In places it looked thick enough already to pose an avalanche threat. I thrashed and groped up to the final cairn, and did the usual tour of the surrounding knolls to fix it as the highest point, a frustrating occupation with time so critical. Returning to the cairn I observed the second ritual of thrusting a brochure under its snow-caked rocks in the fullest confidence that this one would not be discovered for a long while; but amazingly Rory Dutton of Aberdeen plucked it out and returned it less than a fortnight later.

There remained a headlong plunge into Glen Shiel on a bearing that had to be true, for already the light was fading. My reserves were low, and a single skin bivouac bag would hardly provide a recuperative shelter in these vile conditions. On the slithering descent the dry powder pellets turned to heavy wet flakes as the air warmed with loss of height. Though the compass looked correct, success was not certain until emerging beneath the cloudbase at 250m I happily perceived the main road snaking along the valley bottom. Escape seemed assured, but the day's diary of events was not yet complete:

> I approached the River Shiel, first surprising a large herd of deer, and then being mobbed by nigh on 200 Cheviot sheep, all expecting a feed I suppose. With this escort of 400 luminous eyes I searched vainly for the bridge marked on the map. The more welcoming lights of the van mocked at me from the far side. After ten minutes pacing the riverbanks I was forced to the reluctant conclusion that it didn't exist. Near to tears with frustration and exhaustion I pulled off boots and socks, rolled up salopettes and waded into the inky black waters, the blizzard still raging overhead. Two hungry farm horses then chased me the last 200m to the road, but that at least warmed me up a bit.

Joy was understandably puzzled by my delayed arrival:

> Sitting at our rendezvous I saw his torchlight not more than a quarter of a mile away, but was at a loss to understand the delay of forty minutes before he staggered in, looking like a stray dog, and quite obviously choked with emotion. No doubt; this had been a hard day.

Unfortunately my emotions soon spilled over, but into sudden temper rather than tears. For a couple of minutes I could not articulate a single phrase. Then Joy dared to venture a comment, not perhaps well chosen at *that* particular moment, but made with the best intent:

'There's plenty of water at hand if you'd like a good wash down.'

'That's the last bloody thing I need', I retorted, and sank into silent brooding.

It took a pot of tea and a good half-hour to unwind sufficiently to apologise for this indecent outburst, and to realise that today was the greatest victory of the winter so far – five Munros stolen from the fury of its worst storm, a cause for celebration rather than anger. Just thirty-two days and already 113 summits. It seemed unbelievable.

We passed the night cosy and secure at Shiel Bridge, awaking to a long list of road closures and another grim weather forecast. Quite happily the day was abandoned to travelling and in the event this proved sufficiently problematic. With the arrival of deep snows our game in the West Highlands was now up, and it seemed the right time to get over to the Cairngorms, and strap on the skis.

Though a mixture of rain and sleet was falling by Loch Duich, it quickly turned to heavy snow as we crawled up to the Cluanie Inn. Joy was especially mindful of yesterday's drama and drove with patient care, berating those oncoming drivers who sped along the hard-packed snow at something approaching 40mph. The inn itself was besieged by a convoy of vans and lorries, their drivers anxiously querying the conditions, or else reporting their own adventures. The landlord supervised operations with great enthusiasm. He must rarely see such custom outside the tourist season. Many of the truckers were glad to abandon their journeys and return home to Inverness or Fort William, while others rather fancied the idea of a few days marooned on Skye at their firm's expense.

We stopped to fix our new snow chains, showing off our superior preparedness for the conditions to the group of spectators by the inn, at least until I realised they didn't fit our wheel size. Disentangling the mass of hoops and links, we crawled out from beneath the chassis caked in snow and with reddened faces to continue the drive in more subdued mood. The crossing to Invermoriston was marginal. We were lucky to get out at all and if anything the roads worsened as we approached Inverness.

No sooner had we entered the 'capital of the Highlands' than it was declared by the RAC to be completely blocked on all sides. We drove a few miles down the main A9 towards Aviemore to discover the truth of this broadcast, but it was not a groundless warning. More than 10 miles short of Slochd Summit the police turned us back, and it was plain to see that the drifts were hopelessly deep. By underestimating the greater severity of the blizzards on the east side of the country the change of plan had badly misfired. Trapped in Inverness with not a single Munro within 20 miles – what a predicament! Chain-stores, supermarkets, fresh fish, limitless Calor gas supplies, and even a rapid-cycle launderette – none of them offered much solace. Indeed, it seemed an embarrassing irony that our mountaineering expedition had ground to a halt in the middle of a city.

8

SKIING FOR SURVIVAL

23–27 January:
Ben Wyvis – Fionn Bheinn – Monadh Liath – Creag Meagaidh

The whaleback bulk of Ben Wyvis floats proudly on the northern horizon above the fertile plains of Strathconon, a noble skyline featuring in many Highland panoramas. As a mountain, though, it lacks exceptional qualities and has merited scant attention other than from those groups who have at various times proposed its development as a downhill skiing resort, or mooted the construction of a rack railway to the summit. It was designated an 'easy half-day' in my winter route-plans, an 8-mile round trip from Garbat to provide a light respite from the greater challenges of the north-west.

But now Wyvis quite innocently acquired a role that was crucial to our further progress. Twenty-third of January dawned sharp and frosty, the lights of Inverness twinkling brightly across the Moray Firth from our parking spot at North Kessock. The snow-bearing depression had winged away towards Scandinavia to be replaced by a strong north-west airflow, fresh and bitingly cold but moistened by the North Atlantic and therefore dangerously turbulent. On seeing clear skies I was anxious to move, for if a second day was lost my hard-won advantage would be all but swallowed up. But with a maddening obstinacy the roads remained emphatically blocked. The strengthening wind was obviously drifting the snow mercilessly, scorning all efforts at clearance.

However, there was a corridor of escape. The A835 was open up to Garve, and above Garve lay Wyvis. We made no delay, and were ready to go at 7.30, but then the van refused to start failing us for the first time. We were now meeting enough hurdles to turn the venture into a giant steeplechase! I methodically cleaned and sprayed the points and plugs and with bated breath tried the ignition again. To our delight the engine fired – pure magic to a mechanical misfit like myself.

Up in the hills fresh snow lay in aerated suspension to a depth of ½m. The drive was slow and cautious. Ours was clearly one of the first vehicles to penetrate the route beyond Garve, which anyway was broadcast as blocked a few miles further at Aultguish. Listening to the radio reports such as '12,000 Highland consumers without electricity for the second night' and 'Helicopter dash to hospital for snow-trapped mother-to-be', was it being just a little imprudent wilfully dashing off into the mountains? But surely Wyvis would not offer any serious resistance. Anyway, we were both dying to try our new cross-country skiing kits.

The farmer at Garbat looked askance as we marched purposefully past his gate thrusting skis and sticks forward with military precision. He was most concerned over when the council's snowplough would arrive to clear his driveway, and he must have doubted our sanity on hearing my confident declaration that with skis Ben Wyvis would be no problem. But perhaps he had one eye on the black squall clouds sailing down from the north-west.

Joy noted the lighthearted tone of our approach to the mountain:

> Today the prospect of a new mode of travel using a different set of muscles was very appealing. The forest trees were stilled by their heavy mantles of snow, and absolute silence prevailed apart from our own panting as we pushed our tracks over the virgin ground. Soon we were forced to strip off, so tough was the effort, but this was a fresh experience and really exciting. I had to laugh at Martin's vain attempts to cross a 2 metre deer fence with his skis on . . .

Once on the open slopes the snow was wind-crusted and firmer to ski. An isolated square copse at half-height on Wyvis's southern shank is probably a test planting, and provides an ideal landmark by which to stage the ascent. Just before we reached it the first squall hit. Blinding hail pellets and a gusting wind enforced a 'heads down-hoods up' attitude. We carried the skis up the final steepening to emerge on the summit ridge no more than half a mile south of the highest top, Glas Leathad Mor.

> A wild scene opened up, snow-plastered hills to our west, lowland expanses shining golden in the sun's glare to the south, and another squall cloud quickly racing down from the north. We were enveloped in the storm as we skied up the final ridge.

Skied up! What on earth made me suggest putting on our skis when about to be plunged into a white-out? Only the childish desire to use our new possessions at every opportunity!

> Visibility fell to zero, and we edged along together, myself eyeing the compass every few steps. The buffeting wind made us stagger from side to side. Yet I foresaw no problem other than finding the summit trig point on this broad easy ridge . . .

Every few steps that gale could be pushing us perilously off course. And this *broad easy ridge*: had I forgotten about the headwall of Coire na Feola just to the right? Or conveniently ignored the knowledge that cornices can form above slopes as gentle as 20 degrees? The uniform screen of whiteness filling my vision at that moment was a good reflection of the vacuum that must have occupied my brain. Joy recounts what followed:

> Suddenly I slipped over what seemed to be a small bump in the snow; but found my skis hanging in space poised over what in fact was a considerable drop! Martin held out his ski-stick to help me back to my feet, but before we could conjure a single thought I heard a dull crack and was immediately carried off downwards.

The slope shuddered and I knew that a cornice had broken but in the next moment all logical thought was engulfed by a spasm of terror. Once my weight hit the scarp below, I suddenly became aware of riding downwards on a moving carpet of snow.

> Avalanche! The grim word rocked my senses. I struggled desperately to keep upright and stay on the surface, alternately swimming and clawing in the amorphous flowing mass, but powerless to get free. As the slab crumbled into huge blocks, I was certain that my skis would get trapped, twisting and snapping my legs like matchwood. Beyond that was the imminent prospect of being buried. Then came the appalling thought that Joy was somewhere below, and a cruel pang of remorse for leading my own wife to her likely doom. As I was gripped by such torment, and still fighting desperately to keep afloat, the avalanche finally halted. A lifetime of emotions had crammed into a mere ten seconds. I was left half-submerged in the debris, but seemingly in one piece. Apart from a madly thumping heart, a deathly silence and a ghostly whiteness reigned once more . . .

Relief at surviving uninjured and incredulous attempts to grasp what had happened were instantly replaced as my thoughts flashed back to Joy. After struggling to my feet, a long look about revealed no sign of her, only chaotic debris stretching on all sides. The worst seemed probable.

I embarked on an exploratory search downslope, then thought to yell her name. A faint voice answered back and 30m away I found her, prostrated in front of a block the size of a small car. Immediate fears that she was injured were lifted by a quick check of limbs and joints. She was merely stunned with shock, and understandably so, having imagined that she had made a solo plunge, leaving me back on top of the mountain:

> Hearing Martin's voice provided an indescribable relief. With his assistance I got to my feet. The cloud had cleared a little and looking back up I saw that the slope was devastated across a width of two, possibly three hundred metres – stripped completely bare to its grass surface. Above it hung the broken jagged edges of a cornice. It took some minutes to sink in that an enormous avalanche had occurred.

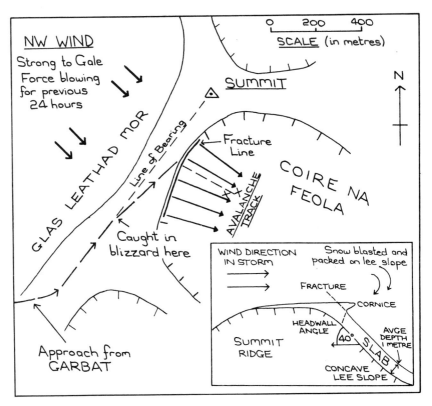

BEN WYVIS : ANATOMY OF AN AVALANCHE

We stood there, two awestruck witnesses of the remains of a full-depth slab avalanche, the fragile slab created by deposition and packing of wind-blasted snow on this lee slope, and triggered simply by our own weights as we fell with the cornice. It was an 80m climb back to the ridge. The angle at the top could have been no more than 35 degrees. Deadly conditions had evolved on this innocent ground in less than two days of blizzard.

Climbing back up I realised that we must now seek the crucial summit cairn, surely only a few metres distant. Joy was not an active participant in the search, but just clung close to me, her eyes staring wide with fear. The skis were safely strapped to our sacks. True to expectations the trig and cairn emerged from the shifting mist 150m further on.

In descent we kept safely to the windward slopes, and hurried down to avoid catching a further squall. The lower slopes and forest rides were skied, but with little pleasure. Our friend the farmer was still out and about at Garbat but we didn't stop to converse. Acute embarrassment would only have deepened my personal shame over the day's events.

At 4pm, and a staggering six hours after setting out, we thankfully reached the van, but Joy at once noticed that the spare wheel casing had somehow detached itself from the chassis. So my mind was straight away forced back to the trying necessities of the present, and the next half an hour was spent lying in the snow refixing it. Only then did I climb into our sanctuary and over a soothing pot of strong tea, together we unscrambled our nerves.

Humiliation was the foremost feeling. Danger stalks the winter hills however competent or cautious the climber. An element of untamed risk has to be accepted as an essential part of mountaineering. But today, through small but thoughtless errors of judgement, I had literally stepped over the reasonable margins of safety. Even the easiest hills should be accorded a proper respect, and our lucky escape made me determined that henceforth on the Munros unchecked confidence would never again be given full rein*. The oft-used quote: 'Eternal vigilance is the price of freedom' can be applied perfectly to climbing. And history has proven the predictability of avalanches given certain combinations in recent weather and snow conditions. There have been several 'black days' with concurrent incidents on different mountains, for instance 15 February 1982 when there were four separate accidents, with three fatalities, on Ben Nevis and Creag Meagaidh. And what is predictable should be avoidable.

Later that night just before getting to bed, as I sat idly thumbing through the pages of Munro's Tables, my eyes fell disbelievingly upon the Gaelic translation of Ben Wyvis – 'Wivis, locally Weevis; Gaelic Fuathas; perhaps the hill of *terror*.' So much the better if I had done this piece of homework before our ascent. It was a sobering revelation on which to sleep.

We stayed at Garve. The road system was still disrupted and the continuing sweeping snow showers seemed likely to keep it thus. Ten miles along the A832 above Achnasheen lay the lonely dome of Fionn Bheinn, another Munro whose praises are rarely sung. It was too conveniently placed to ignore, so instead of making a headlong rush back towards the Cairngorms this easier option was gladly grasped though it would add only a single summit to my tally. Frayed nerves needed knitting slowly back into place, and a modest day was well chosen.

My only previous memory of Fionn Bheinn reaches back to 1966. An eleven year old tends to underestimate the scale of the world about him, but his enthusiasm knows no bounds. The mountain held the dubious distinction of being marked as a spot height on our 'National

*In tragic coincidence a lone ski-tourer was killed in an avalanche on Ben Wyvis on 31 March 1985 just two months after our own experience.

Benzole' touring map – my sole geographical aid on this family holiday at Beauly – and as such it formed a mighty and unknown objective. Brother Richard and I left musing parents at Achnasheen and headed directly up the long heathery slopes. After forty minutes we topped the first main rise expecting to see the summit just beyond, but to our dismay the mountain still loomed large and distant, its brown crest swathed in clouds. Already tired and fearful of incurring parental wrath by a late return, we turned tail. Ambition was unrewarded but my heart glowed with the magnificent scale of it all. These lofty summits really seemed untouchable. Nearly twenty years and many mountains later, I was at last able to stand on the top. The link with boyhood passion was somehow reassuring.

Today the Nordic skis were an unqualified success, enabling a round trip of three hours, although the descent was difficult to control and quickly exhausting. The snow cover exhibited a baffling variability, regularly switching between packed powder and wind-crust and making a joke of my minor pretensions to skiing ability. Early snow flurries gradually cleared, and a sparkling sunny day developed, sparing the horrors of another white-out. Only a light playful mist shrouded the final dome.

After lunch it took three and a half hours of tense driving on ice-rutted roads to reach the Spey Valley. The immediate memory of the avalanche had receded a little and an anticyclone looked to be settling in. We parked just above Newtonmore that night in a slightly happier mood.

Above us lay the Monadh Liath, or 'grey hills', the upland expanse betwixt Speyside and the Great Glen. It has four Munros which are conveniently grouped on the south-eastern rim, forming a series of craggy edges above Newtonmore and Laggan. Behind them stretches an endless chain of barren moorlands, a country devoid of appeal save to the seeker of anonymous solitude and the connoisseur of sporting game. Only the Corrieyairack Pass, which carries General Wade's Military Road through its bounds from Laggan to Fort Augustus, sees much walking traffic, whilst names like Strathdearn, Coignafearn and Dulnain would arouse a vacant stare from most keen hillwalkers, even though they define an area quite as great as the Cairngorms. As it lies wholly around the 700 and 800m contours the Munro-bagger is spared the effort of penetrating this hidden wilderness. The fringing four provide quite sufficient a challenge to the will and stamina, as well as a potential navigational nightmare, and it would be wise to pick them up on a clear day.

Concern over whether my skiing muscles and techniques would withstand the rigours of the proposed 21-mile tour dictated a predawn start, so we poked our noses out into 16 degrees of frost at 7am. Joy came as far as the first summit, A'Chailleach, but we were unable to keep a compatible pace. Whilst her fishscale-bottomed skis refused to grip on any angle much greater than 10 degrees, my stick-on skins were so tractive as to tempt the ascent of near-vertical drifts, often resulting in hilarious backward tumbles. Reaching the crowning tumulus fifteen minutes ahead I had plenty of time to fully absorb the serene beauties of the dawn. Up north the icy sugar-loaf of Wyvis captured a sideways glance, and as my gaze swung back to the sweeping plateau of today's route, I thanked my guardian angel for this glorious weather.

Over the tender undulations of the next 12 miles the skins were kept on continuously; not a style prescribed in any of the technical manuals. However, it spared the time and bother of refitting them at every change of slope, and they retarded my downward velocity to a graceful glide. The more conventional alternative would have been to delve into the array of multi-coloured waxes which were hidden in the depths of my sack, but that would have brought problems of choosing the right wax for the ambient snow temperatures, and then applying it in the correct thickness – all this requiring a practised expertise which I do not possess, or otherwise becoming a frustrating game of trial and error. Also, the wind-bared ice and surface hoar on the exposed plateau would have rapidly stripped off the most liberal coating of wax. Even my skins of brushed nylon exhibited a distressingly shredded condition by the day's end. Whether you opt for waxes or skins, or even use the simpler but limited fishscale models, the light-weight Nordic ski with the metal edges for control on ice seems infinitely the most efficient mode of snow travel for the rolling hill country of the central Highlands. The surprising and delightful 4mph at which I traversed Carn Sgulain, Carn Dearg, and all the interven-ing bumps and tops to Geal Charn, supports the recommendation, but my final descent to Glen Shirra without the skins revealed the one major proviso. Without the facility to lock down the heels that is available on the heavier Alpine ski-bindings, long downhill stages demand excellent technique and control.

Yet despite frequent spills into the fathomless depths of powder snow drifts I reached the road at Sherramore at 3.30 in cheerful spirits, almost beating Joy to our rendezvous, for I had seen her roll along from Laggan Bridge only a few minutes earlier.

'Not finished already?' she exclaimed, and then regaled me with the catalogue of her misfortunes: a breathless sequence of frozen battery, ice-caked windscreen, insurmountable drifts, and a tow from a farm tractor as the final face-saver. A good-natured argument followed over who was having the tougher time on this trip.

A deep silent frost was still hugging the shaded floor of the glen, and a check on the temperature revealed a startling −12°C. Any thoughts I might have harboured that Joy was exaggerating the travel problems were soon dispelled when we commenced our journey to Glencoe, where we were due to meet a large and distinguished support crew for the weekend. The single-tracked road to Laggan would have made a good luge track, more suitable for the bobsleigh than the motor car. However, the twenty-minute delay suffered in redirecting a saloon, which was hopelessly skewed across a side entrance, was but a mild precursor to the mayhem which greeted us on arrival at the main road. A juggernaut with a full load of timber was stranded on the right-angled corner where the road climbs steeply up from the Laggan Bridge. The queuing vehicles on either side were manoeuvring into a complicated jam. Tows were being attempted to no avail, and after half-an-hour the spectacle became a touch tedious, as well as uncomfortable for the evening frost was piercing and forced us inside. Faced with a 40-mile detour via Newtonmore and Dalwhinnie to avoid this impasse, we decided to cook our evening meal on the spot, in vain hope that a solution might be found in the meanwhile. We took the van off the road, and set about defrosting our water, milk and food. Half-way through our hearty platefuls two snow ploughs arrived. By dint of one towing in front and the other bodily shunting from behind the lorry was slowly inched around the bend, and by the completion of dessert the way was open once more.

Full of admiration for the skill and tenacity of the men of the Highland Regional Council we restarted our drive, and did not reach the Clachaig Inn until 9pm. Here we were to step from seclusion into the full glare of public attention.

The day's success on the Monadh Liath had helped to patch up my confidence to face the inevitable strain of the coming weekend. The skis were working to great effect, and at 119 Munros in 36 days once again my nose was in front of schedule, but with a string of long committing journeys in the Grampians stretching into the future there was nothing to justify the least hint of complacency.

On a snowy winter's night there can be no greater contrast to the icy world outside than the hot and noisy interior of a Highland pub. The Clachaig was doing great business with a lecture in progress in the lounge and a boisterous bunch of climbers squeezed into the bar. In the euphoric atmosphere induced by the sweating throng and the liberal consumption of alcohol, the hushed snow cover which mantled every cliff face to an impressive depth was temporarily forgotten by most. Epic adventures were related with gusto and great plans boldly laid down for tomorrow. Up above, though, the white peaks of the

Coe stood in gaunt silhouettes, towering impassively above this melting pot of human aspiration. Within this stark difference perhaps is contained the real appeal of the bar-room gathering – its offer of a temporary haven safely insulated from the harsh reality of this 'savage arena', as Joe Tasker so aptly described it.

It was for us a minor culture shock walking straight into this hive of activity. We had for the past thirty-seven nights sought our comfort in the relative calm of the van, with the powerful heat of our radiator and the soothing tones of Bach and Mozart on our cassette barring intrusion from the hostile elements without. Yet now there was an obligation to be sociable, for the entourage by whom we were joined held such notoriety that it was acutely embarrassing to be its focus. The twin aims of the assembly were to promote our appeal for Intermediate Technology, and provide some suitable publicity photographs of our clothing and equipment in action, and of course there would be plenty of help on the hills.

Hamish Brown had kindly travelled over from Fife for the weekend. It was with some trepidation that I had broached my plans for the expedition to him. He might well have felt that my venture was merely an attempt to usurp his own achievement of the continuous summer round, or else even a cheap imitation. But no; after explaining an initial misgiving that the calendar season could never exactly correspond to the duration of true winter conditions on the mountains, he quickly warmed to my idea, and now was a willing participant.

Chris Bonington, justifiably Britain's most famous mountaineer, was up in Scotland with a busy schedule of ice-climbing, lecturing and publicity work, so it was a privilege that he was prepared to devote a day to help. On seeing him at the end of his lecture he greeted me with the enthusiastic advice: 'Gosh, you'll be so fit you just *must* get out to the Himalayas at the end of this!'

The words made me feel disappointed that there were no such expeditions pending. Indeed, at that moment I could have fancied an 8,000 metre peak or two, just for a bit of variety.

Richard and Nick Crane would be the endurance experts of the party, always ready to stretch their remarkable stamina and will-power to new limits if offered a sufficiently crazy challenge. Richard had of course run across the Himalayas in 1983 with his brother Adrian (they are an energetic family the Cranes) and more recently with cousin Nick had cycled up Kilimanjaro, a stunt which was another great fund-raiser for Intermediate Technology. Lesser known is Richard and Nick's narrow failure to beat the 'three peaks' cycling record – climbing Ben Nevis, Scafell Pike and Snowdon, and cycling the 420 miles between them in a total of little over forty hours. The pair arrived after tortuous journeys from Aberdeen and London respectively, Richard pitching up out of the darkness at something after midnight.

To this group a sizeable supporting cast must be added. Steve Bonnist, our constant mentor throughout the enterprise, was on his first-ever visit to the Highlands. A typically impressionable American, he could not hide his boyish excitement, but the scene in the Clachaig bar was a disappointment to him.

'I was expecting to see men dancing in kilts and haunches of venison roasting on spits in here', he observed.

Alan Thomson was to be there and climbing photographers Brian Hall and Alan Hinkes completed the team. It was Hamish who coined the term 'circus' to describe our gathering, though not, I hope, in the sense of a troupe of clowns!

The photographers demanded some dramatic scenery with a sensational foreground – the Mamores ridge would have ideally suited their needs – but this idea was rejected with my declaration that skiing was the only feasible mode of transport given the deep drifts, and that a smoother set of mountains must be chosen. Not a popular decision, this one, since only half of the party possessed skis, but as it transpired very wise.

Creag Meagaidh would perhaps provide a venue to compromise everybody's requirements. Meagaidh is both the highest top and the collective name for the grand massif of five Munros which flanks the northern side of the Spean Bridge–Laggan road for a dozen miles. Its fame is owed to the perfect series of corrie bowls which are scooped out of its southern slopes: Gall, Moy and in particular Coire Ardair.

Though vegetated and shattered in summer, Ardair's headwall gives magnificent climbing when winter conditions develop. Placed mid-way between Nevis and the Cairngorms it steals the merits of each, the moist air of the Ben to build the ice, and the continental chill from the east to keep it frozen, and so can provide superb sport when both of its competitors are 'out of nick'. At first climbers were slow to see potential in the place, but it offered a new area of exploration in the middle and late 1960s after the major lines of Ben Nevis had all been taken.

For the walker or skier the range provides a 17-mile plateau crossing, closely akin to Ben Alder in style. If the whole party climbed Carn Liath, the first Munro, the cliffs of Ardair would provide a majestic backcloth for photographs. Then the skiers, namely Chris, Hamish and myself, could complete the traverse, which would give a most productive day.

After a disturbed, restless night we were up at 6am. This was the most frigid morning so far. Inland at Aberarder farm the temperature

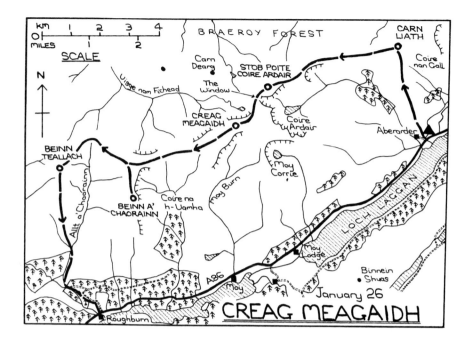

must have been 8 or 10 degrees below that in Glencoe where the sea's proximity held it at a balmy −10°C. We all shuffled about in the shade sorting and sharing out equipment. Steve needed to be dressed from head to toe ready for his first Munro. He dashed about telling everybody that he was about to scale the icy fortress of 'Craig Maggie', his sense of humour lost on most of the audience, who were feeling blue enough with cold.

A group of climbers arrived back at the cars, already repelled by the drifts at 9am. 'Impossible!' was their conclusion on the conditions for walking. If that comment was discouraging, then the following events left us in disarray. First Chris arrived to report the overnight theft of his Nordic skis from his car roof-rack. Then Hamish let his dog 'Storm' out of his dormobile only to watch him disappear under the thick snow cover in the adjoining field. Hamish and Storm are devoted companions, veterans of many a Munro-bagging campaign. As it was clear that Storm could not join the party, Hamish regretfully decided he must return after a few hours.

So, unbelievably, the majority of my planned day would be in solitude. It was a motley but cheerful crew of ten that crawled up to Carn Liath in laboured staccato style, three on skis, one on snowshoes, and the rest thrashing about on foot. I suppose Chris could console himself that the 800m knee-deep plod to the summit was excellent training for his forthcoming and ultimately successful attempt on Everest. Frequent interruptions for photocalls on the ascent were followed by a prolonged barrage of pictures on top. My mood slipped into an introverted gloom as the time raced by.

At the disturbingly late hour of 1pm the camera crew allowed me to get away to commence a frantic dash across the plateau, leaving the others to more leisured perambulations valleywards. The next five hours were a blur of fleeting perceptions. A perfect winter's day sparkled all about, the Highland outlines from Affric down to Drumochter revolving on the horizon with every turn and twist of the skis as they smashed through ice hoar and wind-crust towards Beinn Teallach, the goal by nightfall.

The precipices of Coire Ardair were impressively framed from across 'The Window' gap – a wispy trelliswork of snow-caked runnels, smears and lofty balconies, delicately beautiful but today unsafe or even impossible to climb. The Window is a narrow notch on the plateau edge formed by glacial overflow, and provides the only easy descent into the coire after completing climbs on its headwall. In bad visibility many climbers have failed to find it, and have been forced to make an exhausting 12-mile trek northwards into the headwaters of Glen Roy to secure shelter. Meagaidh in winter is a mountain deserving of the greatest respect.

My skis were removed only once that afternoon, in order to nip out to both the south and central summits of Beinn a'Chaorainn. Both tops have an equal spot height, and each successive edition of the Tables frustratingly swops the main Munro between the two. At sundown I reached Beinn Teallach in a dishevelled state, a broken ski-stick bearing witness to one of many tumbles en route, and lathered in a sweat which quickly froze on stopping. Yet the surrounding scene displayed a still composure that held my gaze for a minute. Down south, Loch Treig resembled a bath of silver mercury, and over to its right the Nevis range formed a defiant silhouette.

Beinn Teallach is the most recent addition to the Munro's Tables, promoted by the Ordnance Survey from 913 to 915m in the 1984 revision of the local 1:25000 map. The change went unnoticed until spotted by a youngster staying at the Fersit hostel during a rainy day spent poring over the maps. Now of course everybody is climbing it, its former obscurity lost for ever.

Whatever the quibbles over its Munro-status, Teallach's southern slopes must provide one of Scotland's finest off-piste ski-runs. The tracks of today's other visitors snaked off down in neat symmetrical patterns. Though trying hard to copy them, my fatigued legs rapidly lost all co-ordination, and embarrassingly I superimposed a series of sweeping snow-plough furrows regularly interspersed by craters all the way down to the Moy plantations.

Leaving the slope looking like a detonated minefield, I slid and

The Creag Meagaidh 'circus' on the summit of Carn Liath: Joy and Martin in front with (standing, left to right) Chris Bonington, Hamish Brown, Steve Bonnist, Richard and Nick Crane (*A. Hinkes*)

shuffled the 1½ miles back to the road, too tired now to be bothered putting the skins back on. Although I was considerably overdue at 6.30pm, the layby fixed for our rendezvous was deserted. A shivering, cursing wait of half-an-hour left me wondering how such an exhausting effort could possibly be repeated tomorrow. The Mamores had earlier been discussed again, for our photographers had not been nearly satisfied by the Carn Liath setting. Meanwhile, Joy was sitting in an identical layby 2 miles up the road, and worrying where on earth I had got to; that is, until she took a ride down, and collected both me *and* my black mood!

Richard Crane was with her, and applying his 'quadrathonal' mentality obviously thought that a little more exercise would cheer me up. First he generously invited me to join him in an attempt that spring on 'the Bob Graham Round' – the notorious twenty-four hour fell run over forty-two of the Lake District's fells. If that suggestion wasn't enough to choke me, we were all then cordially requested to help start his car, an abysmal wreck of a Cortina which was dumped at Ballachulish. Repeated failed attempts at a push-off left us lying flat on our faces in the snow. By now I was too mesmerised to care that one of my climbing ropes was then commandeered for a tow-start.

107

At 9pm at last the Clachaig's lights swung into view. A wave of sympathy spread from the gathered team at the sight of me so hollow-cheeked and sunken-eyed. All proposed schemes for tomorrow were quietly laid aside, and after a welcome bath in the hotel, Joy and I were kindly left to get our meal and recuperate. Writing up my diary at midnight I reflected:

> A day which I could have accomplished alone in eight hours has occupied fourteen, thanks to driving, photography and the inevitable delays of organising such an unwieldy group. I know I have an obligation to be helpful to sponsors and pressmen, but my limits of tolerance have been reached!

The weather turned quite viciously overnight. At dawn the temperature hovered back on zero and a south-easterly gale was whipping plumes of spindrift off the slopes. A blizzard looked imminent. Over breakfast our party sensibly decided to disperse forthwith, most being anxious to escape the Highlands before the snows commenced.

How disappointing and ironic that such a strong team had been unable to offer practical support. In fact there was a profound relief in driving off back towards the Spey Valley and a return to our untroubled routine. Yet the exercise had not been wholly fruitless. Several new friends had been met, and their sincere parting wishes for our success gave a long-term boost to morale.

We passed the shores of Laggan for the fourth time in two days, branching off to land in Dalwhinnie minutes before the main A9 was closed by drifting. The locals strongly advised us to retreat to Newtonmore. I breathed a long sigh of frustration and slowly acquiesced to the prospect of another lost day, the second in a week. The Drumochter hills would have to wait a while. Strangely, the snowstorm failed to materialise, but the wind-drifting was sufficient to close the roads. Lack of sleep soon knocked me into horizontal posture once parked in the shelter of the town, and the rest of the day was happily idled away regathering our strength and wits.

Meanwhile, on the slopes of Ben Nevis others less fortunate were engaged in a battle for life itself. The sad news was broadcast next morning on the radio: 'Two climbers have been killed in an avalanche in the Red Burn area of the mountain . . .'

In an instant we were back on Wyvis. Through the joys of the Monadh Liath and the farce on Creag Meagaidh our thoughts had turned full circle.

(*right*) Skiing through the Garbat woods towards Ben Wyvis

(*overleaf*) The 'Rough Bounds' viewed northwards from Sgurr nan Coireachan (Glenfinnan). The skyline Munros are (left to right) Meall Buidhe, Luinne Bheinn, Sgurr na Ciche, Garbh Chioch Mhor (see Chapter 6)

9

THE ATLANTIC STRIKES BACK

28 January–1 February:
Drumochter – Loch Treig – Mamores Ridge – Ben Sgriol

The Drumochter hills are by reputation dull and drab, and disfigured by the road, railway and pylon lines which scythe through the central pass, carrying the lifeblood of the Highlands north to the Spey. Such unkind repute encourages me to adopt a perverse stance and take a positive view of their qualities. They are fine hills for ski-touring, and nicely divided into two groups of three and four Munros, one on each side of the pass, easily accessible and with a helpful starting altitude. They provided two days of useful but non-committing progress ideally suited to a spell when the weather was arguing inconclusively with itself.

The eastern trio is substantially the longer day at 17 miles due to the isolated position of Meall Chuaich, which we climbed first. Although our start was delayed until 8.30 when the main road was opened up to Dalwhinnie, a thaw was beginning and, coupled with yesterday's blowing of the snow, conditions were already lean for skiing. Still dwelling on the news of the avalanche tragedy the plod up into the summit mists was devoid of pleasure, and it was hard to leave Joy to continue with only sad thoughts and self-doubts for company. The snow had settled into a sugary slush, dirtied by streaks of blown dust and speckled with the protruding fronds of heather. A brief thaw certainly wipes the shine off the winter scene.

Thick mist and the confusing repetition of ridge and furrow on the middle slopes, together with the absence of contrast in the light, left me troubled to find the tiny cairn atop Carn na Caim. From there to A'Bhuidheanach Bheag is a 3-mile sea of confusion. The ground ebbs and swells with wave-like regularity, whilst the boundary fence twists in apparent discord with its marked route on the map, and disappears altogether on some sections. My navigational sense was further bemused by the impossibility of judging one's speed when travelling on skis. Even on Scotland's modest heights an altimeter is a useful tool

(left, above) On the slopes of Carn Liath (Creag Meagaidh) with 'The Window' notch on the left and Stob Poite Coire Ardair to its right *(H. M. Brown)*; *(below)* Beinn Mheadhoin's summit stack (see Chapter 12)

of orientation to the skier when distance can't be gauged, and would have helped me greatly now.

A sharp descent fixed a position below the final rise, but on the summit plateau I still got wholly lost for nigh on an hour. One should be glad that the top sports a trig point which certifies arrival, for there are three identical bumps and my wayward steps visited the lower two more than once apiece before they chanced upon the central and highest with only a scrap of daylight left. I imagined the laughter of tomorrow's visitors when they saw my crazy web of tracks. In the excitement of the search my earlier sorrow was dispelled. Such 'dreary pudding-shaped humps' can still surprise and intimidate, and should never be discounted.

As I skied out of the cloud, a fiery sunset was dropping behind Beinn Udlamain. The van waited on the road below. Drumochter Pass was resplendent in that golden hour.

The western group of Munros are higher and more pronounced. They throw down a pair of square-shanked offshoots above the pass. These dark and surly beasts are twinned, with powerful inspiration, the Boar of Badenoch and The Sow of Atholl, and tower in constant watch over every passing traveller, dominating the scene while their parent summits remain unheeded.

With the thaw continuing our skis were left behind, and apart from the wet and sloppy initial approach to Sgairneach Mhor the decision gave no regrets. The ridges over Beinn Udlamain were clear of cloud and almost bare of snow, firmer and faster than the tops of yesterday and enabling our brisk completion in five and a half hours. A strong westerly hurried us along but conditions overhead stayed kind, in dull contrast to the traumas of the previous week. As the grouse, ptarmigan and hare emerged from temporary hibernation, the moors were once more restored as a living habitat. It was difficult to believe that just three days ago we had endured temperatures of −15°C. From A'Mharconaich, the third Munro, Joy dropped down beside the Boar, and brought the van to Balsporran Cottages where my descent from Geal Charn met the A9.

'Sitting on the fence' at Drumochter had been a canny tactic to allow some recovery from the Meagaidh epic, and to let the weather define its intent; but at the same time had soaked up two more of our diminishing selection of accessible day-routes. We were losing choice and it was time to be committed to something more substantial. East into the Cairngorms, or back west for the Mamores? The loss of good ski-touring conditions swung the choice to the west, even though we might be heading straight into the teeth of some hectic Atlantic storms.

An orange neon glare suffused the sky above the Fort in a night of thick and hanging cloud, and showers blustered long before dawn. Hopes for the Mamores were scotched again, and another long drive had been made to no avail. What was left under the weather's duress? Our ploy of 'flexible response' had all but lost its flex, at least as far as Lochaber was concerned. An option was needed which would leave the Mamores and Grey Corries ridges untouched, not only because these were seen as highlights of the expedition but also as they are each best tackled in a single push.

Stob Coire Easain and Stob a'Choire Mheadhoin, which stand in spacious isolation above Loch Treig, were our day's salvation. The van might have driven itself back east that morning, having spent the last six days in taxi service between the Spean and Spey.

Fersit is the nearest public road from which to gain these twin domes, but the climb along the north-east spur of Mheadhoin is not advised for those who like their mountains short and sharp. The spur is gained by a bouldery tussle up from the lower shores of Treig and, excepting the craggy nose of Meall Cian Dearg, gives a gentle pull of some two miles to the top. And then, if the further and slightly higher top of Easain is also taken, one must reverse the linking ridge on the return journey.

It is far better to assail the pair in a rapid climb from Leacach bothy to the west, and use the long declivity of the north-east spur for a striding descent. Thus a graceful crossing is achieved at a 4-mile saving; and indeed this was my original scheme. They would have coupled neatly with an epic saga on the Grey Corries to make a well-balanced two-day outing. This combined traverse forms the northern leg of Ramsay's Round, and would have spared the toilsome miles of forest tracks to gain the Leacach direct from Spean Bridge, which sadly seemed the only way of access to the Grey Corries in the wake of today's round trip.

How dispiriting to make a 10-mile trek and in the doing create an extra 7 miles for the future; and especially in a sleeting downpour which gave us our first complete soaking since Mull, all of thirty-two days previously. Up above 1000m the snow still lay unbroken, and a dense mist produced many minutes of white-out:

> Whenever the cloud closed in we felt stranded and vulnerable. I looked at the map. All reason said we stood on safe slopes, yet we could not bring ourselves to move until a clearance gave back our vision. We relived our Wyvis nightmare several times on the north-east ridge . . .

Our psyches were still quite badly bruised from the avalanche experience, and this irrational lurking fear would not be a happy load to carry for the rest of the winter. At least the day had sustained some impetus, and did not dissuade my ardent pursuit of the Mamores. The winter mountaineer must be a stubborn suitor. By dusk we were settled back above Fort William on the old military road which curves around the Mamores' western end and down to Kinlochleven. Tomorrow there was effectively no choice.

'I will go, and maybe take a drubbing for my trouble', I wrote that night.

The Mamores Ridge holds an unequalled cachet to the winter mountaineer. Wedged between Ben Nevis and Glencoe it is centrally positioned in his most-sought crucible. Though not as long as, say, the Cluanie skyline the ridge is twice as complex, a switching saw-toothed edge with a clutch of pointed summits and several Munro outliers. The inclusive traverse gives eleven Munros at a cost of 20 miles and 3050m (10,000ft) of climbing from end to end, offering the perfect level of exposure and technical difficulty to test but not deter the unroped walker, and its quality is such that few climbers would deny themselves a day away from verticality to march its crest.

However speed and endurance need to be harnessed to firm conditions and preferably a full moon if a complete one-day traverse is sought in winter, all of which gave me scant chance of success.

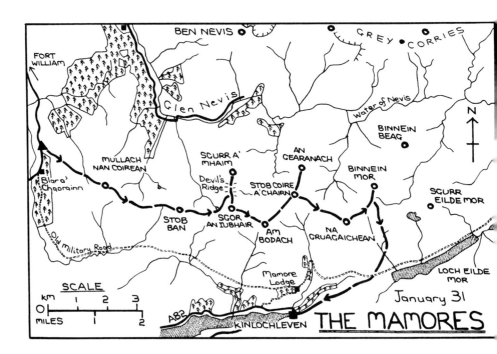

Throughout the night galeswept rain hammered against the van. Only slight moderation was promised by the early morning weatherman and so:

> I set out at 7am with no real hopes, but determined to go as far as I could. Somewhere along the central ridge I would move from 138 to 139 Munros and the half-way mark would be attained. This was lure enough to keep my nose to the grindstone . . .

Certainly this was a day when without such incentive no sane climber would have stayed up much beyond the first Munro, Mullach nan Coirean. My climb from the west was simple, and saved 120m of ascent on the alternative start from Glen Nevis.

A sharp shift of climate, perhaps signifying a cold front passage, was keenly sensed on the following ridge to Stob Ban. Dawn had been dank and mild and the dwindling snowfields wringing with moisture on the initial climb, but come the switch of gale from south-west to west a drier, cooler airstream took command. Within an hour the thaw was stilled, slush became ice and wet rocks donned a verglas coat. Plodding suddenly turned to skating, but there was one constant in all this, the whistling wind which did not drop a single knot.

Squall after squall was thereafter hurled against the mountain tops throughout the day, each one visible from miles afar as a black and blotting mass of cloud. The first caught me coming down off Stob Ban and caused a serious loss of route:

> I withdrew my nose into my hood as the stinging hail commenced, and ploughed blindly downwards. About 130m lower I sensed the wind was meeting me head-on. 'Goodness this is strange weather,' I thought, 'it's turned into an easterly!' But then came painful realisation, confirmed by compass check, that I was some way down the south-west ridge. There was no route round, so biting my lip, I could only climb back up . . .

Sure enough, the take-off point for the eastern edge is not distinct, and it is only at the central hubs of such a pronounced ridge as this that navigation is problematic. With the error any slim chance of my finishing the 'integrale' finally disappeared.

The central section of the Mamores contains its most dramatic moments. In particular the slender crest and rocky notches of the Devil's Ridge on the northwood detour to Sgurr a' Mhaim give a delight which far outweighs the fag of diverting from the main axis of the chain. The peak itself cuts an impressive pyramid above the eastward turn of Glen Nevis, from which it is an unbroken climb of 1050m, steeper than that from Etive to Ben Starav and a treadmill if you aren't fit.

Hardly less exciting is the second scrambling detour out from Stob Coire a'Chairn to An Gearanach, but like the Devil's Ridge the steep

The squall-lashed Mamores; An Gearanach from Stob Coire a' Chairn

terrain would not forgive a slip when the snow is hard. Ice-axe braking is the one basic skill which every winter walker should learn, perfect, and practise regularly (though ideally not on the brink of a cliff!) for the axe is usually his sole means of security on such wind-swept edges.

An Gearanach was the vital 139th Munro for me, and only with its safe completion was a break for food allowed. During a lull the piercing note of the factory siren down at Kinlochleven's aluminium plant could be clearly heard as if to justify my own lunch-stop, but the bellowing wind was soon refuelled and drowned all other sound. It battered my back over Na Gruagaichean, but as the ridge swung north towards its highest point at Binnein Mor each gust would strike broadside and leave me clinging on to axe or boulder. Yet the buffeting storm was wildly thrilling, and how preferable were the driving squalls of snow to the unremitting wet of yesterday. You can wrap up well, stay warm and dry, and give your all; and the gale may chance to blow a gaping hole through the thickest cloud, fixing the gaze on the infinite mosaic of snowpatch and lochan on the moors below.

Binnein Mor thrusts a fierce spearhead above the upper reach of Glen Nevis and, like Sgurr a' Mhaim, stands proud of the main ridge crest. By this, the ninth Munro, my all was given, so two were left for an extra day, the final outposts of Binnein Beag and Sgurr Eilde Mor. It was galling that despite my hard-won bag of nine, a day would be lost to time, but the two leftovers at once solved my remaining Lochaber problem, for they could be contiguously linked to the Grey Corries just as yesterday's hills had been intended. But for now they would be left untouched. It would only be proper to finish the winter on Ben Nevis itself, and by these two hills I hoped to approach the climax of the trip, six or seven weeks hence.

A net of stalking tracks rings the eastern end of the Mamores, and from the foot of Loch Eilde Mor a peaty path drops down to Kinlochleven's housing suburb, making the descent quick and clear even in the gathering gloom.

'A desperate day!' was Joy's pronouncement.

'But marvellous too', I rejoined, though it was hard to explain exactly why.

There can be few finer pieces of mountain travel in the Highlands. How the ridges up in the north-west would compare was a matter for keen conjecture.

The pendulum of our fortunes which had yo-yoed perilously all over the Highlands in the past two weeks now swung back further west. Out of the twenty-six Munros between Glenfinnan and Glen Shiel which comprise Section 10 of the Tables only Beinn Sgritheall (or Sgriol to use its English corruption) was outstanding. From there the northward quest could be resumed.

The weather appreciably worsened on the way to Shiel Bridge, the broken showers merging into prolonged downpour. No mercy was to be shown for my presumptuous capture of the Mamores. But help and company were already on their way. Driving up from Manchester through this lashing night was a team of four fell-runners from the Dark Peak club, ready I hoped if not for 'hell' then certainly for five days of 'high water'!

Chris Dodd was already a good friend, and a vital cog in the bureaucratic workings of the British Mountaineering Council, having administered its training courses for the past three years. As a runner he was the first man to go under twenty-four hours for the completion of the eight 4,000ft Scottish peaks in 1980. Martin Stone and Pete Simpson were familiar only by reputation. In particular, Pete has a notorious penchant for solo self-supported mountain runs. Rumour has it that only an unscalable deer fence prevented his achieving a solo twenty-four hour circuit of Ramsay's Round. Roger Canavan, the fourth member, claimed no pretensions as a mountaineer, having expended most of his youthful energy as a cycle road-racer. Could this crew succeed where Brown, Bonington et al had so recently failed?

Neither of us could relax into untroubled sleep that night:

Perhaps it was the unease of knowing Chris and friends would arrive at 3am or later and have to set up camp in this awful storm while we lay in warm dry luxury . . .

Their welcome at Shiel Bridge was every bit as hostile as my imaginings. 'Tent-pitching heroics' was Pete's description whilst Martin Stone was up at 5am to refix a flysheet that was about to take off. None of them got a wink of sleep.

Their experience typifies the lengths to which the Sassenach devotee will go to snatch a weekend in his beloved Highlands, fully knowing that the weather may issue a callous rebuff. The London-based climber Mick Fowler has acquired legendary fame simply for driving the 700 miles up to Torridon and back in three days, never mind climbing new winter routes of the utmost difficulty during his thirty-hour stay! So what brings them north with such determination? Our first day on Sgritheall was a very modest outing, and almost washed away, yet so unique in quality as to give lasting merit . . .

The mountain stands in splendid isolation on the Glenelg peninsular, guarding the mouth of Loch Hourn and looking down the Sound of Sleat to Rhum and Eigg. The twisting 15-mile drive from Loch Duich over Mam Ratagan and round to Arnisdale is a revelation in itself, and adds an exploratory flavour to the day. The road passes by Gavin Maxwell's gate at Sandaig, which was his home and literary inspiration, and 2 miles further as it drops by the ancient woods of Coille Mhialairigh one can conveniently embark on the steep climb to the peak, as we did. The south-west ridge is met at 600m and thence a rocky scramble gains the top. A route direct from Arnisdale can also be made with equal strenuosity, for Sgritheall gives no quarter on its seaward side.

Our timing of the climb was inspirational for we pinched the only dry two hours of the day, yet still cowered gratefully out of a screaming gale in the summit shelter. Down by the shore the emerald field strips and whitewashed cottage row of Arnisdale made a calm and ordered foil to the turbulent sea and racing clouds. Together with its guardian mansion house, the hamlet is a perfect Victorian enclave of fertility and civilisation, an almost indecent contrast to the surrounding wilderness from which it was hewn.

On the descent the storm returned with a vengeance. Peals of thunder and lightning bolts backed up by volleys of hail hurried us down to the road. Never was this contemplated on a winter climbing holiday! Suppressed and checked throughout the last month, the Atlantic cyclones were striking back in full fury.

The evening assembly at Cluanie Inn was awkward and tense. The lads were back under canvas and coping gamely with the flood, whilst we remained aloof in our 'castle':

> A sense of pity and the obligation of decency sorely presses us to offer our facilities to them, but how could we manage to dry and feed an extra four when we ourselves need some space and peace to recover our wits for the next four days . . . I'll be relieved to get to Affric hostel where we can share as one.

Our reticence was quickly noticed by Martin Stone:

> He is quite reserved at first but I suppose he gets used to solitude, and we must appear an intrusion . . . he and Joy kept their distance from us at the north end of the Cluanie causeway.

And the tension? The northward quest would tomorrow take us through the gap of An Caorann Mor and into the hills of Glen Affric for three lonely nights. After sixty hours of unbroken pounding in the storm we felt cornered and trapped. Hope of an end to the tempest diminished the longer it continued.

10

ROAMING THE BIG GLENS

2–7 February:
Affric – Cannich – Strathfarrar

Can these possibly be the rainwashed mountains of yesterday? The convex swell of Carn Ghluasaid stands before us glazed in ice, and the ridge proceeding onto Sgurr nan Conbhairean is clothed with pristine whiteness. The air, so sharp and dewy, draws deep fresh breaths, and the sun is already alight on the lower slopes. There is an iridescence of rejuvenated colour in every distant view. But most outstanding is the profound silence in which each croak of the grouse and ptarmigan echoes harshly over the moors and the occasional passing of a vehicle over the Cluanie watershed filters up to reach the tops as a long faint drone.

The abatement arrived unannounced as late as 7am. The final dark hour of tumult had induced an utter despair of executing the Affric trip, and a dour battle conference was about to be convened to ponder the non-existent alternatives; but no sooner did the wind subside than we all commenced a frenetic sorting and packing operation. This chance could not be missed.

The Affric section was not only tough and remote but also presented the most fascinating tactical puzzle of the winter. Anything less than an efficient solution to its twenty-four Munros would involve many extra miles of traversing and load carrying. The district does however have an ideal base right at its centre in Alltbeithe Youth Hostel which, like that at Ossian, is unstaffed but left unlocked in winter. If all sallies to the summits are made from here then a tent is not needed, and much weight saved. This leaves the problem of both reaching and quitting the hostel, whilst still collecting a handful of Munros en route. Because of the latitudinal axes of the ridges in the area, this condition can be satisfied only by going in from the west side at Cluanie or Glen Croe and emerging at its eastern roadheads. And here is where a support team is indispensable, for it is 60 miles to drive between these termini.

So the plan was hatched that Pete and Martin, ostensibly as the best-trained of the team, would help me over the Conbhairean–A'Chralaig ridges, whilst Joy, Roger and Chris ferried the transport round to Loch Beinn a' Mheadhoin in the lower Affric glen, and then took unpaid 'sherpa' duties to get eighteen man-days of food and kit the 8 miles up to the hostel, where we would rejoin. I had chewed off several pencil ends to establish this as the optimal scheme!

The six Munros of our day included the highest yet the least frequented of the Glen Shiel ridgetops. They lack the elegant continuity of the Five Sisters, but in the crenellated southern approach to Mullach Fraoch-choire possess the most spectacular bit of walking in the district.

Surging with joy from the morning's climatic miracle, we attacked the whole route with gusto, even the long ankle-twisting traverse from Sail Chaorainn across the northern slopes of Conbhairean to gain the Bealach Choire a'Chait, and the taxing climb from there to A'Chralaig. For me it was great to be speeded by fit lads, who roved across the hills like a pair of unleashed hounds. However, Pete's choice of footwear created quite a stir:

> If it was disturbing to see him set out in a flimsy pair of fell-running shoes, then I was absolutely horrified when he stopped to strap his crampons to them. 'No boots, Pete?' I queried. 'But *these* are my boots', came the riposte. Was he blithely ignorant of the Scottish winter, or else a hardened expert who had pruned his needs to a minimum, and for whom a touch of frostbite held no fear? Without knowing him I couldn't tell, yet boldly predicted the crampons would soon fall off . . .

But Pete was unabashed, and later concluded: 'My Walsh "slippers" gave excellent blister-free service all day and worked fine with crampons, for all the derogatory looks of the Berghaus-sponsored elite . . .'

Only on the pinnacled crest of Mullach Fraoch-choire was his composure ruffled, and a little coaxing needed to see him safely over, but though they flipped and flopped from side to side those crampons never once left his feet.

From the 'Mullach' the hostel is just a simple jog down its northern spur. However, the plucky spike of Ciste Dhubh, lying west across the head of An Caorann Mor, should not be missed even if Munros are not your goal. With a serrated summit ridge and the diamond-shaped slice of its southern cliff, the peak has the ideal mountain form, albeit on a miniature scale, and provides an ample incentive to the 580m toil of its eastern ridge. The top cairn occupies an enviable pulpit on the brink of the precipice and gives a fine appraisal of the upper Affric strath. The array of broad grass braes and sprawling ridges leaves the impression that these are outgrown hills, which as yet lack the bared teeth of fully-matured mountains, a soft rather than savage scenery.

The descent to Alltbeithe is short and quick. We ran down wide fields of névé, and splashed the final valley mile in darkness, subtly scenting a warmer salty flush in the air which would likely bring back

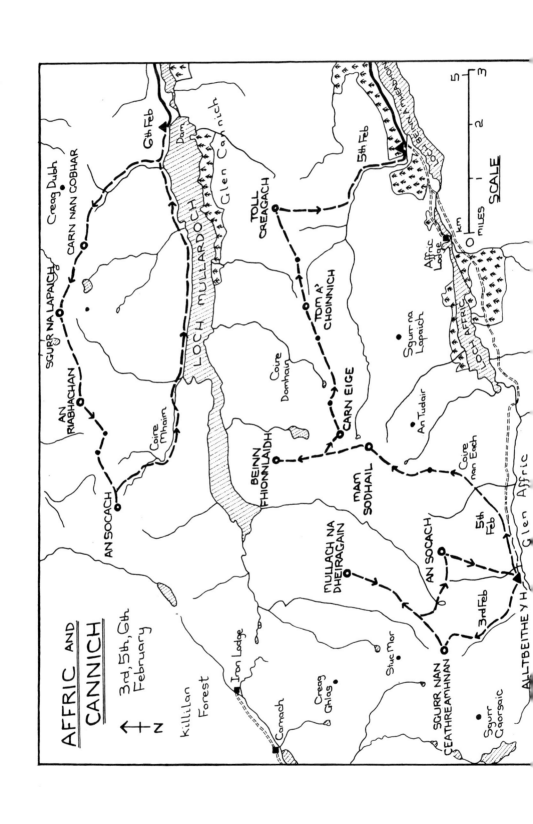

AFFRIC AND CANNICH

3rd, 5th, 6th February

N

Killilan Forest

Canach
Iron Lodge
Creag Ghlas
Stuc Mor

SGURR NAN CEATHREAMHNAN
Sgurr Gaorsaic
ALLTBEITHE Y H
3rd Feb
5th Feb
AN SOCACH
Glen Affric
MULLACH NA DHEIRAGAIN
MAM SODHAIL
BEINN FHIONNLAIDH
CARN EIGE
Coire nan Each
Coire Domhain
An Tudair
Sgurr na Lapaich
LOCH AFFRIC
Affric Lodge
5th Feb
BEINN A MHEADHOIN
TOM A' CHOINNICH
TOLL CREAGACH
Glen Cannich
LOCH MULLARDOCH
Coire Mhaim
AN SOCACH
AN RIABHACHAN
SGURR NA LAPAICH
CARN NAN GOBHAR
Creag Dubh
6th Feb
Dam

SCALE
MILES
0 1 2 3
0 1 2 3 4 5 km

rain, until assailed by the acrid odour of smouldering peat, which took our steps unerringly to the hostel. Indeed, the 'sherpas' had taken occupation and were, in Pete's words, 'impersonating kippers' as Roger conclusively disproved the theory that there's no smoke without fire. Despite the risk to health there was happy camaraderie in the kitchen that night. Now installed at Alltbeithe, we would take some shifting.

Having squeezed 2315m (7,600ft) of climbing into the 15 miles of yesterday, the stay at Alltbeithe provided a pleasant interlude, tantamount to a mid-term vacation for myself. The half-way highlight having by now faded, the next thirty peaks might have been a gruelling struggle, lost in an eternity where indeed 'there is no sight of a beginning, and no prospect of an end'. But with good company, an exciting choice of hills, and by stepping down the pace a little, a mental vacuum was effectively avoided.

As sensed the previous evening, the weather had turned to a spongy drizzle by dawn. All six set out at 9am for Sgurr nan Ceathreamhnan, a name which leaves one's jaws ajar, but held in highest esteem by every dedicated gangrel. Simon Stewart inevitably had been captured by its aura:

'Aye,' he had sighed, 'Knoydart's getting packed with tourists these days, but it's at the head of Affric that you'll find the real hillman, up on peaks like "Keroanan". . .'

Viewed on the map the mountain has the most beautiful structure of all the Munros. The summit trails a sweep of crescent ridges like tails of an advancing comet. A sense of graceful motion is captured by the looping contour threads. Underfoot these long northern and western ridge spokes can, however, seem interminable. The north-eastern arm is itself of sufficient bulk to possess a lower Munro at its far end, Mullach na Dheiragain. The 2-mile trek to get there is the ultimate test of the Munro-bagger's resolve, for it must be then reversed nearly in full. Yet the visit is necessary to savour the full extent of Ceathreamhnan's virtues.

In mist we took some time to decide which was the highest point of Dheiragain. My 1:25000 map was dug out as the final arbiter. Then by contouring round Coire nan Dearcag a second visit to the top of Ceathreamhnan was avoided on the return journey, and we emerged direct at the linking bealach to An Socach, the third Munro of a compact round. It gave a mere 120m climb before we could gaily bound back to the hostel which is directly below.

Martin and Pete put on a fine display of downhill running on these slopes, their precise control harnessing a frightening speed. We four others had more sense than to try to emulate such a practised

125

The Affric ensemble on top of An Socach: (front, left to right) Martin Stone, Pete Simpson, Roger Canavan; (back) Joy Moran and Chris Dodd

skill, and anyway could leave them the job of getting the kettle on. A freshening wind had cleared the rain, and our clothes were nicely aired by our return.

It was hardly noticed until this second night that we had a fellow inmate in the hostel. He briefly emerged from retreat in a separate bedroom at teatime, a dapper young fellow dressed in white tennis shoes, flannels and sports jacket – surely a miscast from a Wodehouse plot rather than mountaineer. A suspicious reticence kept us guessing at his purpose and identity, but we learnt he was in the second week of his stay and was 'supposed' to be at university in Kent. If he was indeed a runaway he could not have found a more secure hide-out from the wrath of tutors and distress of parents, and we wonder if he is still there yet!

The second day's sortie from the hostel proceeded further west to Beinn Fhada and thence to A'Ghlas-bheinn. Whilst the ascent of Ceathreamhnan is available solely from the hostel base, this pair can be tackled with equal facility from Morvich at the head of Loch Duich. Fhada is the main attraction, possessing the largest girth of any hill in the area. The two southern wings each extend in an unrepentant barrier of 5 miles. One pursues the length of Glen Lichd whilst the other stalks the Fionn Gleann down to the confluence of the River Affric and there is no appeal at any point throughout their endless screes and grasses. The northern side evens the score, being scoured by a series of cirques and chasms, two of which have carved a rapier-edged spur that climbs direct for 600m to the summit point.

This ridge was our unanimous choice but its pleasure was spoilt by another moping morning. However Martin Stone is always bubbling with bright-eyed schemes for future marathons, and at the foot of the spur reminded us that we now stood on the watershed of Britain. The indeterminate mass of peaty channels by which we were encircled hardly seemed the spot for such a historic declaration, but of course he was correct. To our right the Abhainn Gaorsaic now gathered every pool and runnel, stealthily amassing volume and strength in its 5-mile meander, to spout forth in a single 110m drop over the Falls of Glomach and speed away to Loch Long and the western seas. And yet the crucial point of birth of such a stupendous torrent is a barely perceptible bog. The Western Highlands watershed repeats this pattern throughout its length, being dissected by east-west glacial breaches which bear the waters in both directions from low summits.

But to return to Martin, the purpose of his revelation was far from geographical tuition, but rather to tell us about his planned 'British watershed walk' which would follow the precise divide between the North Sea and the Atlantic from Caithness south to Land's End.

'I've traced the route on all the maps, it's the last great challenge', he pronounced.

Well, maybe; but while the straths and bens of Scotland would make a superb setting for its initial stage perhaps the shine might have worn off by the time you are crawling through canal ducts in the middle of Birmingham. No doubt it will be done though.

The link from Fhada to A'Ghlas-bheinn is disrupted by the precipitous gap of Bealach an Sgairne which is one of the principal ports of entry to the Affric wilderness. We spent some time searching a means of access from above, and settled finally on a safe northwards detour. A'Ghlas-bheinn is then gained by an ever-rising series of knolls, which put one in mind of Haystacks, the Lakeland favourite.

As we strolled back towards Affric with shirt sleeves rolled up in a drier afternoon it left me uneasy that these fell-men might be thinking my exploit just a little soft. For after all they probably *ran* the 12 miles of this walk every day at home! But Pete's thoughts were at that moment quite the reverse:

> The day was the most sociable of all; I just wished this lifestyle could go on. But jealousy is futile emotion – I've had my chances and stuck with the safer income of the city. But these days will be long remembered – time to enjoy the hills, to walk with a different person on every stretch and talk on a closer personal level . . .

For me there was even time to take an hour's sleep before dinner. Harder days now lay ahead but I emerged from this cure feeling a new man.

Planning for the final day in Affric was another game of chess. At least the transport was in place down the glen and my route of egress already settled along the northside ridges from Mam Sodhail to Toll Creagach, 18 miles and 1950m (6,400ft) by the map. However, everyone naturally wanted the chance to walk the tops, especially as the skies were clearing and the breeze swinging back to the east to bring a return of frost; but unfortunately there were several tasks to share such as cleaning out the hostel and portering three substantial loads down to the road.

The most admirable quality of the fell-running fraternity, apart from their hardiness, is a spirit of mutual support. The foursome had no self-seeking motive in being here. Their stated job was 'to help me over' whatever Munros I chose, and they had displayed unquestioning deference to my every preference on route, pace and timing. This is their customary style. Each member of a club will take his due turn in the limelight whilst his mates give total commitment to help him achieve his challenge.

And now there was no hint of rancour as the 'straws were drawn'. Joy was not allowed to stand down. 'No; you must have the day with Martin', they protested, appreciating that this was a rare opportunity for her to relinquish her own supporting role. Martin Stone drew the lucky lot to join us. Pete and Chris would ferry loads, but make a short dash to the highest peaks en route, while Roger cleaned the hut and took the biggest sack directly back, willingly taking on the least glamorous job of all.

Bathed in pinky sunlight the snow-streaked hills bore the freshness of an Alpine spring this morning. We three took a rising traverse from the valley floor and then kicked up the sequinned snows of Coire nan Each to debouch on Mam Sodhail's southern spur, as the sunlight spread into its fullest radiance. There could be no doubt about the weather:

> I knew I was lucky. The average winter may produce ten such days so I could count my share already, and here was February hardly begun . . .

Mam Sodhail and Carn Eige used to confuse me as a lad. At 1,180 and 1,183m they are the highest peaks west of the Great Glen, but each atlas or touring map would name one and not the other in identical location, leaving me under the delusion that they were the same mountain. The twin rooftops of the west are in fact only three-quarters of a mile apart, and though Eige is just the higher, Mam Sodhail was preferred as a major station in the Principal Triangulation of the British Isles and so is named on maps with equal frequency. On its summit we took our snack by the remnant of the stone tower which was constructed in the 1840s to assist the survey.

Originally 7m tall, it is still an impressive monument at its present height of 3m.

Carn Eige's conquest was deferred until we had visited the northern offshoot of Beinn Fhionnlaidh, which has a status parallel to that of Mullach na Dheiragain though is not so far removed from its parent peak. Both these outliers overlook the deserted head of Loch Mullardoch, facing directly my hills of tomorrow.

By happy chance we met Chris and Pete on Carn Eige summit and lunched together. In all these four days we had the hills to ourselves. The ongoing ridge has some slender sections as far as Tom a'Choinich, with fine northern exposures over Coire Domhain, but thereafter slowly casts aside its armour to finish tamely on the rounded dome of Toll Creagach, the fifth and final Munro. Mam Sodhail has a parallel but shorter eastern arm which contains the Top of Sgurr na Lapaich. Viewed both from our own highway just to the north and especially from the lower glen, Lapaich possesses sufficient aplomb to be accorded the sixth full Munro of the range. The combined circuit of these two ridges would make the centrepiece of any Affric trip.

From Creagach we dropped directly southwards into the afforested hearth of the lower glen. Yes; perhaps this is Scotland's most lovely. The wooded mix of ancient pine and modern fir is intertwined to a velvet luxuriance, and its rich fragrance reached up to draw us off the frosted tops. We were loath to go inside once down and stood by the van vacantly gazing over the orange millpond of the river until the sun was lost.

Sadly, our companions' stay was now concluded. Four hundred mindless miles of motorway to drive tonight, and by 9am tomorrow they would be back in front of office desks and computer screens. The thought aroused no trace of envy. My accountant's hat had been hung up long ago. When we had all regathered Joy and I made a large fresh meal to fuel their journey which we hoped would be a small gesture of thanks for their fine support.

The northern ridge of Glen Cannich from Carn nan Gobhar over Sgurr na Lapaich to An Socach vies with that of Affric for height and continuity – such similar groups of hills yet with wholly different impact on successive days. At first the absence of company was keenly sensed. No human buffer was there to shield the stark loneliness of these empty hills; and then there was the glowering weather. Under a blanket of leaden cloud and in a biting easterly wind, today's thin crests exuded only menace. And to complete the change, my strides today were ever westward bound, each summit one more step from the Cannich roadend until at An Socach only the wilderness expanse of Killilan Forest lay in front. There is no sanctuary over there for a dozen miles, and Glen Cannich's woods were fully nine behind me:

> At times I wished myself in the shops of Inverness with Joy, but then thought better of such envy for here my chosen battle was right at hand – steering my compass through every turn of An Riabhachan's 2-mile crest, then seeking its vital western exit down the shrouded rocky scarp below. Inside my mittens my finger-ends were still frozen white, making the final link to An Socach a trial of endurance. Clench them, shake them – 100 . . . 200 times – keep the blood flowing . . .

The crowning trig on Socach was touched, then fled. A tingling warmth returned down in the sheltered folds of Coire Mhaim, but the long trek back remained.

This punishing walk towards nowhere formed the final act of the Affric scheme, and was certainly its least attractive portion. But the only shorter means of access to the ridge would have been a camp at the head of Mullardoch, set up on completion of the Ceathreamhnan traverse, an exciting thought but risky in its logistics. So having chosen instead to make the Lapaich group a one-day circuit I now set my head square into the wind for a gruelling return beside the gloomy loch.

Mullardoch, Monar, Cluanie and Quoich – these four great waters have all been dammed and raised for hydro-electric power production and in the doing their pre-existent nets of tracks have been disrupted. On Mullardoch as much can be sensed from a glance at the map. Zig-zag tracks career off the tops to plunge into the waters, sometimes re-emerging several miles further down the shores. New walking thoroughfares have sadly not been established. The stalkers wisely now prefer a boat to get to the upper reaches, which gave little con-solation as I ploughed between the remnant paths.

The loch was the most sombre of all the wild places seen on my travels. It evokes deep sadness and powerful inspiration on a brooding day like this. One thinks of all the woes and trials of Highland history; only the mournful skirl of the pipes is lacking, but there are no people here to listen. Not even in summer would a piper be paid his worth. It left me craving warmth and company, and comfort too, for the wind had sapped all strength. At 4.15 I rounded the final headland and passed the boat houses and jetty. But though Joy was waiting by the terminal dam with her glowing complexion and a flood of news, it was all too hard to grasp, still less respond, in my tired and humbled state.

Strathfarrar is the third of the big glens between the Shiel and Carron. Its private road meanders with the river for a dozen miles of sylvan charm as far as the Monar dams. Up above them the steely sheet of the loch snakes west for 10 miles more. Five wild Munros lie about the West Monar Forest at its upper end, but being nearer to Strathcarron than the Farrar roadend these would be left for the later Torridonian campaign. But just north of the lower glen is a further ring of four summits which were a brief finale to this present phase of western exploration.

The estate restricts public access via the road to daylight hours, and then the numbers of vehicles are closely controlled:

> Having sensibly arranged permission from the factor by phone last night we took a couple of hours extra sleep and made a late start up the glen at 9.30. By approaching first the easternmost peak of Sgurr na Ruaidhe once again the wind was behind us on the tops. In today's strong breeze this really felt like cheating, and with the snows frozen to rock-hard consistency we fair flew over Carn nan Gobhar. Yesterday's clouds had lifted and the air and views were invigorating, especially down over Beauly and the Moray lowlands. While Joy went down to the van from Sgurr a'Choire Ghlais, I collected the last Munro, Sgurr Fhuar-thuill, then ran down the Allt Toll a'Mhuic with the help of a good track to meet the road by Inchvuilt. These rounded friendly hills had taken just 4 hours and 20 minutes, and I still felt fresh and buoyant. In fact I'm right on top of my game, now four days up on schedule with 167 done in 49 days. Maybe now I can take the Cairngorms in a single bite and put the issue beyond doubt.

This burst of euphoria, despite its bravado, can claim justification remembering the real trepidation on setting out from Cluanie six days previously. This vast forest of high hills had elicited my greatest respect, and to complete their summits without hitch or delay was an unexpected boon. Which is not to say that the area failed to match its imagined reputation. The three glens – Affric, Cannich and Farrar – in their lower parts are the most enchantingly beautiful that we saw, yet each has birth in an upper reach of awesome wildness. And the summit ridges can fulfil what must be every mountain walker's dream – to stride unfettered over narrow crests for day upon day without foreseeable end, a master to all he beholds.

11

IN BLEAKEST MIDWINTER

8–16 February:
Feshie – Tilt, Shee and Clova – Lochnagar – Mount Keen

The air was thick with dust and grit, gathered up into spiral clouds, then flung full length across our tracks. Only a skin of ice still clung to the ground, and the booming wind echoed round the corrie. Each blast would send us skidding backwards clawing for a rock to hold. There was no hope without crampons. Grasping vainly at the flying straps with mittened hands, our minds too numbed to tie the knots properly, the job of fitting them took ten minutes. Helping each other to our feet we staggered forward . . .

All this, and we hadn't even left the car park! Coire Cas on Cairn Gorm – one day the skier's sunny paradise, the next a bowl of white hell. Yet even this morning there were a few brave souls scattered over the nursery slopes, loath to admit defeat despite the frank impossibility of standing up in balance. But for me there was no point in persevering against insuperable odds. The simple climb to Cairn Gorm summit would have asked my all, never mind the planned continuation to Bynack More, and at this stage if a scheduled route could not be met then energies might as well be saved for tomorrow.

The White Lady Shieling was far enough to say we'd tried without getting into trouble. We retreated inside its deserted restaurant for a minute's breather before going back, glad of a secure shelter or so we thought. But not even the shieling was immune to the power of the storm. During the following night it burnt to the ground, due to a tiny wall fire fuelled and fanned by the rising gale. Had we bought a cup of tea we might have been the last customers.

Yesterday's plan for a four-day swoop on the area's seventeen Munros was but a fond memory, and even today's idea of doing the northernmost two now a tattered banner. After I had respectfully jockeyed around them for the last three weeks why did the Cairngorms have to smite me in the face on the very day I took my battle there?

That night as the storm reached its zenith we sheltered in the pine-woods by Glenmore Lodge. The skies were a clear pale blue at dawn, but looking over to Cairn Gorm, the plateau was shrouded in the same purple cloud that had accompanied yesterday's hurricane. These lenticular or 'fisheye lens' clouds are a sure sign of turbulence on the tops. The access road to the ski-roads was blocked by the blown snow, and yet we tuned to the radio to hear these fairy-tale pronouncements:

'Mountain weather for the Cairngorms: sunny intervals and scattered snow showers, wind south-east fresh to strong . . .'

'Ski-reports: Cairn Gorm: main runs all complete, vertical runs 1,800ft, wide snow cover, surface icy . . .'

Anyone sitting at home in Glasgow listening to those bright and breezy predictions might have been half-way to Aviemore at the time we gave up hope and drove round to Glen Feshie (see map on page 150). Not even the specialist forecasts are able to assess the remarkable local intensity of a Cairngorm storm. The gentle plateau topography welcomes any south-easterly airstream with open arms, giving a perfect take-off board from which the convergent winds jet down the northern corries at a destructive velocity. It is sound advice to double the quoted windspeed and stay off these hills when a sou-easter is in flow in winter.

But sitting in lower Glen Feshie, bathed in sun and seeing only a soft breeze at play in the treetops, it was still hard to accept defeat, and furthermore, two full days without progress would cut my hard-won lead by half. What if gales kept up for a week? The final straw was to see a party of middle-aged ramblers set off up the track from Achlean towards the Carn Ban Mor. They were probably going nowhere near the tops, but my pride was sufficiently pricked to follow their suit at 2pm.

Sgor Gaoith was the aim, the higher of the 'Sgoran' twins which overlook the head of Glen Einich in a 2-mile barrier of cliffs. The approach from Feshie is a simple stroll, but for chance of meeting that cliff-edge in a white-out, a serious undertaking. Only a lucky clearance in the cloud on the approach gave me the slightest hope of safely finding the summit. Whenever the shroud was drawn the surface drift of the snow produced the mesmeric effect of a moving quicksand. All sense of balance, slope and direction was destroyed. Even free of cloud it took a tense half hour to find the precipice and skirt its edge to the highest point. Because the top is unmarked, back-bearings, map-sections and other navigational tricks were employed to prove it, using the gloomy sheet of Loch Einich below as the only sure reference point.

The sortie had hardly brought a rich reward for all its risk, but in a war of attrition, no summit would yield easily.

*

The storm was recharged in energy come the start of its third day, wiping out every hope other than to struggle up the other Feshie Munro, Mullach Clach a' Bhlair. Joy sensed my desolation and joined the fight.

Without permission to drive on the private road up the west side of the river, Achlean farm was the nearest starting point. A sheltered valley approach to a full-blown tempest is if anything worse than the battle up top, and so it was on the 2-mile trudge to Carnachuin:

> The pasting that was coming to us was all too clear from the headwind funnelling down the glen. Despite the bitter cold I was sweating with apprehension. Every little discomfort, the rub of the boot, my streaming nostrils, or the whip crack of the wind in my hood, was saying 'give in and go back' . . .

But once the first steps upward were made this sickly fear and cowardice vanished entirely. I was heartily glad of the broadly bulldozed track which led us up almost onto the summit plateau where it was lost under the snowfields, for once forgetting my dislike of such scars on the land.

Our objective stands at the south-west corner of the Moine Mhor, or Great Moss, the moorland expanse which marks the western bound of the Cairngorms range. Originally five Munros lay in close proximity to the Moss, barely decipherable on the criterion of 'separate mountains', but since 1974 three have been rightly demoted to Tops to leave Sgor Gaoith and this Mullach of today as the definitive hills of the area.

On the final steepening the wind threw itself upon us. There was no cloud as such, only a 10m cowl of blowing snow through which a blue sky was occasionally glimpsed, but once enclosed within its wrap:

> . . . I could only recall the 20,320ft summit of Mount McKinley in Alaska for a proper comparison to the severity of these conditions – gusts of 80 or 90mph blowing us over, and a wind-chill temperature below the minus thirty mark with real frostbite potential. Behind me Joy's face was masked by a cake of frozen breath which had grown between her trails of hair. We took turns to break the wind, making quick dashes forwards in the clearer lulls until the paltry pile of summit stones was found . . . And oh, the relief of getting back to the glen with its stands of pine, farms and cottages – so welcome now that we had survived our task.

After the ethereal splendour of the morning, our later visit to the Aviemore Centre was quite inappropriate. Its concrete façades and manufactured entertainments made us wonder which indeed was the alien world. We bought a paper and commiserated with the groups of would-be skiers who mooched around the lifeless precincts, then left

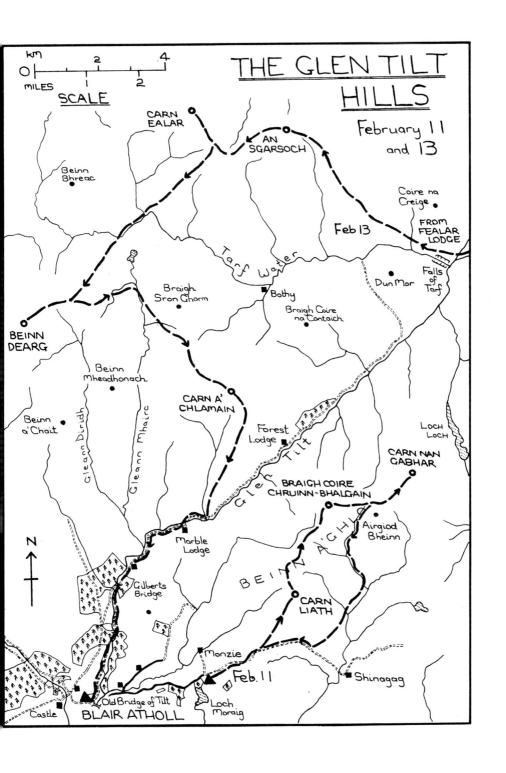

THE GLEN TILT
HILLS
February 11
and 13

SCALE
km
0   2   4
MILES
1   2

CARN
EALAR

AN
SGARSOCH

Beinn
Bhreac

Coire na
Creige

FROM
FEALAR
LODGE

Feb 13

Tarf Water

Braigh
Sron Gharm

Bothy

Dun Mor

Falls
of
Tarf

Braigh Coire
na Contaich

BEINN
DEARG

Beinn
Mheadhonach

Beinn
a'Chait

Gleann Diridh

Gleann Mhairc

CARN A'
CHLAMAIN

Forest
Lodge

Glen Tilt

Loch
Loch

CARN NAN
GABHAR

BRAIGH COIRE
CHRUINN-BHALGAIN

Airgiod
Bheinn

N

Marble
Lodge

Gilberts
Bridge

BEINN A'GHLO

CARN
LIATH

Monzie

Feb. 11

Shinagag

Old Bridge of Tilt

Castle

BLAIR ATHOLL

Loch
Moraig

to soothe our worries by the frozen shores of Loch Morlich. Two simple summits which one could be round in four hours of good weather had soaked up three whole days. What next was in store?

The curtain rose brightly on day four, everywhere at least except the Cairn Gorm plateau. All ready in boots and gaiters, and with flask and sandwiches packed, we drove up Glen More confident at last of doing the Cairn Gorm–Bynack round. Yet to our infuriated despair as soon as the forest opened up, there were the same stormclouds covering the tops, and the ski-road was still blocked, precipitating an urgent dilemma. To risk waiting could mean the loss of another day and the onset of total demoralisation, yet time was short to go elsewhere.

On decisive impulse we drove off at full throttle over Drumochter to Blair Atholl. Cairn Gorm was handed its just victory, but surely the central Grampians would be more tolerant of our presence. The forecast was optimistic. Atlantic and Scandinavian airmasses had been tightly wedged over northern Britain in the last three days but now were disengaging from their tussle, and a gradual moderation of the wind could be expected. At Atholl a minor road turns left from Bridge of Tilt and climbs steeply to the open braes by Monzie farm. At 9.45am it was late already.

From here for 20 miles north and east to Glen Dee lies the heart of the Grampian chain, an empty moorland deserted by the finer touch of Nature's brush, abundant only in its barrenness, and under winter's snows enough to sink the strongest spirit. So great is the expanse that it completely fills the 'Braemar' Ordnance Survey sheet. With the maps spread out, the eye is arrested less by the summits of the area than the meandering watershed lying at its centre between the Geldie, Tilt and Feshie catchments, their discordant drainage evidencing major glacial interference. The rivers Tilt and Feshie captured parts of the headwaters of the Geldie, which were blocked by glaciers in the main Dee valley during the Ice Age. Each has since carved a lower gorge of impressive depth, but left the Geldie bereft of erosive power. The linkage of the three glens enables through treks to be undertaken between Braemar, Badenoch and Atholl, which are lengthy but very popular in summer.

Only one mountain group stands aloof from these arguing waters – Beinn a'Ghlo, the highest ground of the Grampians save for Lochnagar, and a steeply sculpted mass of rounded tops and three Munros. In our disorganisation it formed the only close objective for a day's round trip, travelling over the summits from Carn Liath to Carn

(*right*) Sundown in lower Glen Affric (see Chapter 10)

nan Gabhar and descending by the eastern flanks towards Shinagag until a farm track leads back west to Monzie.

Joy watched me set off in full expectancy of a hard struggle and a late return, but conditions aheight were unsavoury rather than murderous, and no real hindrance to progress. At last the storm had eased its grip. The snow was confined to the lee-slopes, where it had been set like cement by the wind, giving a quick approach, and on finishing the trio a running descent down the drifted course of the western stream of Airgiod Bheinn. The following traverse to the Shinagag track was a contrasting slog in knee-deep heather. All the way along a 'snowcat' vehicle shadowed my steps, bringing the fear that it was stalking *me* rather than the hinds which are culled during the winter months. However, it finally passed on the track with a pair of beasts strapped to the sides, the bodies lifeless yet still steaming from the heat of their final flight.

That evening we entertained a distinguished visitor from the colonnades of Fleet Street. We were viewing the press suspiciously, knowing that all publicity would help the charity but fearing that glorified reporting would demean our enterprise to the level of a stunt with ourselves as a pair of performing puppets. 'Tough Training for Bonington!' was one typically silly headline that followed our capers on Creag Meagaidh. However, we were instructed by IT to be on our very best behaviour tonight, for our guest, Mike Herd, was the sports feature writer for the prestigious *London Evening Standard*, and so intrigued on hearing of our doings that he had made a special journey to investigate. From both stature and dress it was clear that his avid love for sport was safely couched in the armchair, and his swift removal from Pitlochry's four-star Atholl Palace Hotel into our sweaty cabin for dinner came as a rude shock. Yet he displayed a delightful charm and interest throughout the ordeal, even expressing the hope of taking a little air with us on the morrow at Glen Shee.

There are two further groups of Munros in the vicinity of Glen Tilt, a string of eight beginning on The Cairnwell summit, and the ring of four around the Tarf Water to the west of the main glen. Each group would give an arduous day of nigh on 25 miles with perforce an overnight bivouac between, somewhere in the glen's upper reaches. Here as nowhere else the Nordic skis were needed, but without continuous snow there was no choice but to go on foot, and quickly too.

(*left, above*) Lochnagar: Black Spout Pinnacle and the summit cliffs; (*below*) Ben Macdui from the top of Beinn Mheadhoin (see Chapter 12)

SIR HUGH MUNRO probably didn't know what he was starting best part of a century ago when he painstakingly mapped and listed the 277 Scottish peaks that are more than 3000 feet high.

Since 1891, the year in which the worthy knight completed his task, the Munros, as they have become known, have been a target for British mountaineers. Some men have made it their life-time objective to climb the lot and three have actually scaled all 277 in one spring-summer season. But no-one has succeeded in reaching every peak in a winter.

Some climbers have thought of it and abandoned the idea as impossible or just plain crazy. But right now, as you read these words, somewhere up on one of those peaks a young Englishman is clawing his way into the record books.

At the last count 29-year-old Martin Moran had reached 184 peaks. Winter in the mountaineering calendar last 90 days, starting on December 21 and finishing on March 20, so there are 93 peaks still to be climbed and 35 days in which to do them.

Moran, born on Tyneside, is a chartered accountant who realised his destiny was not to sit in an office keeping somebody else's books. Instead, it was to climb mountains to a height where the cold, glittering across the snow, seems to freeze the air itself.

He has had his wish these past few weeks because the winds on the Scottish summits have been between 60 and 100 miles an hour and the temperature 35 degrees below. You take your glove off to scratch your nose and you have frostbite. And it is easy to lose your hearing, sight and, worst of all, your sense of balance.

"I was on a ridge the other day which should have been easy, but the wind was so fierce I had to crawl. The wind was throwing me about, playing with me." As the man said, mountaineering is a judgment game and sometimes the stakes are life and death.

Club-footed

Most of us would have stayed in the office, content to dream, but not Moran. He and his wife, Joy, a kindred spirit, sold their house to raise the £2500 needed for vehicle hire, petrol, food and equipment. Then they took the high road. . . .

I met them parked, in snow of course, just north of the Pass of Killiecrankie. That day, despite feeling club-footed from the numbing cold, Moran had reached three peaks in the Grampians and was planning the next day's assault.

Four mountains — An Sgarsoch, Càrn Ealar, Beinn Dearg and Càrn a' Clanain — ascents of 5000 feet and 22 miles of walking, much of it, in knee-deep snow, like exploring virgin land.

MARTIN and JOY MORAN . . . sold their house and took to the high ro[ad]

Moran's theme Climb every mountain . . .

MICHAEL HERD reports

smoke or eat meat. He is bespectacled and studious-looking. Come to think of it, he looks like an accountant so what the hell is he doing climbing these mountains?

There are two reasons. The first is to raise £50,000 for the charity Intermediate Technology, which works in famine-and poverty-stricken countries. That was the agency, you might recall, for which Richard and Adrian Crane ran 2000 miles along the length of the Himalayas. Moran calls his venture ——— [Lim]its for Surv[ival]

hoping it will give me a reputation. For instance, anyone who comes to Scotland will say: "Martin Moran must know the Munros like the back of his hand. We'll go to him. It must increase my knowledge as a guide, mustn't it?"

He knows his way up the sides of a mountain, does Moran. He has climbed in the Himalayas and Alaska and conquered the north face of the Eiger. "But I can tell you this winter assault on ——

up, there was a blizzard and w[e] had white-out condition.

"I didn't expect anythin[g] to happen but Joy stepped o[n] to a cornice, an edge, of ic[e.] It broke away behind her an[d] I fell off with her. The cornic[e] hit the slope 20 feet below an[d] it avalanched."

There was a low-pitche[d] rumble and suddenly th[e] Morans were sliding, rollin[g,] tumbling down a 200ft slop[e] surrounded by blocks of sno[w] large enough to maim or bur[y] them.

By some miracle, and u[p] there you don't argue abou[t] who's pulling the strings, the[y] finished, uninjured, on top o[f] the snow. They had survive[d] wha[t] mountaineers describe [as] a full-depth, wind-slab av[a]-lanche 300 yards wide.

As a cynic weaned on pro[fes]-fessional soccer in whic[h] cheating is par for the cours[e] it occurred to me that th[e] Mor[a]ns could stay in [the]——— van

Mike Herd's feature in the *London Evening Standard*

A start was made from Cairnwell to use the 665m height advantage of Scotland's highest road pass. Tomorrow's route would finish back at Blair Atholl, so Joy could not be with me for need of moving our transport; and more was the pity, for this is the sort of country where company is at a premium.

Mike came up Glen Shee to see me off. No amount of persuasion would take him ten paces off the chairlift car park. After briefly sniffing the chilly morning air, he wished us well, dived into his car and hastened back to breakfast at the Palace. Yet our antics left a suitable impression for he wrote a most entertaining article to our favour which must have left many a Cockney commuter scratching his head in wonder.

On a bleak midwinter morning the rim of the Glen Shee pistes from Carn Aosda to The Cairnwell is the edge of civilisation. Below, hordes of skiers are already disgorging from cars and buses and rapidly turning the slopes into ant-hills, whilst over to the west is an unbroken desert, imported direct from the Arctic tundra. An Socach, Glas Tulaichean, Beinn Iutharn Mhor, Carn an Righ – they are all obscured by a haze of merging snow and cloud. The foreground plane of mottled moor is powdered white, blotched by peat, and destitute of form and feature. One searches for a gauge of scale, and maybe a twisting clough or shooter's box is spotted, but is it one, two or three miles away? Even map and compass are confused, and slow to give the answer. All this and still a further horizon beyond are to be crossed within the next few hours.

Pace yourself, set your watch, divide the daylight hours and ration out the snacks. Then knuckle down and don't stop or you'll lose heart . . .

At 5.30 a final spurt saw me onto Carn Bhac, the eighth Munro, right on the target I'd set on Cairnwell. Fealar Lodge, high on a tributary of the Tilt, was 2 miles to the south-west and would likely provide a barn or at least a wall for shelter. As darkness fell, the haze cleared and a keen frost pinched, so I hurried down towards it. Quite abruptly I was stopped in my tracks at the sight of vehicle headlights flashing nearby. The beams seemed focused directly on my path and I felt a real fear of being hunted. There was no bothy here, no other reason to come. This was surely not a chance encounter! I even switched my own torch off as I cautiously approached the nest of buildings.

A generator was humming by one of the cottages and in a lighted doorway a bearded figure waited.' I had unwittingly arrived at Scotland's highest permanent habitation, and one of its most remote, 500m up and 8 miles from the nearest public road.

Stepping into the light, Jimmy Lean the shepherd looked me up and down until his eyes gleamed in recognition.

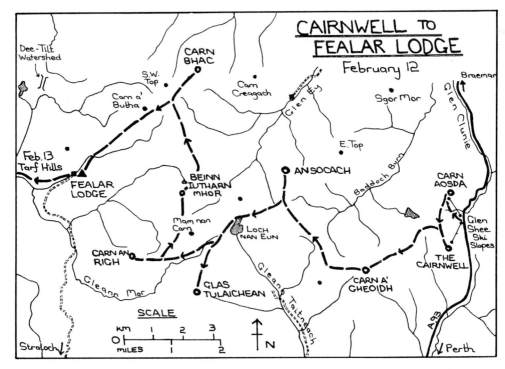

'So you'll be the chap who's doing all the Munros this winter', he
declared with pinpoint accuracy. Now I know how Doctor Living-
stone felt! He ushered me inside where his wife Dorothy already had
the kettle boiled for tea. While I gladly drank they engaged me in an
hour's non-stop chatter. I was the year's first visitor at Fealar.

'We read you were in the Cairngorms and wondered when you'd
come this way', said Dorothy.

Their winter lives are divorced from all normality. On a Monday
morning Jimmy takes their daughter down to school at Straloch in the
snowcat, and, if conditions allow, will pick her up on Friday but: 'In
1984 she had to stay down for six weeks at lodgings in the big snows.'

Both their sons were working on estates, one down by Atholl, the
other over west in Glen Garry. There is no television and a radio
telephone is the only outside link, but you could sense their peace, and
a contentment in each other's company.

'Winter is a quiet time', he said. 'Just the sheep to feed and a bit of
stalking . . .'

At length he saw my eyelids drooping.

'Well, you'll be needing a bed then . . .' He took me over to the
shooting lodge where a choice of six rooms for the night was offered!
So instead of curling up in an open sheep pen, I dropped towards
slumber stretched out on a double bed, browsing through the back
copies of *Country Life*, and feeling quite a distinguished guest.

The two-day wait in Blair Atholl was not an easy time for Joy. Outside, the village life gave a picture of normality which threw a disturbing mirror against her own existence. Suddenly a home and job were missed:

> I saw the men leave for work, watched housewives go shopping, small children hanging at their skirts, heard the endless idle chatter in the village store – their lives struck me as so mundane at one moment, and at the next I was aching with envy and longing for my own home, and sorely missing that secure job I had gladly abandoned last year. With Martin away, and nothing to do, the point of our venture just vanished from my thoughts . . .

Joy had to wait until 7pm for my return. We both felt subdued that night, for the Ring of Tarf and a 7-mile walk out down Glen Tilt had sorely tested my own dedication to the task. In all, the walk from Fealar Lodge was 28 miles, and both terrain and weather were raw accompaniments throughout.

The atmosphere of the snowy Tarf would be hard to match for its sheer intensity. Apart from a walker's bothy in the centre of the Ring, any marks of humanity that do exist are obliterated under the snow. You can be transported back to any era of the choosing and really live out the dream for a few hours. Sound is also absent, for even the wildlife has deserted the moors in winter. Of course the waddling ptarmigan and fleeing grouse are there in plenty, but their cries are harsh and only emphasise the intervening silence. Occasionally a white hare dashes through the tussocks. The deer have sought low grazing, and there are no stampeding herds to stir the spirit. Few of the rarer birds are around, though a flutter of snow buntings may be spotted if you are quick of eye. Even the wandering sheep are missed when absent.

The traveller must plot a skilful route through this country, holding to the hardened snowfields, frozen peat and burnt heather. Today, this meant avoiding the drifted north-west slopes, and pursuing either the exposed crests or icebound streambeds. However, the tougher ground could not be dodged for ever. After a heathery climb up from the Falls of Tarf, An Sgarsoch and Carn Ealar and even the 6-mile valley crossing to the granite crown of Beinn Dearg were firm and fast, but on the western flank of Carn a'Chlamain, my luck ran out:

> The snow looked firm, but just as my balance rocked forward into each new step I would break through the crust and plunge to the knee; so I would aim for the heather but there found only hidden ditches and tangled tussocks which would send me searching back for the snow. As passage was deflected and retarded, the remaining miles grew into an awesome burden.

Anyone who has trekked the Pennine moors under the snows,

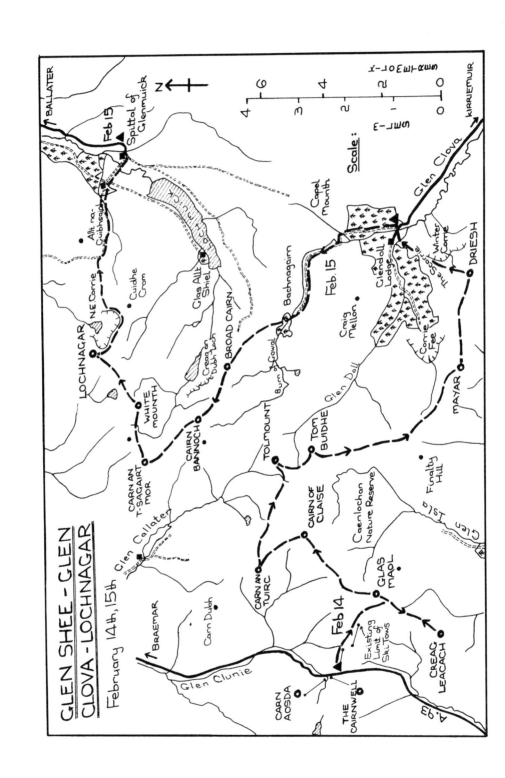

GLEN SHEE – GLEN
CLOVA – LOCHNAGAR

February 14th, 15th

Scale:

BALLATER

Feb 15

Spittal of Glenmuick

N

Allt na Guibhsaich

Cuidhe Cром

LOCHNAGAR

N.E. Corrie

Glas Allt Shiel

WHITE MOUNTH

Сreag an Dubh Loch

BROAD CAIRN

CAIRN BANNOCH

CARN AN T-SAGAIRT MOR

Glen Callater

BRAEMAR

Carn Dubh

Glen Clunie

CARN AOSDA

THE CAIRNWELL

Feb 14

Existing Limit of Ski Tows

CARN AN TUIRC

CAIRN OF CLAISE

GLAS MAOL

CREAG LEACACH

A.9.

Glen Isla

Caenlochan Nature Reserve

Finalty Hill

MAYAR

Tom BUIDHE

TOLMOUNT

Burn of Gowal

Bachnagairn

Craig Mellon

Glen Doll

Feb 15

Capel Mounth

Glendoll Lodge

The Scorrie

Corrie Fee

DRIESH

Winter Corrie

Glen Clova

KIRRIEMUIR

especially the great bogtrots such as the Derwent Watershed, could echo these sentiments with heartfelt sympathy.

The final plunge into the fault-line trench of the Tilt brought a sudden end to the wilderness. The lower glen is richly ornamented by woodland copses, sweeping drives and pretty cottages, a charming end to any trek however great the fatigue, and even on a dark night.

East of Cairnwell pass the Grampian sprawl bears a further eight Munros before its next major incision at Glen Clova. We drove around to Glen Shee immediately on my return through the portals of the Tilt. The weather was holding its improvement and early morning snow showers only briefly veiled a clear blue sky which at last gave some definition to the distant views.

From the head of the ski-tows we detoured south to the walled top of Creag Leacach before traversing the piebald dome of Glas Maol. The top is currently a bone of contention between the skiing and environmental lobbies. An application has been permitted to extend the tows very nearly to the summit to give an appreciable expansion of the Glen Shee ski domain. However, this will encroach on Caenlochan National Nature Reserve, the breeding ground of dotterel and other rare bird species, and seems to breach the Scottish Office Ski Guidelines*. It is unlikely at this stage that the decision will be overturned, but happily the development is subject to several clauses protective to the environment.

For more than fifteen years the capacity of Scotland's downhill ski facilities has been static. Since the plan to extend the Cairn Gorm lifts towards the Lairig Ghru was defeated in 1982 the pressure of increasing demand has become uncontainable. On any fine winter weekend the Scottish resorts are completely overwhelmed, with disgruntled skiers spending the majority of their expensive day waiting in queues. Yet despite this, and for all the fickle weather, they are still prepared to come.

Although Glen Shee has a large untouched potential, it is in the west on Aonach Mor in Lochaber that new development is now imminent. An access road was given planning consent in early 1985 and all parties have pronounced a cautious blessing. Yet the scenic impact of a wholly new scheme may be severe, and the skier will lack the reliable snow cover that is guaranteed in the east. During the 1984–5 winter season, albeit an exceptional year, the Glencoe slopes were closed for lack of snow for all but three or four weeks. However,

---

*The Guidelines state a 'presumption against any significant intrusions into the National Nature Reserves'. In this case the extension is conveniently not being treated as a *significant* intrusion.

Fort William is the undoubted winner, for it desperately needs the new jobs and income which the project promises.

If we were all on Nordic skis the problem would be solved at a stroke. Now there was a bright thought as I trudged away *on foot* towards Tolmount! Yet today the snow was deep enough that I pined for them. Joy had dropped down from Carn an Tuirc to bring the van to Clova.

Mayar and Driesh are Clova's local Munros, and the last of my day. Their shapely summits were a welcome sight during the feature-less tramp from Tom Buidhe and gave fine glimpses over the scoured edge of the glen. Coire Fee and Driesh's Winter Corrie have good climbing here, especially in the lower grades, and are the local haunts for the denizens of Dundee.

Thirty-two hours on the march out of the last sixty had taken toll of my energy. On the steep descent of The Scorrie my knees collapsed like jellies. I slithered down to level ground then swayed light-headed to the roadend car park. But Joy did not arrive for another hour, harassed by the snowy roads, still depressed from Atholl and suffocated by a head-cold. All the ingredients were there for a blazing row, and I glibly tossed the spark by demurring to fill the water con-tainer. The crumpets just requested were promptly hurled rather than served to me, and I was soon outside breaking the ice in the river, my ears still ringing from the retort. After two months cooped like hens it was testimony to our mutual patience that this was our first serious flare-up.

Lochnagar has a greater tradition and romance than any other Scottish mountain, its quality being immortalised in Byron's stirring verse:

> England! Thy beauties are tame and domestic,
> To one who has roved o'er the mountains afar;
> Oh for the crags that are wild and majestic!
> The steep frowning glories of dark Lochnagar.

Notwithstanding the summer visitors, the mountain is the true 'monarch' of Balmoral. Its north-eastern corrie is a magnificently proportioned granite bowl, 300m in depth, and after Ben Nevis the country's most famous winter climbing ground. From Glen Clova the route to Lochnagar is indirect, but in its circuit of the Dubh Loch valley achieves the finest high-level traverse in the area, and formed the next link in my Grampian route.

At −11°C the overnight air in the glen had been even more frosty than the atmosphere inside the van! Expecting a repeat of yesterday's drifts I shouldered my skis for the 4-mile approach up the glen's northern fork to Bachnagairn. Here the Burn of Gowal forms a delectable wooded gorge which today was choked with columns of shining ice. Beyond is the featureless climb to the plateau at Broad Cairn.

The Lochnagar massif is geologically twinned with the Cairngorms, being formed of the same igneous intrusion in contrast to the varying schists of the other Grampians. The change of rock is quickly noticed. Broad Cairn's gentle northern incline breaks with no warning into the Creag an Dubh Loch, a 250m slice of bare pink granite which cuts the flanks for half a mile. The cliff has taken over from Lochnagar in the last two decades as the spearhead of climbing advance both in summer and winter. A look at its compacted overlapping slabs will leave no illusions of the difficulty.

The skis were on and off across the tops, and mainly off on Lochnagar which was blown down to hard ice:

> This was the first day of calm. Released from the need to fight the cold I relaxed into a drowsy reverie in the sunshine and nearly fell asleep after lunch on Cairn Bannoch!

From Lochnagar my descent skirted the edge of the great corrie then dropped to Meikle Pap and then Allt-na-giubhsaich. This is the most popular route of approach, revealing the corrie with stunning immediacy and enabling its inspection from below as well as above. The final pitches and exits of Eagle Ridge, the Parallel Gullies, the Black Spout Pinnacle Face and many other great climbs may be identified and admired by the walker sauntering around the rim to the summit tor of Cac Carn Beag.

Glen Muick was soft and tranquil on my arrival, its bottom flats bathed in the warm sunlight of middle afternoon. The square-cut glen is a perfect piece of glacial architecture and with the brooding loch, which spans it from side to side, has a compellingly wild aspect. The Spittal of Glenmuick is merely 7 miles from Clova via the direct Capel Mounth track; but for the driver is a nightmare journey of over 80, and gave Joy one of her most hectic and trying days; witness her diary:

> I was the first vehicle down Clova, the road a sheet of ice and the ditches waiting open-mouthed to catch a slip of concentration. At Kirriemuir there were two radio interviews to do, and between them a frantic round of shopping. Then to the garage – petrol, oil, water, tyres and propane gas. No gas – so on with the drive and find it en route. The minor road to Glen Shee once again was dangerously drifted. It took three hours to reach Ballater where I arranged to collect Steve Bonnist from the Aberdeen bus, and located our fuel before proceeding up Glen Muick. There was an hour before Martin was due, just time to prepare the van for our guest and make an evening meal. Nothing had touched my lips since 7am!

Beyond Lochnagar the Grampians slowly lose their momentum and only at Mount Keen is the 3,000ft contour again attained. But although it is the most easterly Munro, there are a further 30 miles of moor and glen before the Aberdeenshire coast is met. The hill is most easily ascended from Glen Esk to its south, from which an old mounth road crosses close to the top. By comparison, the way from Glen Muick over Cairn Hillock has a long stretch of peatland to cross before the final cone, which is a painful plod in deep snow. Though only a 12-mile return distance this was not for me the respite desired before our return to the Cairngorms. But the weather was superlative, the burning sun making us glad of cream and glasses. Yet every patch of shade was like a three-star freezer. A whole week of sub-zero temperatures had now elapsed, so still the snowdrifts lay unbonded.

We were joined by Steve, who was in Scotland to make arrangements for the coming climax of the journey. At a total of 198 Munros, the finish was not *so* far away. But as we sat at lunch just beneath the summit all complacency was shattered by the arrival of two hardy-looking walkers on the top. One of them thumped the summit trig point and exclaimed: 'Ah ha, just one more to go!'

So at last we were to meet him! The anonymous competitor, whom I had often imagined secretly at work these last two months, always sneaking on a step ahead, was now ready to take the winter Munros glory, and render my own venture a nonsense. Bonnist blanched; all his charitable efforts were about to crumble. Our curiosity soon became unbearable. I ambled over as though to pass the time of day . . .

'Doing the Munros are you?'

'Aye, and only Ben Lomond left', came the triumphant reply.

'Taken long then?' I must have been visibly twitching in anticipation, but his bearded countenance broke into a roar of laughter.

'Oh, the better part of twenty years, I'm afraid to say!'

However entertaining the episode, it later raised a more serious reflection:

Why the fear of being upstaged? What if he *had* said 'two months'? I might have cursed and brooded for a day or so, but would I ever think of giving up? Of course not, and all power to him if he had done it! The prime motivation for me must be personal challenge. The lure to be first is only a secondary spur, and though undeniably a strong incentive, I hope it will never be my lord and master.

Even taken in isolation, the last hard days had brought great fulfilment, for a solo crossing of the Grampians is a test of will, and a lasting restorative for the mind.

12

THE CAIRNGORMS COMPLETE

17–21 February:
Beinn Bhrotain – Braeriach – Ben Macdui – Ben Avon – Cairn Gorm

The River Dee has the pre-eminent claim on the drainage of the high Cairngorms. The trickles of the melting snows give its birth 1250m up on the Braeriach plateau. This tiny sub-Arctic stream plunges down and through the greatest corrie of the massif, then gathers the tributary waters of the Derry, Luibeg and Quoich to its girth, and broadens into graceful maturity through the Forests of Mar and Balmoral. Comparing the claims of the other major rivers, the Spey all but ignores the range apart from the collection of the Feshie, whilst the Avon seems so embarrassed by its capture of Macdui's waters that it rushes out of the mountains without a pause. Deeside therefore undoubtedly forms the most natural and grandest route of entry, which has long been a pilgrimage to all who seek the lonely plateaux.

Already repelled in our attempt from the north, it was now imperative to gain a foothold on the range by this southern approach, even though it meant stretching my endurance to the limit on each clear day that followed. The non-stop Grampian traverse had only just regained the ground lost in the windstorm. Now there was a chance to capitalise on that effort. A three-day round from the Linn of Dee roadhead could encompass all the fifteen outstanding Munros of the massif given a continuation of the excellent conditions. We chose to start from the west with Braeriach, Cairn Toul and their sub-sidiaries, and packed our sacks late into the night.

The twilight temperature of $-13°C$ sent us off towards White Bridge at a swinging quickmarch. Its sudden stimulus was much required, for we had risen in a soporific stupor, due partly to fatigue but mainly as a result of my mistakenly setting our alarm for 4.30 instead of 5.30. Mornings were tough enough already without such catastrophe, but an early start would no doubt pay us back by sunset.

The Cairngorms are the 'blue hills', although they are actually composed of red granite. However, the tundra landscape of the high tops does have a distinctly bluish wash when viewed at a distance, in refreshing contrast to the brown heather moors of the nearby Grampians. The effect is especially pronounced in winter when the snow's refraction adds an icy tingle to the hue, and it inspired a

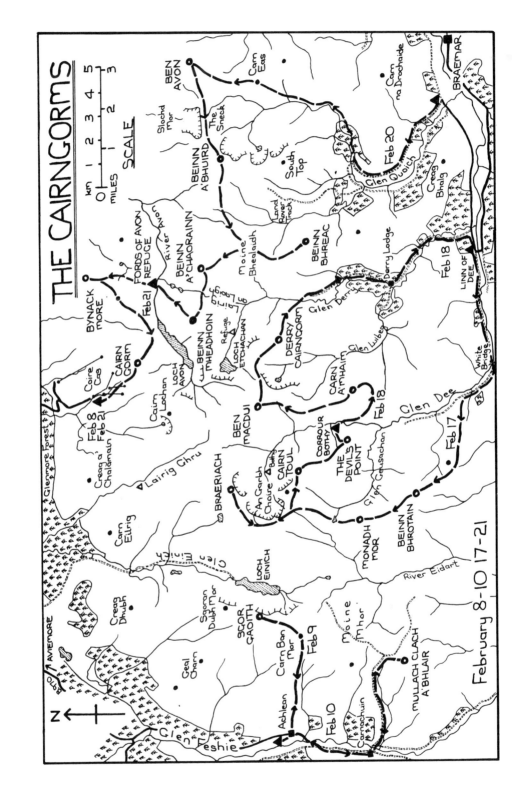

THE CAIRNGORMS

SCALE

km 1 2 3 4 5
miles 1 2 3

N

February 8–10 17–21

growing vigour to our ascent of the patchwork slopes towards Beinn Bhrotain that was climaxed by the rise of the sun over Lochnagar. Streams of cloud idled at the higher levels and threw our silhouettes into foggy shadows and ghostly spectres, but the summit pierced these mists into an azure sky, against which the white sweep of the highest plateaux made a brilliant relief.

Bhrotain and Monadh Mor led us around the skyline of Glen Geusachan and onto the featureless back of Cairn Toul. Lunch was taken at Loch nan Stuirteag before the climb. Again, no wind disturbed our rest, but the sun had faded above a coverlet of cloud which infiltrated from the west. The Tarf and Feshie hills were close in view. Mullach Clach a' Bhlair was but a dull and dingy bump on the Great Moss, hardly seeming the scene for our 'Alaskan' battle just a week ago.

After a tiresome plod the crest was gained near Einich Cairn, where An Garbh Choire makes its deepest bite into the plateau. This is the Cairngorms' greatest amphitheatre, a mile and a half in width and with a nest of hanging corries etching its 4-mile rim. As recently as 1810 the coire may have held a small glacier, a suggestion based on the dating of lichen on its terminal moraines, and there are still permanent snowfields through most years. Though we are now in a phase of climatic warming, it would take only a slight reversal to bring the Ice Age back to the Cairngorms.*

In direct contravention of the climbing rules we left our sacks on the edge to make the long detour to Braeriach. It is a dubious tactic and should be entertained only in settled visibility, but on countless occasions through the winter saved me vital time and strength. The Braeriach–Cairn Toul circuit is the most exhilarating plateau walk in the Cairngorms. In winter it is part of the 4,000ft tops ski-tour which gives a hard but magnificent day's expedition from Glen More, and is usually feasible for many weeks of a normal winter due to its high elevation. But though the cover on the tops was now complete, the surface was icy and with the snow-base as high as 600m the skis would have been more a hindrance than a help.

Joy found the head of An Garbh Choire an intimidating spot:

> The cornices hung over the edges like huge jaws ready to snap; their sight enough to make me shudder. As the cloud spread and the light flattened I became more than a little anxious to get back to the sacks and off the plateau . . .

She might, however, have taken a leaf out of Richard McHardy's

---

*Gordon Manley has estimated that a 2°C drop in average annual temperature, if sustained for fifteen years, would be sufficient to re-establish permanent moving icefields in the high corries, though there is minimal likelihood of this happening in the short-term future.

book of tricks. A few years ago he applied his inimitable panache to demonstrate how the cornices can be tamed to one's advantage. On a filthy day when Richard considered the snow conditions too dangerous to join his mates on a climbing route on the corrie walls, he ambled alone up an easy gully onto The Angel's Peak and over the plateau. Trying to find his way back in the mist he walked straight onto a snow edge which collapsed and carried him down for over 300m, stopping conveniently near the Garbh Choire Bothy door. Up he stepped, miraculously unhurt, and wandered in for an early tea, quite unruffled by a plunge which made our avalanche on Wyvis look like child's play. Such style must take many years of practice!

The summit wedge of Cairn Toul in both its shape and perched position is the finest top in the Cairngorms, but we hurried on, for it was the next and last Munro of the day which held a special significance for Joy, but:

> With the abundance of beautiful Gaelic names for the Scottish peaks why should I get landed with 'The Devil's Point' for my 100th summit of the season!

From the Point it was an initially steep but fast descent to Corrour Bothy. How welcoming it is when your night's refuge lies directly beneath, fully in view and is a simple descent in the last daylight. Corrour had a few other visitors as is usual, for it is a popular staging post on the Lairig Ghru route, but we squeezed in and were laid out on the floor by 8pm, the prospect of a glorious ten-hour sleep banishing all concerns of cornices and approaching blizzards.

Answering Nature's call half-way through the night, my torchbeam struck a myriad of floating flakes and a barrier of white fog outside. I hurried back to my warm cocoon of sleep and dreams but later, as the milky light of dawn filtered through the bothy windows, reality had to be confronted. To be trapped in a bothy by a blizzard was the most disastrous scenario that could be envisaged for us, but now we had to face the situation and juggle the options:

Plan A: stay put and stretch supplies for the extra day that would now be required to get over Ben Avon – hungry and very boring.

Plan B: retreat to the van; 6 miles down, a comfortable rest, then 6 miles back with more supplies when the storm cleared – 12 miles of extra effort and still a day lost.

Plan C: go on over Macdui's four Munros, leaving Cairn Gorm for a separate day; stop at the Hutchison Hut in Coire Etchachan tonight and hope to do Ben Avon tomorrow – *if* it improves.

A and B were safe but woefully depressing. C was the daring option but rather risky. However, since there was no perceptible wind at the bothy and as the Macdui tops were all familiar to me, it quickly gained my preference. But Joy was set against Plan C from the moment of its inception, and immediately withdrew. Having inspected the map of Macdui in great detail she was already well acquainted with the Coire Sputan Dearg, the Loch Etchachan cliffs, and the Loch Avon basin, and there was not a hope of tempting her anywhere within five miles of their edges in a white-out, whatever my claims to navigational skill!

Now realising that the next two days would be spent in solitude with only a compass needle for comfort, my own resolve was lost. The decision had been reached on hard-baked rationality and bound me fast, but underneath it I was all along banking on Joy's company. Our parting on the crest of the Luibeg path was therefore charged with such emotion that anyone would have thought I was setting off for the North Pole. Joy hated seeing me embark on an exploit that she herself declared unsafe:

> In the dense mist we rearranged the loads, Martin standing like an iceberg, his solemn face no doubt hiding only bitterness at my letting him down. As he walked off towards Carn a' Mhaim, my tears began to flow and I cried despairingly 'take care!' A faint 'aye aye' floated back but he was already swallowed up by the cloud and beyond recall.

Joy, however, was unaware that this steely exterior was only a front to my own anguish. Had my true emotions escaped, Macdui would have been missed, and doubtless regretted later. But for the first time in sixty days my enthusiasm for the tops ran completely dry:

> With no heart for the task, every step of the ascent was a torture. I ate my lunch long before a mid-morning snack was due, but this only left me more in want of succour. And frequent rests simply put me further behind the cursed clock! I passed into the throes of yawning depression for a good two hours before accepting my rotten lot.

The top of Scotland's second highest mountain is a gentle and feature-less dome. My navigation proceeded first on directional bearing and then by gauging distance travelled. From the head of the Tailor's Burn to the summit is 750m at 300 degrees, which converts to 450 of my double paces. Counting sheep may induce sleep, but not so counting steps in a white-out. When the total is reached and no trace of the top is visible, then comes the time to worry; but it is preferable to have a vain confidence which says, 'Perhaps they've moved the cairn' rather than dissolving into a 'Help, I'm lost!' panic. A block search of each surrounding hundred metre square eventually brought success. Absolute self-belief is one's only ally in the search.

Sitting beside the crowning tumulus my sympathies went out to the aspirant mountain guides who were that week undergoing their winter climbing assessment at Glenmore Lodge, for no doubt today would have been chosen for their navigation test. Suddenly I realised that not so far away there were other tormented souls even less fortunate than myself, for I vow that a month of isolation would be preferable to a foggy day finding spot heights on the Cairn Lochan plateau, with a Lodge examiner breathing down your neck.

During my own test in 1984, Choe Brookes and I had suffered near disaster. Inevitably, white-out conditions prevailed and on this day a bitter 60mph wind added to the pleasures:

'OK, Martin, you do the next leg – take me to that ring contour south of Coire Domhain', ordered the grim-faced Bob Barton who has been the scourge of a generation of hapless candidates. As I prepared my bearing, a sudden gust of wind tore the plastic-coated map out of my hands, and flapping like a concertina it disappeared into the cloud. I received a long frost-caked stare from Bob that could only spell 'FAIL'!

'Over to you then, Choe', he said. I felt like jumping over the nearest cornice at that particular instant.

But just as Choe unfolded his own map, another blast of wind swept across (does the Lodge have a divine hand in these matters?) and though he fumbled gamely, it too was plucked from his grasp. Long silent seconds and then the 'coup de grace':

'Well, perhaps we could borrow *your* map please, Bob?' I was polite but obviously desperate, but an emphatic 'No!' was the reply.

Meanwhile Choe saved our bacon by digging out a tatty old one-inch sheet, fortuitously brought along as a spare, from the bottom of his sack. Clinging to it for dear life we got Bob off the plateau and escaped with only a severe censure.

Yet we should be glad of the rigorous standards of mountain training which Glenmore Lodge has set over the past twenty-five years, whether we be guides, instructors, teachers or youth leaders. In the five years between 1979 and 1983 there were only 29 serious rescue incidents and 12 fatalities in the Cairngorms and Grampians in winter – no cause for complacency, but viewed against the rapid increases in the numbers of hill-goers, a remarkably low frequency of occurrence.*

*However, the annual numbers of incidents for the whole of Scotland rose from 60 in 1974 to 157 in 1984. Full accident statistics are published annually in the SMC Journal.

(*right, above*) The upper Feshie hills from Beinn Bhrotain; (*below*) The cloud-wreathed plateau of Ben Avon from the summit slopes of Cairn Gorm

That the current level of accidents in winter is no greater is in large part due to the Lodge's work.

And now my own training was applied in full measure to traverse round the head of Coire Sputan Dearg and onto Derry Cairngorm, all the way in white blindness:

> Already it was 3pm. Beinn Mheadhoin, the fourth Munro, would take at least one and a half hours and leave very little light for finding the hut. A wind was rising fast and a blizzard looked to be in the offing. In fact all the makings of a major epic were gathering together. And then came the thought that tomorrow was a momentous occasion – my thirtieth birthday – and would undoubtedly be better spent in rest and celebration with Joy at Braemar than shivering in a stormbound 'howff' sans food or fuel.

The extra 5 miles of a retreat by Glen Derry were brushed aside by my overwhelming urge to get down. Nor was any disgrace felt after having valiantly forced myself over three Munros; so the earlier agonies were superseded by a carefree homewards romp.

My descent dropped steeply down the eastern flanks. In the upper Derry straggling survivors of the native pine forests bent and groaned in the wind, which whistled unchallenged through the glen. The trees seemed to be withering under the storm's assault, shrinking back to leave a snowy desert in the higher reach. Only down by Derry Lodge does the forest thicken sufficiently to give warmth and security; and at dusk was filled with sheltering herds of deer. The return walk raised my total mileage for the past week to 140. No wonder my knees were wincing on the final stretch of icy track. But what a surprise there was in store for Joy:

> Having heard the snow and gale warnings on the 6pm forecast, I was settling down for an evening alone feeling very morose and sorrowing for my desertion this morning. Then I heard footsteps crunching up to the back door which thankfully was locked just in case of intruders; but unbelievably it was Martin's voice which called out. I opened it and there he stood grinning broadly: 'Thought I'd come back for my birthday!' he announced and jumped up in.

The names of Ben Avon and Beinn a' Bhuird are synonymous with long hard days in the hills. Even by the exacting standards of the other Cairngorms these eastern tops are depressingly remote. The ascent of both main Munros in a single day demands a dour determination, winter or summer, but is nought compared to the crossing of all their subsidiary tops, which on Ben Avon alone involves a journey

(*left*) On the crest of An Teallach looking up Gleann na Muice to the Fisherfield Munros (see Chapter 13) (*A. Thomson*)

of 6½ miles all above the 3,000ft level. Not surprisingly, the four great corries of Beinn a' Bhuird have lagged behind Lochnagar and the Loch Avon cirque in their winter development though they yield little in quality to either. A productive visit here requires at least one overnight bivouac or camp beneath the cliffs.

The storm had proved neither severe nor prolonged, but was enough to make me glad to be off the hill. It left a couple of inches of fresh snow on the tops and gave a day of drizzle as we rested down at Braemar, but over the next night the stars were reborn, and all was set for my final bid. To see the Cairngorms complete at last would be a sweet success.

Glen Quoich provides the shortest access to Ben Avon, yet it is still 10 miles from the road at Linn of Quoich to the summit. The upper part of the glen, where the water meanders between sandy banks under a canopy of Scots Pines, is of exquisite beauty. Yet it had a forlorn atmosphere, for the widely-spaced stands with their stunted growths and fallen branches give a strong breath of decay. Slow climatic change is largely responsible. Warming weather and most especially increased rainfall have caused a progressive acidification of the soils, and while the peat moors burgeoned the trees have died off. However, the overgrazing of deer has greatly accelerated the process in the last two centuries. Only by fencing the remaining areas to keep the deer off the new seedlings, and by expensive ploughing to drain the ground, could the spiral of decline now be reversed. It was these great old forests that first inspired my own love for the Cairngorms, and many a long mile can pass unnoticed in the enchantment of their company.

Joy came with me to the final trees. Looking up at the beckoning tops as they glowed pink with the sunrise, she was understandably envious of my striding off towards them, but was spared a tough 2 miles breaking trail in the fresh drifts of the open valley.

The new snow gave me some misgivings, for there was a long day ahead; but the tops were once again coated by a solid crust of ice to give a perfect walking surface. Bhuird's array of corries captured all my attention on the long pull over Carn Eas, and conditions must have also been good for ice-climbing judging from the opaque smears and streaks in their major clefts and gullies.

Ben Avon's summit is a striking granite tor some 15m in height, a fine example of the many such 'warts' which outcrop on the eastern plateaux. Their formation has long been a mystery, but by latest opinion they are dated to a pre-glacial period when the region experienced a sub-tropical climate and deep weathering under the soil mantle attacked the granite joint-lines. The embryonic features were then exhumed during glaciation, and have survived only on the plateaux tops which were spared erosive destruction under the ice.

The Sneck saddle provides a neat connection from Avon to Beinn a'Bhuird. The trough of Slochd Mor and the Mitre Ridge of the Garbh Choire are excitingly positioned on its northern side, but the scenery deteriorates profoundly on the dull eastern side of the mountain. A Land-Rover track has been driven to a height of 1100m on this flank to assist in deer stalking and occasionally provide vehicular access for spring skiing.

The gentle slopes of the Cairngorms are particularly vulnerable to disfigurement by bulldozed roads. Only since 1980 have landowners been required to obtain planning permission to drive new tracks above the 300m level, and then only in the specified 'National Scenic Areas'. Yet it is clear that these procedures have been little heeded. Whilst many new roads have appeared, only a handful of planning applications have ever come before the Countryside Commission. Not only are these tracks insensitively routed, but most are improperly drained and will likely trigger severe future erosion, while their economic necessity has never been properly demonstrated by the owners.

At least the ski developments visibly benefit a huge number of users. However, it is unlikely that a lift system will ever be constructed on these remote eastern tops, and long may their snows remain the domain of the ski mountaineer. Linking Ben Avon and Beinn a'Bhuird to the four-thousanders creates probably the ultimate quest to the long-distance tourer, the traverse of the 'Six Tops'. A one-day crossing was first made in 1962 by Adam Watson, and more recently was done in a round trip from Derry Gate by Raymond Simpson and Rob Ferguson in 1983 in nineteen hours of skiing with five hours' sleep at Corrour Bothy.

A broad moss, the Moine Bhealaidh, separates Beinn a'Bhuird from the central Cairngorms, and rises to a Munro at each end of its 3-mile stretch. These two, Beinn Bhreac and Beinn a'Chaorainn completed my scheduled route, but to their west on the far side of the Lairig an Laoigh, Beinn Mheadhoin was still outstanding from the curtailed Macdui round. Though it increased the day's mileage to 27 and ascent to 1920m (6,300ft), the 400m climb out of the Lairig felt effortless. My day off had created ample new reserves of stamina to call upon, and so I won the race to reach the summit tor before the sun was lost. The Cuillin apart, this was technically the most difficult top of the winter, only 12m but at least grade II under a half-inch coat of verglas. The sunset, however, moved me to a rapturous diary entry that night down in the Fords of Avon howff (see overleaf):

Shifting mists had draped themselves across the high plateaux, through which Mheadhoin's summit stacks protruded, and were fired to the deepest bronze. The glory of the Cairngorms was at its apogee this evening . . .

The Avon refuge is an oblong wooden cell covered with a tarpaulin wadding and weighted by granite blocks, and even on a clear evening was not easy to find. The appellation 'howff' denotes the most rudimentary form of shelter. Some of them, like the Shelter Stone, are simply natural caves with a walled-in entrance, whilst others in the Cairngorms have been specifically constructed for mountaineers. By contrast, the typical 'bothy' of the West Highlands is an old croft restored to habitability, usually by the diligent effort of the Mountain Bothies Association, and guarantees a higher level of comfort. But this howff was kept spotlessly clean by fortnightly visits from the Nature Reserve warden and was quite sufficient for my basic needs.

The final link of Bynack More and Cairn Gorm took only four hours on a warm and balmy morning. The views were still lovely, but just a slight anticlimax after the perfection of the previous evening's sunset. We are never satisfied it seems, always fixing our expectations at the highest level. But it was also a tedium with my own company which made me less receptive to the surrounds. On the tops during the last twelve days I had met only one pair on Lochnagar, a school group on Einich Cairn, and of course that bearded apparition on Mount Keen. Yesterday the sight of a lone ski-tourer on Beinn a'Bhuird had warranted a quarter-mile detour to meet for a minute. Hopefully he shared my feelings and was not abashed to be forcefully accosted and engaged in conversation. This was the February school holidays, and yet the hills seemed empty. Outside of the popular haunts this sense of loneliness in winter is still quite genuine.

The pistes of Coire Cas were suited more to ice skates than skis this morning. A nervous throng of skiers were gathered at the top of the White Lady runs, unwilling to make an irreversible commitment. Only the occasional expert or dare-devil clattered off downhill. For myself, crampons were a godsend to ensure a safe descent.

The emergence from yonder wilderness was the winter's greatest breakthrough. Suddenly freed from the Cairngorms' clutch, I was back in the car park where their story had begun so dramatically two weeks ago. Our steps now hastened north and west. Twenty-seven days was generous allowance for the sixty-four remaining peaks and among them lay the crown jewels of all the Munros; small wonder the buzz of excitement with which we finally left the Spey Valley.

160

13

NORTHERN HEATWAVE

22 February–3 March:
Sutherland – Assynt – the Fannichs – An Teallach – Fisherfield –
Inverlael – Torridon

The empty quarters of Sutherland are steeped in the sad history of the
Highland Clearances of the early nineteenth century, to which the
relict mountain peaks of the area were the silent witnesses. On first
acquaintance the solitude of the straths is inspiring, but as John
Prebble has reminded us: 'if their history is known there is no satisfaction to be got from the experience'.

His account of the Clearances was my sole literary company during
the expedition, hardly a well-chosen tome for the light entertainment
that I required at nights. Yet the chronicle of forced eviction and
emigration of the native communities under the imposition of large-
scale sheep farming gave a proper perspective to our brief visit to the
far north.

Ben Klibreck and Ben Hope are the sole Munro outposts in this
deserted land, and neither possesses the interest of the nearby lower
peaks of Ben Loyal or Foinaven. North of Ullapool the rule that the
Munros corner the best mountain scenery no longer applies. Furthermore, full winter climbing conditions rarely pertain due to the
proximity of the sea and the lower height of the mountains, but there
is still much to repay a long drive north from Inverness in the dark
months of the year.

Our caravanette had now clocked well over 3,000 miles of Highland
driving, serving us flawlessly throughout, and how vital this was in
these far-flung parts. Often we toasted dear old Mr Jackson, who had
so trustingly placed it in our care, but little did we know that back in
Sheffield he had been living in frantic worry over its safe-keeping ever
since seeing us driving around Glencoe on a Yorkshire Television
news feature!

Gradually the temperature had crept back to zero over the last
three days, and today a major frontal system was forecast to cross the
northern regions, so our reveille at Bonar Bridge found us understandably reluctant. However, on the approach from Lairg the sight
of Klibreck's grassy shield lightly washed by the morning dew quickly
put some polish on our boots. And as a further stimulus the day would
be spent together, a situation becoming increasingly rare as we

covered the more remote regions, where Joy's mobile support with the van was usually necessary.

The messenger clouds of the advancing depression enveloped us on the upper slopes during the climb from Vagastie, which is the shortest route to the main summit. Ice floes ringed the lower lochans and tumbled down the rocky western flanks, but having come straight from the piercing glare of the snow-smothered Cairngorms, it seemed to us that winter had neglected these hills.

Before continuing our drive to Ben Hope we stopped at Altnaharra and admired the retrospect of the mountain. What little snow remained gave graceful highlight to its folds and curves, but though very fine, it was difficult to see resemblance to the vivid metaphor which the impassioned Prebble had drawn, standing at the nearby ruins of Grummore settlement: 'Klibreck takes the naked shape of a sleeping woman, the milky smoke of burning heather for her hair, and her head turned away from Strathnaver.'

The rain held off that afternoon, a welcome reprieve but perhaps a mixed blessing, for the longer a storm is delayed in arrival, the more intense and protracted its eventual passage. From Strath More, Ben Hope rises in two precipitous tiers, with the intervening screes clothed in birch-wood. A mile north of the Dun Dornaigil broch a break in these defences leads onto the gentle southern slope from which the top is a long simple stroll. Standing on the summit and viewing the grey northern sea stretching beyond the last ramparts of land, one realises that the Highlands have finally come to an abrupt conclusion. There could be no self-deception when confronted by this sight. The imagined 'infinity' of mountains sadly does not exist, and so Ben Hope left me with a sense of disillusion. At least there was the consolation that the end had been a long long time in coming.

Turning away from Ben Hope our homeward journey down the western seaboard commenced, and Assynt was the first port of call, a region of a geological diversity that is unequalled in Scotland. The world's oldest known rock, the Lewisian gneiss, forms the foundations of the land, on which rise the monumental quartzite and sandstone peaks of Suilven and Quinag. Ben More and Conival, the only Munros in the area, lie over a band of Cambrian limestone, which contains the country's longest cave system. This is a fantastic landscape, far removed from all normality, and it combined with some weather of the most bizarre variety to give us a chequered stay:

> The rain had started soon after we reached Inchnadamph, but only in the morning did it become clear that this was no ordinary storm. I sleepily wandered out of bed at 7am only for the back door to be snatched from my

grip, and flung open by the wind. The usual check of the thermometer showed a plus 10°C overnight minimum which made me glance again in disbelief. Though clad only in pyjamas, I then took the brave step from the lee of the van into the open, where a fierce stream of water sent me scurrying back to shelter. Clouds of rain were pelting the mountain-sides, and the trees were blown close to horizontal. I had little compunction in taking the day off. If anything the storm only strengthened towards the middle day.

Already the burns were in a torrential spate, richly echoing Norman MacCaig's fine words:

Black hills are slashed white with this falling grace
Whose violence buckles space
To a sheet-iron thunder.

Reeling under the power of the tumult we cowered inside for the whole day. The gales in the valley possibly surpassed those we had witnessed on the tops above Glen Feshie, but by amazing contrast the air was 20°C warmer, plucked straight off the tropical seas it seemed, and giving the highest temperature of the season. No ordinary storm? This was no ordinary winter.

The rain still sprayed the hills but without such fearsome wind on the following morning. We were on our way up Gleann Dubh at 7am, an untowardly early hour considering our round was only 10 miles, but after a day pinned indoors we were dying for some action. The upper glen cuts through the limestone layer, and its river, the Traligill, has a subterranean section. The sinks and pavements, short-cropped turf *and* the slippery mud all seemed misplaced from their 'home' in the Yorkshire Dales. Inside the Cnoc nan Uamh cave entrances the underground stream was brimming in spate, and roaring mightily as though a giant turbine was churning up the flood.

The upper bastions of Conival are a mass of disintegrating quartzite. Instead of aiming for its northern ridge we attacked the western screes direct, a route of unrepeatable horrors. The rock has broken down to blocks the size of coal, with the consistency of brittle coke and all the stability of a slag heap. In its decomposition rich deposits of glutinous clay are formed, and today were bulging with saturation. Carelessly I stepped onto one swollen mass and watched engrossed as it belched into life and became a mudflow which slowly gathered volume for 50m down-slope, compelling Joy to jump smartly from its path. Our avalanche education was now complete.

After a blustery crossing to Ben More Assynt and back, the descent of Conival was equally demoralising, even by its easier northern route. We sloshed down Gleann Dubh, wringing out our gloves every two minutes, so wetting was the rain, and gathering a caking of slimy mud up to our knees. Present discomfort, however, weighed little against the miserable outlook at that moment:

> The storm has wiped out winter at a stroke. What chance now to find the Cuillin under snow and ice? Only twenty days of hard slogging remain, devoid of technical challenge, most likely wet and windy; and leaving me without proper claim to a true winter round!

Braemore Junction rates highly among the most desirable parking spots our van had occupied this winter, less for the immediate surroundings than its central position within the formidable encirclement of the Fannich, Inverlael and Dundonnell mountains. All of them are major undertakings, and offer little scope for compromise with bad weather. Whenever it felt that I was sailing comfortably ahead of the wind, up would crop another range of peaks demanding to be tackled forthwith. 'Running hard to stay upright' would well describe the game. The five days allowed for these twenty-three Munros would no more than preserve my four-day lead.

But when the rainclouds cleared, and a crystal coat of hoar-frost settled on the roads at nightfall, the excitement of the challenge was reborn and put me back into pugnacious mood:

> I was keen as mustard to get off – in bed at eight and up at five. The Fannich Forest traverse was, like the Mamores, one of my most cherished aims, and failing to finish the Mamores had only raised my enthusiasm for it . . .

The Fannich range is par excellence the terrain in which to indulge the exploring instinct. Nine Munros, eight high lochans, and fifteen corries crowd its 8-mile breadth. Being isolated from roads on all sides the peaks guard their secrets from the casual observer, but once penetrated divulge a wealth of potential to the climber, whilst the traverse of all nine summits gives a superb marathon walk.

From the Braemore side, tough overland approaches to either end of the ridge place an effective brake to its gaining popularity. Access is more immediate from the south provided that permission is obtained for a vehicle to be taken up the locked hydro road to Fannich Lodge.

The month might have been May so soft was the breeze and warm the sun on the tops, and the going was unhindered except by the odd stretch of ice where the recent rains had frozen in mid-flow. No matter though:

> If spring conditions prevailed then I would match them with a spring-like pace. We started with a rough ascent of A'Chailleach at the west end. Joy came with me over Sgurr Breac, but was (to use her own words) 'glad to let me off the leash' and enjoy a leisured return by the track to Loch a'Bhraoin. After a punishing grind to Sgurr nan Each I swung buoyantly

over Sgurr nan Clach Geala and around the head of the Choire Mhoir, detouring to Meall a' Chrasgaidh then panting up the sugar-loaf of Sgurr Mor. In contrast to the fawns and greens of the other slopes, its East Face was sparkling white with Alpine glory and in ripe winter condition.

Already the final peaks of Meall Gorm and An Coileachan were in my sights, but the second detour to Beinn Liath Mhor sapped the body fluid, and the last two summits gave my first taste of dehydration this winter. It is rare that an appetite deserts me on the hills, but half my rations were left untouched today. And I never usually bother to drink stream water. Sometimes it can upset the stomach, or otherwise coats my throat with a sickly fur that merely fuels the thirst. But on the descent to Loch Gorm I headed for the nearest spring and took a generous fill.

The final 4 miles of heather valley by the Abhainn a' Ghuibhais Li were trackless and trying, but gave me time to stock the memory with a multitude of hidden cliffs and corries for future climbing visits in the range.

The time of nine hours for the round trip of 22 miles and 2680m (8,800ft) uphill was not unduly pressed, and reflected the easy flowing fitness that is built up during two months of exertion. At the start of the trip even a twelve-hour completion would have left us whacked, but now each early finish could be put straight to tomorrow's gain. What deep pleasure it is to feel such physical harmony with the mountains – a sense of power that is hard to win, but so quickly lost once back in city life.

The most famous peak in the Braemore scene is An Teallach. Its sandstone battlements tower out of the Dundonnell moors in a view which has probably lifted more hearts towards the Scottish hills than any other. The mountain forms an effective screen to the wilderness interior of the Fisherfield Forest, and until recently so monopolised attention that its rugged hinterland was almost ignored. But surprisingly the six Fisherfield Munros formed significantly the tougher proposition, for which An Teallach was merely a brief, albeit exciting, prelude. A stay at Shenavall would link the two days and here again was a case of trusting our fate to Nature's providence, for the bothy is notoriously vulnerable to sudden flood.

Access to the Fisherfield ring across the Strath na Sealga can be cut quickly in the absence of bridges, and there are several tales of life and death battles simply escaping from the bothy back to the Dundonnell road. A storm comparable to that in Assynt was all that was needed to stymie our progress, so an especially careful check on the forecast was made before embarkation.

Alan Thomson came up to share the photographic qualities of An Teallach, and two days hence another visit from roving reporters was planned. The media were closing in as the expedition neared completion, and Joy was forced to bear the brunt of their attentions both in

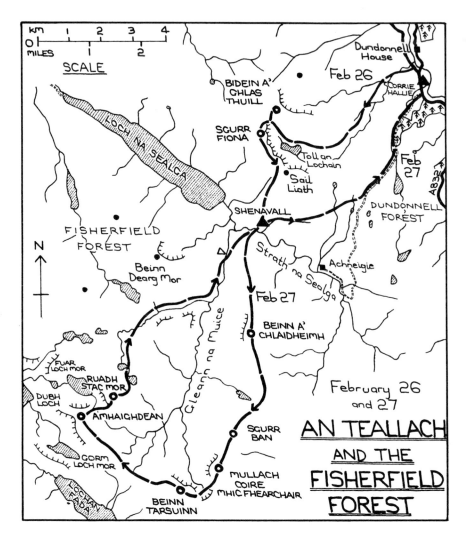

organising a rendezvous and then in feeding and accommodating them on arrival, as if the Shenavall trip itself was not enough to handle. I was justly given a verbal flattening for accepting this second arrangement so soon after Alan's visit. Sometimes we took a perverse delight in dodging the press and deliberately stayed incommunicado for a few days, in which event a bothy formed the perfect hiding place. Between our search for solitude and the needs of publicity there existed the most uneasy peace.

From Dundonnell House a peaty path and then a series of sandstone pavements led us into the Toll an Lochain corrie. To obtain the most impressive impact of a mountain like An Teallach it is necessary to get into the innermost recesses and view the peak from below, an aspect very often missed by the passing ridge-walker. Seen from the lochan shore, the savage cliffs from Sgurr Fiona to Sail Liath rear up to giddy heights, shutting out the sky and leaving the poor mortal feeling trapped and overawed. But then to be able to climb out of the corrie and attain the pinnacled tops provides a thrilling sense of achievement.

For the ice-climber there do exist a few direct winter routes to the tops of Corrag Bhuidhe and Sgurr Fiona though much remains to be done, but the casual visitor should be aware that in winter conditions the screes flanking the cliffs become 45 degree snow chutes, and there are no easy exits from the corrie bottom.

On the same count the complete traverse of An Teallach's crest is a serious expedition under snow and ice, only marginally less difficult than the Aonach Eagach; or so I am told, for today the ridge was bare and dry save for some icy runnels on its shaded sides. A scramble out of the Toll led us to the col between the two Munros, Fiona and Bidein a'Ghlas Thuill, and both were thence quickly gained.

The cautious walker, not wishing to be terrified out of his wits, could approach from the north in winter, bag the pair and retrace his steps without any major palpitation, for all the sensations are reserved for the section beyond Fiona:

> A strong south breeze made us watch to our balance on the tricky pieces. Most obstacles could have been avoided by lower trods on the southern side, though under hard snow these escapes would not exist, but with time on our hands we took the crest throughout. With a brilliant sun and absolute clarity in the distant views there was a feast of filming for Alan. Lord Berkeley's Seat I will vouch for as the most exposed point on the Scottish mainland Munros. Its northern drop overhangs at least for 60m. How will Skye's Inaccessible Pinnacle compare, I wonder? On the final bealach before Sail Liath we parted ways, Alan donning crampons for the snow chute back to the Toll an Lochain, myself dropping off the other side into the shadowy depths of Strath na Sealga and down to Shenavall where Joy had just arrived.

As we sat outside by an old ploughshare, sunning ourselves and supping tea, the mockery of winter again oppressed my mood. Not that a raging blizzard was wanted on *every* day, but even a modicum of snow around would have helped maintain the spirit of the season.

Fisherfield's geology is a bewildering maze of thrust and fault lines, switching dramatically between sandstone and gneiss strata, and gouged by ice into a discordant series of cliffed troughs. The extreme of this chaos is found on the flanks of A'Mhaighdean which harbours no fewer than five lochans, each lying at a different glacial level from Dubh Loch at 180m up to Fuar Loch Mor at 600m. It is a miracle that their waters find an escape at all.

(*left*) At the summit cairn of Sgurr Fiona, An Teallach (*A. Thomson*)

To many this is the inner sanctum of all the Highland peaks, to be preserved unspoilt at any price, even that of curbing the urge to broadcast its merits. It was with Fisherfield in mind that in 1972 the Scottish Mountaineering Club proposed a moratorium on the future reporting of new climbing routes for the whole north-western region*. However, the number of walkers penetrating the area is inevitably growing, and traces of tracks have appeared on the ridge tops; but despite new ownership of the estates there is no immediate prospect of the ructions which recently put the fate of Knoydart in doubt.

Two of the area's six Munros were 'discovered' only as recently as 1974 when the OS finally got to grips with the land in its metric survey. Previously the roof-top ridge of Beinn a'Chlaidheimh had appeared as an oval plateau at the 2,800ft contour, and Ruadh Stac Mor was placed no higher than 2,900ft. Even A'Mhaighdean and Beinn Tarsuinn were below 3,000ft on the one-inch sheet, but amateur Munro-spotters had already proved their status. The additional Notes to the old Tables gave a charming explanation: 'The map of this part was very casual; I think the O.S. had bad weather, and were hurried in order to meet the views of the then laird.'

Bad weather was the least of our worries; more a danger of heat exhaustion presented itself on our round from Shenavall, which forms a complete horseshoe of Gleann na Muice. Whilst all the peaks are individually worthy of extended praise, the walk is overshadowed by the climax of reaching the summit of A'Mhaighdean:

> After the dullest climb of the day up its south-east slope, the mountain broke away into a plunging precipice. In its vast depths lay a host of lakes with the Fionn Loch stretching out at the bottom towards the hazy seaboard. The great cliffs of Beinn Lair and Carnmore glowered above the many waters.

By our mid-afternoon return to the bothy we were gasping for liquid as much as on any summer's day. The 5½-mile evening march to the road at Corrie Hallie served to fortify our impression that the Fisherfield ring was quite some undertaking, even in these perfect conditions. Nigh on a gallon of juice and tea must have passed our lips at the van before thoughts could swing back to the north of Braemore, where a 24-mile traverse of the Inverlael hills awaited tomorrow's effort. And on its farthest skyline the grassy swells of Seana Bhraigh were no doubt sighing in the breeze of night.

---

*The moratorium never gained widespread support and the SMC has recommenced publishing new routes in its annual Journal. However, no comprehensive climbing guides to the region have now appeared for thirteen years, so information remains closely guarded.

The visit of the men from the *Daily Record* proved an unexpected pleasure. They gave us cheerful company over dinner in the van, bringing us right out of our shells and helping the rigours of the mountains to recede. Joy felt acutely guilty at having bemoaned their coming.

But of course they wanted pictures, and nothing less than the summit of a Munro would suffice their needs (or indeed the demands of their editor!) in this respect, so the day was slowly begun with the ascent of Am Faochagach from the head of Loch Glascarnoch. The gentle climb well suited Ken, the photographer, for whom this was a novel assignment, and though the hill itself was more reminiscent of the rolling Grampians than the nearby giants it afforded a magnificent prospect of the snowy eastern faces of Beinn Dearg and Cona' Mheall. What a change this backcloth would provide from the usual adornments of the paper's inside pages!

A fourth fine day brought the heatwave to its zenith. The distant tops shimmered in the haze, and our steps in the peat raised a film of dust. Allowing me to forge ahead, Joy took reporter David over Beinn Dearg, while Ken descended direct, shattered but doubtless glowing with satisfaction.

Dearg is the highest of the Inverlael tops, which are grouped on the western edges of an extensive upland plateau. This dips gently down above the straths of Easter Ross, and is sharply dissected by glacial corries and valleys, which Tom Patey explored for winter climbs during his later years in Ullapool. Their more recent development has been sporadic in nature.

The east ridge of Cona' Mheall was today's token concession to winter, the steep névé on its upper section requiring some step cutting. The ensuing stroll up Dearg awoke a smiling recollection of New Year's Day 1984 when we sought to salvage some reward from the stormbound stay at Ullapool. Our attempt from Gleann na Sguaib was abandoned in a blizzard at the angle of the summit wall only 200m from the top. I had sat there for minutes fighting hopelessly to set the map and compass until the numbing cold enforced an urgent evacuation.

From Dearg onwards my eyes were posted on Seana Braigh even though two other Munros, Meall nan Ceapraichean and Eididh nan Clach Geala, intervened on the 6½-mile crossing. The mountain was as much a symbolic pilgrimage as a real goal – beautifully remote and serene, and standing far beyond all homeward tracks. One must approach with the utmost ardour. Never look behind on such a hill! A just reward is in the sight of its northern abyss, the Luchd Choire, which opens like the jaws of hell from the summit pastures, and then in the heartwarming return into the golden glens of Inverlael:

On picking up the path at the head of Gleann Beag, I instinctively began to run. Instead of petering to a halt in a few hundred yards, (as usual!) the twisting trod propelled me the whole 6 miles back to the road, skipping and galloping through the heather and jumping the pools and boulders in a single flowing rhythm.

The stalker's tracks provide the most exhilarating running imaginable, so different from the naked screes, jarring inclines and the swamps of the undisciplined walker's trails of recent times. Designed and built with love and care these paths seem as indestructible as the hills to which they gently lead.

Very soon after this happy conclusion to our stay at Braemore my yo-yoing mood was back in the depths of gloom. The complaints were by now familiar – 'no snow, just a slog' and so on. They suggested a lack of gratitude for the wonderful last four days, and were quite unjustified considering that a further gain had been made on schedule. But the symptoms were obvious – overstrain, tension and, above all, exhaustion. Together they flout good reason and cloud the perception; a rest day was the only solution.

However, time alone is not a sufficient medication; concentrated effort is needed to relax or else the brain keeps whirring round in ever-decreasing rings, brows remain knitted, hands fidget nervously, and the temper stays short. Somehow one's underlying passion for the task must be renewed. How else did Hamish get round the Munros in his calm and unhurried fashion, but with a deep love and an open mind?

We drove along the seaside road by Gairloch and down to Kinlochewe on another fine, but much windier day. The appointment with the Cuillin Ridge was now pressing, and a series of calls fixed a support team to meet at Glen Brittle in two days' time. In the meanwhile the Torridon peaks were still inviolate. Only by late evening was I back to par and fit to pay them due respect. Piece by piece the planning jigsaw was slotting into place.

Torridon has become the most popularised part of the North-West Highlands, a process encouraged, though carefully controlled, by the National Trust's management of the land, but unstoppable given the quality and accessibility of its three great mountains, Beinn Eighe, Liathach and Beinn Alligin.

Eighe deserves much better than its one full Munro summit, Ruadh-stac Mor, which lies perversely on a northern arm of the mountain. The main ridge axis from Sgurr nan Fhir Duibhe to Sail Mhor has five Tops, which together would have made one of the best traverses of the winter. Instead, my acquaintance was confined to an unrelenting scramble up the scree-striped walls of Coire Dubh Mor to meet the quartzite crest at Coinneach Mhor and then a short sally out to the highest peak. Being detached in position, Ruadh-stac Mor offers a good appraisal of the rest of the mountain, especially the upper bastions of Coire Mhic Fhearchair, whose Triple Buttress is one of the grandest cliffs in Scotland both in size and the symmetry of its structure.

Further to the west Liathach and Alligin look to be sailing like castles in the air. All linkages between the three have been severed by slicing glens, and to get onto the end of Liathach it was necessary to drop as low as 320m. Never is it easy to start again from scratch on the second peak of the day and especially when rain is likely. There was clearly a marked change of weather in the offing. Sheet after sheet of metallic grey cloud had drawn across the sky all morning and progressively dimmed the light.

Thankfully, each of Liathach's two main peaks is now a Munro, committing me to the mountain's full traverse. The ridge between Spidean a'Choire Leith and Mullach an Rathain vies with An Teallach as the finest sandstone crest in the north-west, although little Stac Pollaidh in Coigach should not be excluded from the count. The Fasarinen pinnacles are of the same rough and rounded texture, but are more obviously escapable than those on An Teallach via a sensational trod which winds along a terrace on their southern sides. Nor perhaps are the exposures over Coire na Caime quite so exciting as those above Toll an Lochain, but this personal preference should not detract from the mountain's individual magnificence and, like An Teallach, the crossing should be treated as grade II under snow and ice. After all, this was my third traverse, and there were few Munros which had previously borne my steps more than once.

With the rain holding back and the mist hovering just above the summit level, the northern corries were open for inspection. Their terraced murals, jutting prows and recessed apses form an architecture of cyclopean proportions, and here is much the grander side of the mountain – serious winter climbing when it isn't thawing!

Rather than riding the scree shoot down to Fasag I continued over to the western end of the ridge at Sgorr a'Chadail, a far more pleasing finish and less damaging to both man and mountain. From there a short crossing of Coire Mhic Nobuil would have gained Beinn Alligin, and plenty of time was available to complete the trio, for by this, the second day of March, there was usable light until after 6.30. But whatever the appeal of a notable 'hat-trick' my heart was against it:

> I had thoroughly enjoyed Liathach, but knew that to go on would only overtire and probably drop me back into the depression from which I had just struggled free. Energies also needed to be stored ready for the Cuillin, so I descended to Torridon House where Joy had stationed the van. Alligin will be much more pleasurable come the morning . . .

There was the great difficulty in convincing myself of this on the chill and clammy dawn that followed. The patter of rain alone broke the silence. Up aheight the clouds were steaming off Alligin's buttresses, and underneath a soft white carpet was newly laid – all in all an excellent morning for lying abed behind closed curtains.

However, the rain soon ceased, and only thick mist together with slippery snow troubled my climb up the western side of Toll a' Mhadaidh Beag which leads directly to the Munro summit of Sgurr Mhor. Like Beinn Eighe, Alligin has a superb ridge but only one Munro. My direct attack had little merit other than enabling a close-up view of the mountain's sandstone brickwork, which even to a climber's eye is of a repellent steepness and uniformity. Descending by the same way, a careless trip sent me skidding down the snow for 5m, and brought a jolting reminder of the tenuous margin between success and disaster, for rocky outcrops abounded on this 40-degree slope. My fear of an accident was now becoming slightly paranoiac with the end so near.

Sgurr Mhor has a lesser known but far more apposite alternative name, Sgurr na Tuaigh, 'the peak of the hatchet', which is a clear acknowledgement of the vertical gash chopped out of its southern walls. The cleft is 500m in height and forms an indelible mark of identity in every photograph of the mountain.

Down in a little over three hours, I had then to exercise the 'robotic' instinct which had been carefully cultivated during the winter. Slioch, the queen of Loch Maree, was scheduled for the afternoon, and with just four and a half hours to spare before the last ferry to Skye a speedy ascent was essential. A stirring rendering of Sibelius's first symphony (on tape!) charged my emotions for a second bleak foray onto the tops. Such powerful music roused a dull and sleepy Sunday to the height of grandeur, rewaking the senses to the lonely intensity of the winter hills.

So I strode forth from Taagan farm with sabre drawn and promptly fell waist-deep into a black lagoon by the side of the river! This short-cut, however, saved over a mile on the approach from Kinlochewe village, but would be feasible only during a dry spell.

Despite its bold and turreted frontage the walker's route to Slioch goes round the back of the peak and up the pleasant grasses of Coire na Sleaghaich to emerge on the summit throne where both the lovely length of Loch Maree, and the Fisherfield peaks, are dramatically disclosed. An established track takes one up from the bottom of Gleann Bianasdail to the verge of the coire, and thereafter a line of newly-made cairns is attempting to extend the highway right up to the summit. On such a guileless open climb they threaten an unwar-ranted blight on the natural landscape, and I took the 'law' into my hands by beheading a good many of them as I scampered back down. Vandalism or sound conservation? The two passing walkers who caught me in the act were left to draw their own conclusion. Hopefully they didn't get lost higher up!

We dashed off towards Kyle with the fuel gauge well into the red. Had the Achnasheen garage not been prepared to open, we would never have reached Sligachan that night, but the rush was all for naught. Skye met us with a head-on rainstorm that had our wipers working double time, so the Cuillin were immediately postponed a day. Just then it seemed that the heatwave had been frittered away, and for sure it would not return. Fortune had turned its back at the moment of our greatest need.

14

CLIMAX ON THE CUILLIN

4–7 March:
The Black Cuillin Ridge – Blaven

The infrequency with which the Cuillin Ridge attracts good winter conditions is quite maddening. On those precious occasions it offers, in the words of the usually non-committal SMC guide: *'possibly* the finest single outing in the British hills'. The reservation might well be deleted, for the Main Ridge traverse is undoubtedly the most sought prize in winter mountaineering, and by the same score is probably the least often achieved.

Though the Black Cuillin are often turned white by a sudden cold storm, it is rare that they remain so for long. Encircled by the Atlantic shores, and open to the full attack of the salty sea winds, the snows are usually wiped away within a week from all but the deepest gullies. To create the thick plating of ice on which to climb with speed and safety, several daily cycles of melt and freeze are required to toughen the outer layers, and ideally should be backed up by further accretions of fresh snow. Then, while the climber drops his work and packs his bags, a frosty star-filled night must set the mix, and if he drives hard he might just see those sugar-coated peaks shining in the flush of dawn. In comparison, the actual climbing is the easier part of the escapade, even though there are many grade III and IV difficulties, sustained exposure and an Alpine scale of length.

So with luck and persistence a handful of parties have succeeded, while hundreds remain frustrated. The foursome of Tom Patey, Hamish MacInnes, Davie Crabb and Brian Robertson made the first traverse in 1965, closely followed by Graham Tiso and Jim Moriarty. It is rumoured that there had previously been a dozen unsuccessful attempts. Remarkably, no other crossings were recorded in the following thirteen years, despite the big freeze of 1969, but between 1978 and 1980 several teams captured their chance. Stuart Cathcart even achieved a solo traverse in February 1983, but all have required at least one bivouac mid-way along the ridge.

There are eleven Munros to collect en route from Sgurr nan Eag down at the southern end to Sgurr nan Gillean, its northern spearhead. My dream was to lie in wait on the mainland and pick the teeth of the ridge when they reached the pink of condition. Perhaps by

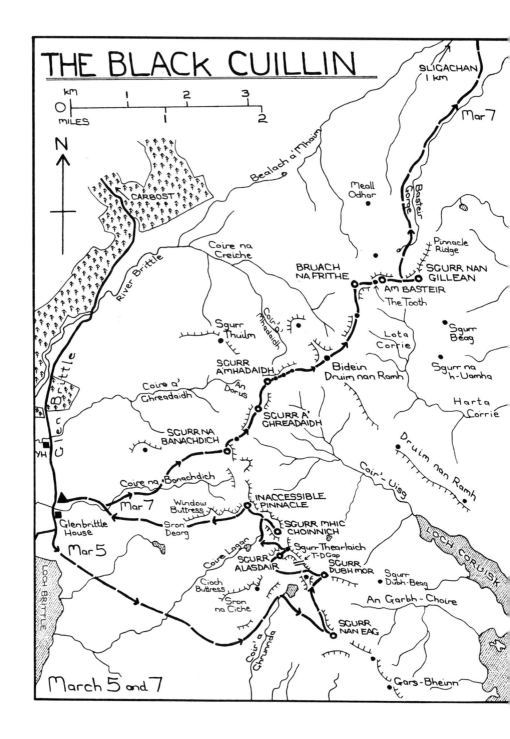

diverting around one or two of the major obstacles, most notably the Thearlaich–Dubh gap and the Bhasteir Tooth, and with a support team at the Inaccessible Pinnacle, the expedition's crux, they could all be done in a single day. But 1985's freakish winter never gave this scheme a chance, though we had waited in eternal hope. So the only alternative was to choose dry conditions and do the peaks in summer style . . .

Which brings us back to reality and a drenching day of waiting at Glen Brittle. While the great ridge stayed in cloud, inaction and boredom whittled away my confidence; and when the weatherman promised only slight improvement, the one-day onslaught was modified to an *attempt* on the southern half of the ridge.

In the evening the arrival of our supporters cheered my hopes – Alan Hinkes as photographer and companion, Alan Thomson to bring a rope and food to the Pinnacle and film the ascent, and finally Andy Hyslop to provide the pacing and route-finding expertise. No better man could have been found for this latter role, since Andy is the current record holder for the fastest summer traverse of the ridge. In May 1984 he achieved a time of four hours and four minutes to claim the title which the legendary Eric Beard had held for the previous eighteen years. Not only did Andy beat Eric's time by five minutes, but he took a more complete route totalling 2450m (8,000ft) of ascent as well as tackling all the difficult sections unroped. An eight-hour traverse would leave most fit men gasping.

He came up from Ambleside, his home in the Lakes, solely for my benefit, even though we had never met. How glad I was of his presence, for my only previous experience of the Cuillin was a brief recce of the Coire Lagan section in December in the final days of preparation. With my faith pinned squarely on Andy's shoulders I was just beginning to warm to tomorrow's challenge, when he shattered the after-dinner silence:

'Well, I suppose we'd better think about a route; has anyone got a map of this area?'

Our faces dropped in horror: 'But we thought that *you* were the map, Andy.'

The climb into Coir' a' Ghrunnda leaves no doubt that one is entering mountains of a different calibre to any others in Scotland. Boiler-plate slabs and dripping black cliffs fill the onward view. Vegetation has abandoned the fight to survive as low as 400m. A wall of cloud hides the upper halves of the peaks, and hangs above a two-tone frame of barren moor and a flat grey sea – the Cuillin grim and brooding, as so often is their wont.

But today there was an added ingredient in the wild scene, not

The 'cloak of treachery': Sgurr Mhic Choinnich, Sgurr Thearlaich and Sgurr Alasdair seen across Coire Lagan from the Inaccessible Pinnacle

expected and certainly not wanted, noticed first as a slippy moistness on the rock, then as a slushy film and finally as a blanket of white deepening with every upward metre. As the three of us emerged by the lochan in the upper basin, the mist kindly lifted to prove the dreaded truth. Glen Brittle's overnight rain had fallen as a 2-in carpet of wet and heavy snow above the 600m level. The higher crags and the ridge itself were plastered on all but the most vertical faces, as though a baker's dough had been unceremoniously dumped on the peaks.

Suddenly we felt a little under-equipped, what with one ice-axe to share, no rope, no spare sweaters and no hot drinks in prospect until the Pinnacle. And was Andy being especially over-ambitious turning out in light fell-boots, skinny tights and a runner's cagoule the thickness of a crisp packet? Crampons, the one piece of kit that we each did possess, would be absolutely useless to tackle this sloppy snow. Could we move fast enough on it to keep warm?

Sgurr nan Eag was a simple scramble from the lochan. In the clearing the sun sparkled over the inner seas of the Hebrides, and occasionally threw a glowing shaft over the hills above Loch Coruisk, but then the mists closed ranks and we saw no more. However, Andy led us faultlessly around the head of An Garbh-choire and directly onto Sgurr Dubh Mor, the second Munro, his intricate knowledge of the terrain mocking last night's consternation over the map request. Already on these steeper screes and outcrops the climbing had become exceedingly delicate. Andy was dismayed that little slabs and grooves which he had run across the previous summer now required a patient cleaning of the holds and a deft balance.

Skirting Sgurr Dubh na Da Bheinn on its north side, we regained the main ridge just below the Thearlaich–Dubh gap. This is technically the hardest piece of the whole ridge, an evil slot with a polished chimney on its north side that is undergraded at 'Very Difficult' even in dry conditions. Most winter parties traverse the ridge from north to south to enable this pitch – and other obstacles like the Bhasteir Tooth – to be abseiled. Not that this was of any relevance to ourselves, and even with a rope the gap would likely have been impossible today.

So we were forced off the ridge back into Coir' a' Ghrunnda, and aimed for the south-west spur of Sgurr Alasdair. This was new ground to Andy, hidden cliffs were massed above us, and of course the compass couldn't help on the magnetic gabbro. An inspired guess took us up a scree gully to meet the ridge below the 'Bad Step', a short 'Very Difficult' wall. Unlike the Thearlaich–Dubh gap this is avoidable a few metres to the right, and a series of snow-filled grooves then gained the island's crowning summit.

Thus far a steady rhythm had maintained our warmth, and spirits were optimistic:

> Even the three peaks completed were an achievement today. Taking the attitude that every additional Munro would be an unexpected bonus, I felt free of any overriding tension. But there was a pressure to go on, for Alan Thomson and Joy would be waiting on the far side of Coire Lagan. Nor was there anything to say that this snow could not lie for a week and the weather outlook predicted that strong winds might soon return. In fact this was likely to be our only decent day!

But events took a more serious turn when we tried to get back on the main ridge at the 'top' of Sgurr Thearlaich:

> The ground became appreciably steeper, with the likeness of a church roof. Tilted slabs masked by snow sloped off beneath our toes into clouded precipices. Gingerly feeling about for something to grip, I suddenly slipped and slid down for 5ft, desperately clawing at the snow until my boots caught an edge and stopped me.

The alarm bells jangled loudly and a hasty conference was convened. Alan Hinkes had been taking pictures all the while from the rear despite my vigorous protests, and there was now too real a chance of his obtaining a notable news scoop. The headlines were too embarrassing to contemplate: 'Charity Climber Plunges to an Icy End!' And then looking at Andy, pale and shivering as he munched at a buttered scone: 'Cuillin Recordbreaker Rescued with Exposure!'

179

Retreat was mooted, and there were no second thoughts, for the ridge from Thearlaich to Mhic Choinnich is one of the trickiest sections, a weaving descent on bubbled basalt followed by a tip-toe traverse along Collie's Ledge. We dropped down the Great Stone Shoot to the floor of Coire Lagan, but the relief was short-lived. Immediately an unpleasant choice was posed. Either we deserted our supporters, or else renewed the 'delights' of the ridge at the following bealach. A sense of honour gave us only the one option, so without a pause we returned to the fray, regaining the crest by a 250m treadmill of scree:

> Hearts in our mouths with tension at one instant, and down in our boots with dread at the next – the day was turning into one long nightmare.

No amount of skill and care can tame the risks of climbing on this sort of snow, for judgement of the underlying ground is impossible. Loose blocks and deep holes as well as the sounder holds and ledges are hidden under one amorphous mass; whole slabs can slide away under your weight as the bottom surface melts. Guidebook grades are meaningless when one treads this cloak of treachery.

We doubled back to claim Sgurr Mhic Choinnich by its easier northern side, then ploughed up the ramps beneath An Stac. The Pinnacle was reached just as the clouds parted company to reveal its wares – thickly daubed in white, as expected. Here then was Scotland's hardest major summit, an eccentric thumb of rock sticking its head above the true apex of the ridge, Sgurr Dearg. It is a fine statue to the dashed hopes of the many Munro collectors who lacked a head for heights. Whilst all the other Cuillin Munros can be individually reached by scrambles that avoid the sensational parts of the ridge, the Pinnacle is obligatory, and therein lies its aura and appeal. Repeated bad weather prevented Sir Hugh himself from ever making its ascent.

There are short and long sides to the Pinnacle. The 'short' is 18m, 'Difficult' and sloping, and the 'long' East Ridge is 45m, 'Moderate' and well described by its pioneers in 1880 as: 'a razor-like edge with an overhanging and infinite drop on one side, and a drop longer and steeper on the other!'

Alan Thomson was ready and waiting with the much needed sacks of food and clothing, but Joy was not around:

(*right, above*) Liathach from the slopes of Coinneach Mhor (Beinn Eighe) across the Coire Dubh Mor (see Chapter 13); (*below*) Hebridean magic: the clouded Isle of Rhum and the shining western seas from Sgurr Dearg on the Cuillin Ridge

(*overleaf*) The rainstorm recedes and a northern heatwave begins: Loch Fannich from A'Chailleach (see Chapter 13)

'I'm afraid she's got a wee bit stuck just down the way, Martin', he apologised. 'I didn't realise she hadn't rock climbed before.'

Instead of pointing down the easy walking approach from Coire na Banachdich, he motioned towards the narrow western spur. Alan had unwittingly taken Joy up by the sporting route, thinking she would enjoy a short climb!

Operations were postponed while I hurried down to find her standing on a narrow ledge before the final knife-edged crest. Having coped with a 'Difficult' gully on Window Buttress with a tight rope and a lot of encouragement, she had been beaten finally by the infernal snow higher up; but on no account was I to be let down. Alan was 'ordered' to go on with both sacks despite her unnerving predicament. By my arrival she had already spent two hours pacing on the spot.

With devotion like that, there could be no excuse for my failing on the Pinnacle, and having helped Joy down onto the easier ridge towards Sron Dearg I scrambled back up. Andy had meanwhile departed for the valley's warmth, pinched by the chill and in no mood for the climb.

'Have you got the hardware?' I then asked, but only a rope and two old slings were produced, enough for a 'classic' abseil from the top*; but without karabiners we couldn't hope to properly secure the ascent. Alan too had been foxed by the snow. He just hadn't envisaged our wanting to protect the 'Moderate' rock arête, which was now unhappily at least a grade III winter route.

So a solo climb it had to be:

Fortunately I often enjoy soloing, partly as a test of self-reliance, but also as enabling a free and unencumbered communion with the mountains. After all, I had already walked most of the Munros alone, but this one was just a little bit more serious.

Alan Hinkes was not unduly deterred by the prospect, so both calling on our reserves of experience, we inched our way up the arête, myself in front with the rope strapped on my back. The mists meanwhile swirled back up from the void below.

At least we could take our time and properly clear each hold of slush, for once this key pitch was complete we would gladly finish for the day. My bare hands stung with cold, and my calves ached at the strain of keeping my toes absolutely still on the slippy holds, and yet I was quickly absorbed by the task. The climbing was a craft in itself, a progress of stealth not

---

*The traditional method which relies solely on the friction provided by wrapping the rope between the legs and over the shoulder – potentially painful and therefore little used.

(*left*) Climbing the East Ridge of the Inaccessible Pinnacle (*A. Hinkes*)

strength, and slowly the Pinnacle yielded, the arête leaning back until we found ourselves crawling the last few feet to the top block. Without ado we fixed the rope and abseiled off, while Alan filmed the sequence through the milky cloud.

The moment of reaching safety after a long and perilous journey is surely the sweetest that the climber knows. Touching terra firma from the abseil brought to us that joyous release from tension. How wonderful it felt to amble back to the glen, hands in pockets. Though the Cuillin were still only half complete there was a brief chance to relax and celebrate the measure of success that we had extracted from the day. And to think that last week had seen me bitterly bemoaning the absence of winter. Well, Skye had given the sharpest retort!

Blaven (Bla Bheinn) is the Island's twelfth Munro, isolated from the Cuillin Ridge, but part of the same igneous intrusion that slowly cooled into the coarse gabbro rock, which so delights the summer climber. In common with its neighbours, the mountain's flanks are seamed with gully clefts, and break into some fine cliffs. The only easy side is to the south-east where a track ascends from Loch Slapin into Coire Uaigneich above which the summit is a dispiriting 500m slog on screes.

It formed a suitable interval to the Main Ridge performance, for next day produced the expected gale and an icy rain. Once in control of the weather the westerly depressions are hard to unseat. Both Andy and Alan Thomson had returned to work commitments, and Alan Hinkes was now my sole partner. The snow that so dominated yesterday's events had almost disappeared. We were assisted up the final slopes by a strange updraught. This was but a small eddy from the blasting tempest that was met on top. Quickly chilled to the bone by driving sleet we tried to hurry down, but soon lost our route. How then do you pick the correct line out of a parallel row of identical gullies, some of which ended in hanging chockstones and vertical chimneys? Twice we climbed back up before locating a run of pounded scree that led to safety.

So the northern six were left to do, effectively the only real barrier to my final success. None of the other twenty Munros posed any comparable difficulty, and there were days aplenty to ride out a serious storm.

With claws sharpened we waited for the weather's signal, and it came on cue at dawn the next day. Just as before the Affric trip, the wind magically subsided, and the mists were fast dispersing when we rejoined the Ridge at 9am on Sgurr na Banachdich. However, the

(*right*) The Inaccessible Pinnacle reveals its white mantle

cooling air of a cold front passage had chased the dying rain and dropped a coat of verglas on the tops in the last hours of the storm; so crampons were essential wear until the day warmed up. The climbing was intricate in the icy parts, but never treacherous in the manner of two days ago. By keeping my head and a steady pace the horn of Gillean would eventually come, and in Alan I had a climber of implacable enthusiasm as well as an inveterate talker to help me there. Each twist and surprise in the route was relished, and there was even time to look about and admire the Cuillin country . . .

The central portion of the Ridge is the least known, and the most complex topographically, so whilst the technical difficulties do not match those of the famous obstacles, it is here that many climbers will find themselves in doubt of the route, perplexed by mist, and at the nearest to abandoning their attempt. This is also the section where winter parties must make their bivouac, and the many walled shelters on the level terraces and cols bear witness to their trials. Patey and party were royally accommodated on Banachdich, having had a cache of food and equipment left in place, while Cathcart on his unsupported solo had a miserable night at An Dorus with a 'howling wind driving spindrift across the ridge'.

Open bivouacs can variously be exalting or murderous but either way are the most intense of mountain experiences, whether you are entertained by shooting stars and a moonlight sonata, or else sitting soaked to the skin and praying for the dawn that never seems to come. It was a disappointment of this expedition that I was denied the opportunity, but the bothies were simply too numerous and con-venient to be overlooked. The Cuillin Ridge apart, bivouacs in the Highlands are usually contrived by choice or enforced by weather, but rarely the sole expedient.

The trio of summits, Banachdich, Ghreadaidh and Mhadaidh are closely linked, but beyond the latter is a long and kinking route to gain the next Munro at Bruach na Frithe. The ridge first swings east over three pinnacled subsidiary tops, then turns north at Bidein Druim nan Ramh which itself has three summits, all deeply incised by basalt dyke lines. On the Bidein at least one abseil is needed in full winter conditions, and Cathcart nearly came to grief here when his rope dislodged from a poor spike. He slid on steep snow for 15m before the line luckily snagged on a flake and brought him to a halt.

Arrival at Bruach na Frithe brings one onto home ground. Gillean has been bobbing on the horizon throughout the central crocodile, but at last has fixed its place and is immediately accessible beyond the Bhasteir Tooth. Andy Hyslop had taken just twenty-six minutes from here to the finish of his record run, despite suffering from a lack of liquid and glucose, for he had not eaten since the Pinnacle. Compare

Andy Hyslop in mid snack on the Cuillin Ridge

the torments of Beatty and Beighton on their north-south winter traverse in 1978. They had taken three hours simply in effecting the abseil off the Tooth when their ropes jammed hopelessly.

No such problems were presented to Alan and myself. Naismith's Route on the Tooth was only a little damp and lichenous, the morning ice having long ago melted in a weak sun, returning us to summer conditions. Though well furnished with jugs and cracks it is nevertheless a remarkably steep and exposed pitch considering that its inauguration date was 1896.

Am Basteir, its Munro parent, lies just beyond, and then only a 'Moderate' chimney bars the ridge to Gillean. We were soon perched on its airy top and enjoying a vast prospect over the tablelands of the northern island which for once glowed soft and warm.

Again we could enjoy a late afternoon descent from the black peaks in leisured satisfaction. A fine day on Skye is as rare in its quality as it is in occurrence, a jewel to be coveted for long months after. As we dropped by the Bhasteir gorge and out onto the moors towards Sligachan there wasn't even a single midge to disturb the pleasure. Whatever the adventures encountered on the Ridge a winter trip to the Cuillin is worth trying for that joy alone!

Alan dined heartily and then departed on his journey back to Newcastle. Later I rang Steve Bonnist and proudly reported that success within the ninety days was almost assured. But suddenly this was not enough:

'We need a definite finishing date, Martin. I've got a battery of journalists and television crews ready to come to Fort William but they need three days' notice, and we must tell *Blue Peter* when you'll be coming . . .'

I instantly totted up the score . . . three days at Achnashellach, two days to the Ben, and one day spare for a storm . . .

'Make it the thirteenth then', I replied. That would be an eighty-three days' total, not bad even considering the luck with the weather . . .

But how can wild mountains be subjected to the beck and command of the media? Could they be so shackled, they wouldn't be 'mountains' as such, and I certainly would have had little interest in climbing them for the last eleven weeks. Driving out of Skye with a full moonbeam lighting the waters of the Inner Sound I was struck by the sudden impulse that I must go out again that night and onto the Achnashellach peaks. Instinct was telling me something, yet with my bed so close at hand and in the sleepy wake of a filling meal, the message was ignored and slowly slipped from view.

15

THE FINAL SURGE

8–13 March:
Achnashellach – Loch Monar hills – Ben Nevis and the Grey Corries

There was no second chance to beat the storm. By 8am the rain was drumming its merry tune on the roof of the van, and the trees at Achnashellach were swaying in time to the gathering wind. Opportunity knocks but once, though exactly when in the night the front arrived cannot be said, for my blissful dreams were undisturbed.

The mountain ranges on either side of Glen Carron filled the last blanks on the Western Highlands map. The glen is a major junction between massive and rounded schistose hills to the south, and the exciting laminations of the Torridonian peaks. On this north side are three Munros, which join with three lower but equally fine summits, Fuar Tholl, An Ruadh-stac and Beinn Damh, to bridge the gap to Glen Torridon itself. All of it is deer forest, a bright and open land of quartz-capped tops and a sprinkling of lochans . . .

But not today. The sky was laden with moisture, and only after prolonged deliberation did we set out at all, winding up the stalker's track and into Coire Lair. At a height of 400m, Beinn Liath Mhor was already half won, but a booming wind rocked us in our steps and forced a crucial pause. Flurries of white wavelets blew across the corrie lochan, and the encircling peaks frowned as black as thunder. And then a squalling rain joined with the gale to drive away my fading resolution:

> No doubt the hills could have been climbed, albeit with a struggle, but though I probed the recesses of my mind, not an ounce of will was there to draw from. With a heavy heart but no delay I called to Joy that I'd had enough.

Plodding back down, I roundly cursed last night's surrender to creature comforts. The moonlight scheme had sounded crazy but it was a flash of intuition which had a chance of success. My want of response marked a symbolic retreat from the fight. And now of course a timely storm had come along to open up the crack, and found me defenceless. All day the tempest clamoured its victory, giving no real hope of a repeal, while with every passing hour, March 13 pressed down its claim:

191

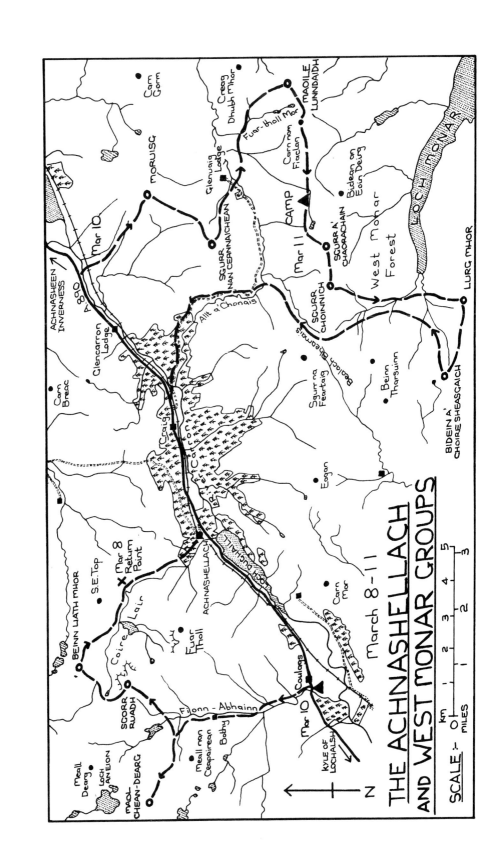

THE ACHNASHELLACH
AND WEST MONAR GROUPS

March 8-11

SCALE:-

km 0 1 2 3 4 5
miles 0 1 2 3

N

LOCH MONAR

MAOILE LUNNDAIDH
Creag Dhubh Mhor
Carn Gorm
MORUISG
Glenuaig Lodge
Fuar-tholl Mor
Carn nam Fiaclan
Bidean an Eoin Deirg
CAMP
Mar 11
Mar 10
SGURR NAN CEANNAICHEAN
SGURR A' CHAORACHAIN
West Monar Forest
SGURR CHOINNICH
LURG MHOR
Allt a' Chonais
Bealach Bhearnais
Beinn Tharsuinn
Sgurr na Feartaig
BIDEIN A' CHOIRE SHEASGAICH
Achnasheen Inverness
A890
Glencarron Lodge
Carn Breac
Eagan
Carn Mor
Coire Lair
S.E.Top
Mar 8 Return Point
BEINN LIATH MHOR
Fuar Tholl
ACHNASHELLACH
Maol Dearg
Loch an Eion
SGORR RUADH
Meall nan Ceapairean
Bothy
Fionn-Abhainn
Coulags
Mar 10
Kyle of Lochalsh
MAOL CHEAN-DEARG

We mused away the afternoon both feeling 'prisoners' of our own making. Until the Munros are finished our lives hang suspended. Our desire for a long unpressured rest, our search for a home, my guiding career up here in the Highlands, nothing can progress. Just five more days of storm and yet I cannot face them.

The following day saw me lowered deeper into the trap. The weather remained foul from dawn to dusk, yet bore the same agonising possibility that I could have gone out had I possessed the courage. Rain, strong wind and cloud are an unpleasant mix, but pose no immediate threat to survival, and so another day was squandered.

Every radio forecast was optimistic for a clearance, but the front was loath to pass away and stayed firmly entrenched over the north-west margins. The remainder of Scotland lay under a stable ridge of colder air, but there was nowhere else for us to escape to, as had been so easy earlier in the winter. The long hours of daylight gave ample time for introspection:

> There is not a glimmer of inspiration in these warm westerly storms, and I've shut off my mind to them, yet underneath I'm clinging to the blithe reliance that they will pass away. To be on Ben Nevis by 10am on the 13th as promised, will demand an enormous effort even in fine conditions . . .

For apart from the three Munros to our north there were seven to the south of Achnashellach, which included the sequestered peaks of the West Monar Forest, Lurg Mhor and Bidein a'Choire Sheasgaich. This pair rival Seana Bhraigh and A'Mhaighdean in the romantic lure of inaccessibility, and the district has no nearby shieling or bothy for an overnight stop. All these ten now had to be squeezed into the following two days and, without a pause, the greater part of the Grey Corries plus the last two Mamores completed on the third. A total of 20 Munros, 62 miles and *30,000ft* of ascent was proposed in three and a quarter days.

Joy was powerless to help me through the barrier:

> On every brightening in the clouds I would make a cheerful report in the hope that Martin might be jolted into action; but underneath I was somehow confident that he would recover by his own devices and make the final surge. From long experience I knew that he works best when under pressure . . .

The rain came in heavier bursts in the evening, yet with thick-skinned optimism we sat in the van drafting and typing the *post*-expedition reports: 'I can honestly say your equipment contributed significantly to my *success* . . .' and other fraudulent presumptions. Bedtime was 8.30, with a play on the radio and still the rat-tat-tat of the rain on the window an inch from my nose.

Four o'clock, and a brief stirring to hear again the familiar sound of the drizzle. At 5am the alarm rings out, crisis point is reached; there can be no turning over and no more excuses. A peep through the curtain shows a shy moon filtering through the cloud, and the wind no longer bellows. Luck is back with us; up like a shot, on with the kit, and out by 6am, Joy striding ahead up the stony path from Coulags:

> The first 2 miles were murderous. Splashing through pools, sinking in the peat, and tripping in the hidden ruts up to the disused bothy by the Fionn-abhainn. The huge effort ahead was painful to contemplate; but then a bright dawn emerged and we left the valley marsh for the white rock ramparts of Maol Chean-dearg. Without consciously trying my muscles started to fire and the awful torpor lifted. The 'show' was back on the road
> . . .

The Torridonian three were being taken in reverse sequence from our first attempt in the hope of relieving the initial anguish of setting out, so my morning's route would finish down Coire Lair. Maol Chean-dearg is ringed by a superb stalking path at half-height, from which its summit cone rises as a jumbled mass of quartzite boulders. The top still lay in mist on our arrival.

Joy's standard-bearing role was now fulfilled, and having reversed the ascent she watched me leap precariously across the swollen burn and romp up onto the 750m western flank of Sgorr Ruadh, happily confident that no further encouragement was required. Then it was a quick trot back to Coulags to make ready for our next stage.

Both Sgorr Ruadh and Fuar Tholl have impressive faces to the Lair basin on their north-east sides. Fuar Tholl's Mainreachan Buttress is considered one of the finest sandstone precipices in the country, while Ruadh's more broken cliffs have several winter gullies and ridges. The latter were first explored by the Reverend Robertson in 1898. In contrast, their south-west slopes are a featureless unbroken sweep. This is the rule with the majority of our mountains. Over 90 per cent of Scotland's glacial corries lie in the quadrant between north and east, which reflects the prevalence of the south-westerly airstream throughout the Ice Ages. This caused maximum accumulation of snow and therefore the concentration of glaciers on the lee sides of the hills.

The airy edge of Sgorr Ruadh was an exciting completion to a gruelling climb. The summit was frosted by a brisk wind which sent the cloud balls scudding across from the north-west both above and between the mountain tops. Beinn Liath Mhor was gained by swinging north around the valley head, and then a steep and stony drop brought me back to the corrie floor and the place of our retreat two days ago. The direct descents on this south-western side of the mountain are fraught with outcrops and scree shoots, and especially in snow conditions are to be discouraged in favour of the longer traverse over the south-east tops.

Joy had worked marvellously to have hot soup and lunch waiting, as well as our camping sack packed, by my arrival at Achnashellach at 11.50. She had also reaffirmed to Intermediate Technology that the thirteenth was still our target. Now there was confidence for you; but the signs were promising. Today had mellowed into a settled sunshine, and my spirit was so vibrant that leaving the van after a thirty-minute break felt no great hardship.

From a dropping point 4 miles up the road past Glencarron Lodge, my steps hastened onto Moruisg, the nearest of the Munros on the southern side. Unknowingly, the two last despairing days had served to replenish my energy. Moruisg, its neighbour, Sgurr nan Cean-naichean, and the descent to Glenuaig Lodge took little over two hours. Joy did not arrive for another ten minutes, having parked at Craig and shouldered a 40lb pack for the 6-mile trek up the Allt a'Chonais glen.

After a quick conference to fix our campsite for that night we parted again, myself springing off towards Maoile Lunndaidh while Joy lugged the load to a height of 600m in the north-east valley of Sgurr a'Chaorachain. My last mountain of the day was also the bulkiest, and its broad summit plateau was sheathed in ice and fringed by corniced corries of which the Fuar-tholl Mor looked particularly impressive. Winter was still fully in control here, an extra 100m in altitude and a further 5 miles inland creating a surprising change in the conditions, and making me glad of having axe and crampons.

The softening of the scenery from the Torridon district was reassuring. Rolling along the southern horizon beyond Loch Monar were the Affric and Cannich hills – already a month in the memory. Indeed, in every direction of the spacious view the mountains were familiar, most of them firm friends, but a few like Wyvis still repellent. Truly the ring was closing and the end was near.

From the shivering top of Maoile Lunndaidh my eyes dropped to the silent shelter of the corrie, and could just pick out Joy's red jacket moving to and fro about our tiny green tent, which was sited on a curve in the burn. If not a bivouac, then at least the winter was granting me one high camp.

Tea was nearly boiled, and quickly feeling the chill of my perspiration, I dived inside to warmth and rest. Propped on our elbows, weary legs glowing in their sleeping bags, and our hearts pulsing as one, we have watched the evening colours fade and the stars light up in the darkening sky; what a perfect haven!

There is still much to do, but the biggest day is off my chest; only six

Munros, but 3570m (11,700ft) of ascent and 23 miles completed without undue fatigue. The pressure has lifted a lot; but who cares anyway? Up here, lying under heaven's vault listening to the choke and gurgle of the tiny stream the hullabaloo might not even exist.

The toughest days of the trip had never caused me undue suffering until the following morning, when the inevitable psychological hangover would catch up and plunge me into misery. Despite my increased fitness this unhappy rhythm had never been dispelled, and today was no exception. Joy's firm pacing dragged me up the first of the four remaining Monar summits, Sgurr a'Chaorachain, heading straight into a gusty wind. There she left me to my own weak impetus, and returned to break camp, then make the 8-mile carry-out to the road.

Without Joy, this winter attempt would have been a folly, doomed to failure from the outset. The injury which thwarted my solo bid in 1980 was perhaps a disguised blessing and in retrospect to ever have considered going without her was naïve in the extreme. Her efforts had been unstinting, and through all the unglamorous tasks which fell to her lot she retained her enthusiasm and enjoyment of the venture. For me, each day's return was given an added thrill by her presence. There is more to living through an expedition of this duration than the animal necessities of food, warmth and a dry set of clothes every morning. But, conversely, our every parting was a little unwilling, however grand the mountains ahead, and rarely more poignant than today:

> Thick clouds poured in from the south-west, and from Sgurr Choinnich I was struggling direct into the wind, fighting myself at the same time.

A descent of the Allt Bealach Crudhain compelled me to a frontal attack of 700m on Lurg Mhor's north slopes. Because the peak was now thick in mist it was essential to hit the summit direct for there was a second top on the undulating ridge which could have confused the issue. On its upper section the slope moulded into a pleasant arête with a half-formed corrie on its left, but reaching the summit gave no sense of achievement, only the grave knowledge that I was a long way from home.

The ridge to Bidein a'Choire Sheasgaich was without difficulties, and by then returning to the head of Loch Monar, my route avoided its rocky north-west crest, which gives the peak a striking profile when viewed from Moruisg or Ceannaichean. The guidebooks generally advise that a traverse of Beinn Tharsuinn be taken to attain these two Munros from the north-west, but for simplicity, directness and shelter my low-level route is perhaps to be preferred, though it was by no means a smooth promenade even on a supposedly happy return and with a wind behind me:

A 2-mile contour, crossing innumerable streams and gullies, was needed to get to the Bealach Bhearnais and the commencement of homeward waters. My ankles were flexed to the right throughout, painfully stretching the ligaments and often turning over in the tussocks. The rain was heavy and continuous and I did it with clenched teeth, a vacant stare and a depressing vision of tomorrow's frolics on the Grey Corries. At 2.30 I reached the road but neither Joy nor the van were there.

Oh, the woe of being soaked, dispirited and deserted; but when Joy turned up twenty minutes later she had her own tale of misfortune. On her return she found that the van's battery was flat; perhaps the lights had been left on. With the help of Gerry Howkins, who runs the private hostel at Craig, the RAC was called. They had only just succeeded in getting it started, and instead of being ready for a composed return to Fort William, we found ourselves late, hungry, wet, very low on gas and above all disgruntled. However, Gerry came to the rescue:

'You look rough, kids', he said. 'Come on in, I've got the water boiling for a bath.'

His huge enamel bath was filled to the brim, a pot of tea was served, and the record-player positioned outside the door to give us the magical melodies of Andean folk songs as we took our steaming dip; the third bath of the winter. Having all but crawled into the hostel, half-an-hour later we floated out, our anxieties dissolved along with the grime and sweat, and forever grateful for Gerry's kindness. We would see it through now, come what may.

Though less than two days away from the end, our routine could not be allowed to lapse. Apart from the growing pile of dirty laundry, we were as tied to the basic tasks as ever. Milk and bread were purchased at Lochcarron, and then a frantic search for the gas commenced. I wedged my foot in the door of the Dornie grocers on the stroke of its closing time at 6.30.

'Yes, we have the propane', the lady said. Our planned cooked dinner was saved, but only just.

Then there was a string of phonecalls needed to fix my route, rendezvous points and timings; but before risking an irrevocable commitment, I wisely waited for tomorrow's weather forecast – something of a shocker, but no real surprise: 'Warm front passage . . . strong south-west wind, gales on coasts and hills . . . heavy showers . . .' Definitely the time for reappraisal.

A westward traverse of the Grey Corries and the Aonachs ridges, culminating in the knife edge of the Carn Mor Dearg arête, is the finest walker's route by which to approach Ben Nevis. Starting from Luibeilt bothy at the eastern end, 9,000ft of ascent are required to reach the Ben, an arduous day in itself, and in winter a serious

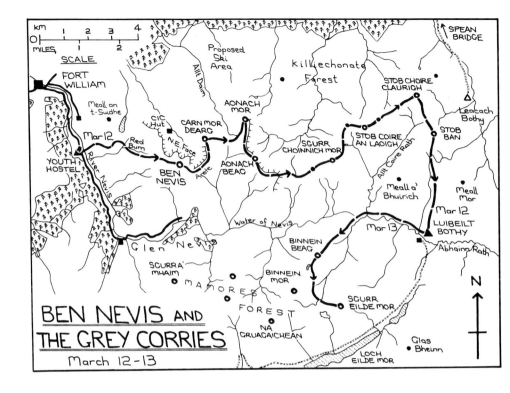

BEN NEVIS AND THE GREY CORRIES

March 12-13

expedition, Aonach Beag in particular having a notorious reputation. Thoroughly comparable to the Mamores Ridge in quality, it possesses the extra stature of leading to Britain's highest summit as well as its greatest precipice, and gives a crescendo of height and scenic magnificence; indeed, the grandest possible conclusion to the winter Munros.

However, in light of the forecast this plan posed twin problems – the difficulty, even the impossibility, of walking straight into the gale, and the necessity of a bivouac somewhere around the Aonachs. My route had first to make a 10-mile crossing of Sgurr Eilde Mor and Binnein Beag even to reach the Luibeilt steading, which is the last available accommodation before the Ben itself. Yet in order to finish by mid-morning on the thirteenth it was essential to press on from here to within four hours' striking distance of the end.

The implications were clear enough to me: a heavy sack with overnight gear . . . fighting the wind to exhaustion . . . soaked by the rain . . . a blizzard on the high tops . . . and *then* an open bivouac at 700 or 800m. Not a chance. Fame is one thing, but martyrdom is quite another story! Yet turning the picture round, a different tale emerged: go west-east starting with the Ben . . . hardest section first . . . blown along the Grey Corries . . . no bivouac pack . . . meet Joy for a warm dry night at Luibeilt and finish at a canter onto Sgurr Eilde Mor.

The rationale was, however, lost on our publicity organisers, Thomson and Bonnist, and the change of mind was met with dismay and acrimony:

'You'll lose all the impact.'

'No one's ever heard of Sgurr Eilde Mor.'

'The press were all planning to climb the Ben, even the TV men . . . we can't change now . . .'

But they failed to budge me, and were left in the panic of re-arrangement while we drove on to our last overnight park in Glen Nevis, my goodwill soured by their seeming lack of consideration of the trials we were going through to finish on time, whatever the route taken. My obstinacy also stemmed from growing disillusionment over the supposed purpose of the publicity – to raise money for Inter-mediate Technology. Yet for all this puppet show, a paltry £2,000 had so far been received. Was it really worth the fuss?

But the very obscurity of the chosen finishing peak possessed its own appeal, and was perhaps more fitting to the experience of the past three months. The popular image still exists that there are no worthy mountains in Scotland besides Ben Nevis, the Cairngorms and the peaks of Glencoe. My express intent this winter had been to explore the wealth of fine Munros outside these glamour spots; and equally to see the most barren and bleakest places, to absorb their strange beauty and cope with their loneliness. So Sgurr Eilde Mor would do very nicely to symbolise this spirit, and perhaps might help to break the myth. But its summit crown was still ten Munros away, and the last week had taught me the one good lesson that nothing can ever be taken for granted.

At 6.45 I set off into a gloomy dawn which morbidly foretold the day to come. Alan Thomson joined me but soon turned back, this was not the light for his photographs and I was hardly inclined to stop for them anyway. Through the winter Alan and I had built a productive working relationship and, more importantly, a happy companionship in our days on the hills. It was a pity that the conflicting demands of publicity and good mountaineering sense should have slightly tarnished the fruition of our efforts. Alan Hinkes came up to help me find the summit, but thereon it was back to my own company.

The 'pony track' to the top of Ben Nevis is the biggest and the most popular ascent in the Highlands, but is probably unrivalled in its tedium, and in winter there is a vicious sting to its tail whenever the mists are down. The benign security of the broad zig-zags is abruptly relinquished as they disappear under the snowfields. One suddenly

The north-east face of Ben Nevis with the Carn Mor Dearg arête on the left, January 1943 (*SMC Collection*)

remembers the two who died in January's avalanche on these simple slopes, and then debouching onto the summit plateau the jagged indents of the north-east face shave perilously close to the line of travel. In this morning's thick cloud and light snowfall the last half mile was a tense affair even though Alan and I between us had climbed all the gullies and faces we sought to avoid.

It seems uncanny that climbers emerging from grade V verticalities can then fail to find the tourist descent. Over-prudence is the usual error; steering too wide a course away from the northern cliffs, and in so doing wandering into the chasms on the western flanks where Five Finger and Surgeon's Gullies are the usual snares. However, the tenuous navigation needed to get off the top in a white-out adds to the challenge and rewards of climbing on the north face.

Whatever the Aberdonians claim for their beloved Cairngorms, it is the Ben which gives the most reliable winter climbing conditions by virtue of its extra height, scale and humidity, especially for the majority to whom 'good' conditions mean solid well-plated ice rather than the snowed-up rock to which the devotees of Lochnagar are so partial. Even during this snowless winter the great Point Five and

Zero Gullies had developed magnificent ribbons of ice, and doubtless had been especially crowded by climbers, due to the bareness of the adjoining faces and the poor fare in Glencoe.

The summit shelter was encrusted by rime ice, maybe not in the proportions of the 7-foot daggers that were once noted sticking out of the observatory anemometer in the last century, but wintry none the less. Careful bearings were now required, for the descent of the south-east ridge onto the Carn Mor Dearg arête is the most treacherous on the mountain. On the left the slope assumes a gradually steepening convexity, which can entice the unwary to a premature plunge over the Coire Leis headwall.

The arête was free of ice, but covered with loose snow. Its graceful sweep was missed, likewise the close-up study of Nevis's great buttresses which are revealed as the corrie head is turned. Today the edge was merely an extended trial of care and patience, thankfully quitted for the easier ground of Carn Mor Dearg's eastern spur, which gives the link to the two Aonachs:

> I sheltered by the ruined wall on the col and ate a cheese sandwich. So far, so good; conditions had been colder and less windy than expected. An ice-blue window appeared in the cloud, raising hopes to an unwarranted pitch
> . . .

This was the first and last sight of the sky. The following climb took me back in the clouds and onto the belly-shaped top of Aonach Mor. Its rough pile of granite stones now guards a heath of lonely desolation, but ten years hence perhaps it will be thrice the size and mobbed by swarms of roving walkers who have dismounted from the proposed gondola lifts to trek into the imagined 'wilderness', much in the mode of a second Cairn Gorm. The 'honeypot' style of development is seen by many as the saviour of the remaining remote tracts; but the sacrifice of Aonach Mor and its hinterland is a heavy price to pay.

As I crept about the bald head of Aonach Beag checking for the highest point, a gusting wind and penetrating sleet commenced. Quickly my spectacles were fogged over and blurred, and so my gropings became tense and unsure. A tiny cairn is rumoured to exist on the top, and many minutes were spent teetering close to the cornice dollops on the eastern edge to prove that it was either a myth or else in hibernation. The extremes of lunacy which the aspirant Munroist will endure! But my own affliction was soon to be cured; just six to go.

Finding the continuing ridge to the Grey Corries brought greater problems:

> The eastern face was one long débâcle without any clear offshoot to tempt me. I spent half an hour wandering back and forth along the edge, losing confidence and getting cold. On realising that my indecision could be a

symptom of mild exposure, I plumped for a steep snow wall close to the compass line, and a further 50m of awkward scrambling led onto easier ground and a ridge of sorts. Shivering noticeably now I stopped immediately to put on all spare clothes and ate the rest of my food. It was 2.30, and there were 6 miles still to go above the 850m level. Time was short; I had to push on, but would I warm up again?

Fortunes rose as soon as the characteristic quartzite screes of the Grey Corries were underfoot. With an increased pace on the easy ridge over Sgurr Choinnich Mor the warmth flooded back, and though battered this way and that by a furious wind, the doubt of finishing evaporated. Occasionally the rain would cease and the gale tore the clouds apart giving wild views of the twisting ridge ahead.

> I was on Stob Choire Claurigh just before 5pm, which gave two hours till darkness. Only the detached subsidiary of Stob Ban remained, a 130m scarp of shattered scree. I crawled up, buckled against the wind and now tiring rapidly, but in quite triumphant mood. It had been a tough battle but at last I knew I could complete the Munros.

The rain became more persistent on the boggy descent to Luibeilt, and darkness came early. At 7pm I opened the bothy door. Joy was slightly concerned, for my arrival was an hour overdue, and this was not a good night for an enforced bivouac. My dripping clothes joined her own on the wires above the fire. There were two others at the bothy very much keeping to their own company, so we were unable to vent our many thoughts. Once warmed and fed we ensconced ourselves in a quiet night of contemplation while the storm rattled on outside.

Inevitably there was excited anticipation, especially for Joy:

> In a few hours a hot bath and a change of clothes were in prospect – a chance to be a little more feminine. But also I felt sad that this strange existence was to be broken. Would we simply drop into a mental vacuum after striving for so long? The idea of returning to the city left me feeling empty and depressed. Far from having missed our former existence, the cosy convenience of suburban life has lost all appeal, and until we have settled ourselves permanently in the Highlands I won't rest happy.

And likewise myself. No exploit in the mountains ever seems to leave the heart at rest, and the Munros were no exception. The direction, style and location may alter, but a love of wild places and the search for their challenge seems only to be increased by hard experience. Devotion or addiction, call it what you will.

Above all, the winter mountains had given a lasting happiness, 83 days that will never be erased from the memory. True, we had remarkable luck in selecting the least windy and snowy season for over a decade, which had helped me to finish a week within the schedule. Compared to the expected 42 days with gales on the summits, my records totalled only 26, whilst precipitation was on average three-quarters of its normal level*. So we had far more than our ration of sunshine and frost. But the great tempests also possess their own awesome appeal, and epics like today's on the Grey Corries will perhaps be the most cherished of all. Indeed, the relative absence of snow and storm was one of my slight disappointments of this 1985 winter.

Doing the Munros in a single winter had been a self-motivated adventure, but how would the achievement stand, stripped of the public glory and assessed on its true merits? The thought was of special concern as we approached the end. Certainly a new record had been created for the fastest completion of the peaks, though the tactics and season were not comparable to anything that had gone before. But its only wider significance, and the real measure of its impact, is whether it motivates others to new challenges, just as Hamish's walk had inspired my own idea.

A continuous journey without motor assistance in the ninety days was far beyond my own capability or conception, but by allowing a full four months from 1 December to 31 March a non-stop winter walk is feasible. And eventually somebody with supreme fortitude, skill and a slice of luck, may overcome the hazards and do this within the calendar season. Then, looking to the summer, the time is overdue for a fell-running attempt. The remarkable feats achieved in the Lake District, Pennines and increasingly in Scotland have shown that there are several men of the necessary calibre – seventy-five days, or even less? And nor should Corbett's 221 peaks above 2,500ft be ignored, for here is an odyssey which would take one from the Border hills to the Outer Isles**. An overdose of 'Munrosis' can blinker the sights to the vast variety and extent of Scotland's lower hills.

But, apart from these extreme endeavours, I hope that as great a stimulus may be provided to those with modest ambitions, or who enjoy the hills in a relaxed fashion, and especially those who presently confine their visits to the lighter seasons of the year. Winter demands a greater respect, prudence and preparedness, but please go and seek, for the pleasures should not be denied and the mountains are still so empty.

✳

*See Appendix IV for detailed weather statistics.
**As this is written, twenty-five-year-old Craig Caldwell is three-quarters of the way through a prolonged attempt to combine all the Munros and Corbetts in a single journey – an effort plagued by the wettest summer since 1897.

At 6am we struggled into damp clothes and stumbled out into a cooler, fresher morning – the usual gruelling ritual of warming up and setting a pace. The hills were lightly dusted with overnight snow, and the dew rose up the grasses to freeze at the touch of the north-west breeze. The thought that I might have bivouacked on Aonach Beag produced a shudder. Both it and Ben Nevis were still clamped under the cloud.

Up on Binnein Beag a feral cat loped across the screes not 50m above us, a lucky sighting which enlivened the toilsome slog from the Glen Nevis watershed. For some reason we were dragging our feet. As the morning haze dissolved, the string of streams and lochans over to the east sparkled into our sight. The air was crystal clear, and pausing on the top we filled our lungs with glad and generous draughts.

Twisting around the shoulder of Binnein Mor by the stalking track and onto the ridge of Sgurr Eilde Mor already we could spot a few figures moving about on its summit, so our finish was not to go unseen. Just 200m to go up the screes and snowbanks above the ice-choked lochan; it was a pity to have to stop . . .

POSTSCRIPT

The cruel fact of life that success counts for all was amply proven on our completion. During the next nine months our appeal total for Intermediate Technology multiplied to £20,000, and through articles, lectures and broadcasts the charity was given a wealth of additional promotion. So the stress and pressure of the publicity (which had sometimes taxed us more than the Munros themselves!) was worthwhile, even though the amount is a drop in an ocean of need.

APPENDICES

I: GLOSSARY

Heights and Distances

The alternating use of the metric and imperial scales in the book deserves an apology and a brief explanation. All long distances are given in miles to provide a consistent measure in line with traditional convention. However, metrication has been attempted in the case of heights. Whilst Munros are defined by their height in feet, the Ordnance Survey is well advanced in its conversion to metric contour intervals and heights in its Second Series maps. The dilemma was insoluble, and a compromise has been struck by quoting all height intervals on the ground and summit altitudes in metres, but quoting daily total ascents in both numbers of metres and feet. The outrageous suggestion (no doubt made with 'tongue in cheek') has been heard from some quarters that with metrication Munros are outdated and should be replaced by a list of 'Metros' (peaks over either 900 or 1,000 metres in altitudes). Given the current boom in the Munros cult, there is scant chance that this idea will ever gain acceptance.

Winter Climbing Grades

Graded climbs on *snow and ice* in Scotland are currently grouped into six classes:

   I Uncomplicated average-angled snow climbs having no pitches normally. They may however have cornice difficulties or dangerous runouts.

  II Gullies which contain either individual or minor pitches or high-angled snow with difficult cornice exits. The easier buttresses (ie, Moderate in Summer) under winter conditions.

III Gullies which contain ice in quantity. There will normally be at least one substantial pitch and possibly several lesser ones. Sustained buttress climbs (ie, Difficult in Summer) but only technical in short sections.

IV Steeper than grade III and of higher technical difficulty. Vertical sections may be expected on ice climbs, and buttresses will require a good repertoire of techniques.

  V Climbs which are difficult, sustained and serious. Also well-protected desperates. May not be possible in poor conditions.

VI Routes of exceptional overall difficulty.

For pure *rock* climbing the traditional British gradings are used where required in the text. These are: Easy, Moderate, Difficult, Very Difficult, Severe, Very Severe, Hard Very Severe, Extremely Severe.

Gaelic Glossary

The reader is referred to the excellent 'Gaelic Guide' included in the current 1984 edition of *Munro's Tables* (Scottish Mountaineering Club) for an introduction to Gaelic grammar, a list of commonly used names, a phonetic key, and the complete translation and pronunciation of all the Munros' names. Rather than inadequately trying to replicate the scholarship of this Guide, only the most common names for topographical features which recur in the text are listed below, as an immediate aid to the geographical understanding of the mountains, and it is hoped the enjoyment of the book.

abhainn	stream	*glas, ghlas*	grey, greenish-grey, green
allt	stream, burn		
aonach	mountain ridge, hill, moor	*gorm*	blue, (of grass) green
ban	white, light-coloured	*lairig*	pass
beag	small	*liath*	grey, blueish grey
bealach	pass	*lochan*	small lake, tarn
beinn, bheinn (ben)	hill, mountain	*mam*	large rounded hill
		maol	bald, bare
bidean, bidein	peak, summit	*meadhoin, mheadhoin*	middle
binnein	pointed peak	*meall*	rounded hill
buidhe	yellow	*monadh*	moor, range; hill, mountain
caorann, chaorainn	rowan tree	*mor, mhor (more)*	big
carn, cairn	heap of stones, cairn-shaped hill	*mullach*	summit, top
		odhar, odhair	fawnish brown
clach	stone	*riabhach*	brindled, greyish
coille	wood	*ruadh*	red, red-brown
coire, choire	corrie, glaciated valley (literally a cauldron, kettle)	*sail*	rounded hill
		sgur(r), sgor(r)	rocky hill or peak
		spidean	peak, summit
creag	rock, crag	*sron*	jutting ridge
cruach	stack-shaped hill	*stac, stuc*	steep conical hill
dearg	red	*stob*	pointed hill
dubh	black	*tarsuinn*	transverse, (a) cross
eas	waterfall		
fionn	white, pale coloured	*toll*	hole, hollow
		tom	small rounded hill
gabhar, ghabhar	goat		
garbh	rough	*uamh*	cave
geal	white	*uisge*	water

NB See Bibliography for suggested further reading and the address of Intermediate Technology

II: ROUTE STATISTICS

An estimated total of 1,028 map miles of walking and 125,580m (412,000ft) of ascent was required to complete the Munros, an average of 12.4 miles and 1515m (4,965ft) for each of the 83 days, or 13.9 miles and 1700m (5,570ft) for the 74 active days, excluding those spent in rest or stormbound. This tallied very closely to my planning estimates. The analysis of daily mileages and ascents shows how varied the itineraries were in their length and duration:

Miles per day	Days		Ascent per day (× 1,000ft)	Days
Rest Days	9		Rest Days	9
5–10	20		Less than 3	7
10–15	23		3–4	11
15–20	17		4–5	15
20–25	12		5–6	7
Over 25	2		6–7	17
			7–8	9
			8–9	4
			9–10	2
			Over 10	2

The daily scores of Munros were likewise widely scattered:

Munros per day	Days		Munros per day	Days
0	10		5	12
1	10		6	5
2	14		7	2
3	12		8	3
4	12		9	3

Joy's final total of Munros on the trip was 120.

The response to the 67 *Brochures* left on the tops was expectedly patchy. Only 21 were returned as requested, and the discovery of a further 2 was proven by way of an irate letter sent to one of the magazines. Of the remainder, it may be assumed that many disintegrated during their weeks of burial in the summit cairns, or else the handwritten request for their return washed off. Happily, 11 of those returned were accompanied by a donation, giving a welcome total of £100 towards our appeal for IT. The longest known survivor was that left on Carn Dearg in Ben Alder Forest, deposited on 12 January and extracted by Tim Young of Cumbria on 29 March.

III: EQUIPMENT, DIET AND HEALTH

Equipment and Clothing

The motto for the success of the Munros venture was to travel light and fast. Yet this ethic had to be harnessed to the equal necessity of being fully clothed and equipped to survive the worst imaginable weather. The compromise between these conflicting objectives lay in 'quality'. By selecting lightweight items of high performance and durability to cover the essential needs, quantity and bulk could be minimized.

Travelling alone for much of the time necessitated an attitude of total self-reliance. In the event of a mishap, no rescue or assistance could be anticipated, and indeed would not have been wished for except in the direst hour of need, so each day's rucksac contained the following items which were considered essential to *prevent* as well as *endure* an unplanned bivouac.

Ice axe (curved pick) and crampons (frontpointed) These items were *never* left behind (though the sharing arrangement on the Cuillin was a regrettable miscalculation, see Ch 14). With the confidence of experience, I knew I could tackle steep ground of up to grade III with just these two items in event of a route-finding disaster. The axe is quite sufficient to fashion an emergency snowhole. Spare crampon strap, rivets and adjusters were also carried.

Headtorch Including spare battery and bulbs.

Bivouac sac Full-length nylon/goretex with zipped hood, weighing little over ½kg.

First-aid kit Including sufficient bandaging, tape and gauze to cope with a major trauma; painkillers (DF 118).

Food The day's lunch (see Diet) plus a couple of spare energy food bars; usually a total of 1,800 calories.

Map and compass A plastic wallet proved an excellent protection against rapid disintegration in wind or rain; if possessed, a spare map was also carried (see Ch 12).

Snow goggles Only taken on the ski-ing days when snow glare was dangerously strong, or when blizzards were likely.

Rucksac Berghaus Redpoint 'Red Wall' – lightweight, with padded-foam back for seat insulation on a bivouac or bothy stay. Nylon bivouac extension above the knees also available.

Spare mittens, wool balaclava, long johns and thin sweater (see Personal Clothing).

Several people expressed surprise that Joy and I did not carry two-way radios to maintain contact and co-ordination. My personal view is that such paraphernalia are an unwanted encumbrance, detracting from the freedom and simplicity of mountaineering. They might have caused more confusion than clarification, especially in times of self doubt when I could easily have been tempted by Joy's voice to abandon a day. In any event, radios would have added little to the 'telepathic' understanding which linked us almost faultlessly throughout the expedition.

With a genuine pang of guilt I must admit that the porterage of the extra equipment for overnight stays at bothies was not usually my concern! However, suffice to say that the usual requisites of sleeping bag, gaz stove, pan, spare socks and vest, candle, firelighter, matches and utensils were carried. 'Epigas' screw-in gas canisters gave long lasting fuel supply at a sustained pressure; but it is wise to check that cartridge and burner are compatible and the seal valves are working before embarking into the wilderness with them, given our experience in Ben Alder Forest (Ch 5). On the occasions when I did carry a full overnight pack (eg, Knoydart, Cairngorms, Glen Tilt) the total burden was never greater than 12kg.

Personal Clothing

This was of course my most important insurance against the elements, and, having found a combination that served me well, my dress was rarely varied. However the kit as listed below, whilst fine for the continuously moving hill-walker might be found insufficient for the roped ice climber who spends so much of his day waiting and shivering on belay stances.

Boots Medium weight, half-stiffened leather boots were worn throughout – mainly Scarpa Trionic SL, but occasionally Scarpa Manta, the latter proving lighter and more comfortable. The boots coped with all terrain from frontpointing on steep snow, to rock scrambling, and jogging on tracks and roads. They did not wear appreciably on the soles (but this is expected when so much of the walking was on frozen ground and snow).

Gaiters Berghaus Yeti Gaiters (with rubber rand on the welt) ensured warm dry feet on nearly every day. However, the rubbers wore out with distressing rapidity, and had to be re-randed several times. By using strong adhesive (eg, 'Superglue') to stick down the toes, the durability was improved to around 3 weeks. It must be remembered, however, that they were being given the roughest possible treatment, often on loose rocky ground. For pure snow and ice climbing, or boggy walking, the Yetis are ideal (if expensive) and they also of course protect the boot uppers from wear.

Jacket A lined Goretex anorak (with hood) seems the perfect outer

garment for fast travel in the Scottish winter. Down-filled jackets are too warm for all but the most severe conditions, and therefore prone to cause excess sweating (with subsequent chilling and energy loss). They are also rendered ineffective when wetted, as so often happens on the winter mountains. Our own Thinsulate-filled jackets only became essential on the days on the Feshie hills during the −30°C windstorm. Otherwise, my Stormbelt Jacket (goretex with a towelling lining) proved warm, windproof and watertight in all conditions. The 'breathability' of the outer material, and the absorption quality of the towelling kept my inner garments fairly dry even when working hard.
Salopettes Stretch-cotton salopettes (French make) were warm, comfortable and very quick drying. By contrast, the Rohan 'Super-Salopettes' (in thicker stretch Helenca) which were occasionally worn, usually proved too hot and heavy for quick travel and are better for serious climbing. With the potential addition of long johns and overtrousers, a light salopette is far more adaptable to the wide range of conditions. However, salopettes have been very slow to gain favour in Britain especially among hillwalkers who seem loathe to discard traditional breeches. In my view these give the problems of heat loss and discomfort at the midriff, together with exposed kneecaps if they are cut too short. However, ladies may have their own reason to disagree with this recommendation!
Overtrousers Goretex, with waist drawcord to prevent excessive sagging, and full-length side zips enabling them to be donned or removed when wearing crampons.
Gloves/mittens and wool balaclava Keeping the extremities warm was of the greatest concern – frozen hands are unable to cope with the simplest tasks, whilst the heat-loss through an exposed cranium is enormous. Spares were always carried. Fur-lined goretex covered mitts were very warm though by no means waterproof; wool Dachstein mitts proved equally warm and retained their insulation better when wet. Sewn wrist-loops guarded against loss when temporarily removed. Thin inner gloves were also carried but rarely worn, mitts providing a better core of heat and keeping the fingers together.
Long johns (Helly Hansen) Only worn on the very coldest days but usually carried.
Fibrepile jacket Remarkably this was often not needed, so efficient was the outer Stormbelt jacket.
Other items Thin spare sweater, wool shirt, long-sleeved vest, ski hat.

Nordic Ski Equipment

This was only used for six days on the expedition, whereas at least a fortnight had been hoped and expected. Our chosen combination of kit, whilst not thoroughly tested, proved light, efficient and ideally suited to the Scottish hill terrain:

Skis Kneissel White Star, 210cm, metal edged, waxable (Martin); Trak Telemark 205cm, metal edged, fishscale bottomed (Joy). The fishscale tread proved ineffective on slopes in excess of 15°, especially on hard or icy snow.

Bindings 3-pin Rottefeller.

Boots Asolo (Snowfield); very warm, vibram soled, and could be fitted to crampons and Yeti gaiters; therefore adaptable to mixed climbing and ski-ing terrain.

Skins Brushed nylon; excellent for long or steep climbs.

Other items Poles, waxing kit (though not used on the hill due to lack of time and expertise), spare-pole basket, screwdriver and repair kit, spare skin.

Camera

Finally, my camera cannot be passed without mention. It was an ever-present companion demanding frequent stops and continual exposure no matter how severe the weather or short the daylight; in use the bane of my life, but with retrospect, and a collection of some 750 slides to illustrate our memory of the trip, an indispensable accoutrement. A Minolta X300 (35mm SLR) was purchased for the trip, with a choice between a standard 50mm lens and a 28mm wide-angle, with which a simple UV filter was used continuously. Apart from the malfunction mentioned in Ch 2 which was due entirely to my own ineptitude, and an occasional falter in the batteries at −15°C and below, the camera operated excellently all winter. With a padded pouch and shoulder sling it was well protected and easily portable. Kodachrome 64 and Fuji 100 films were used alternately, the former giving admirable reproduction of pure snowscapes, whilst the Fuji better captured the complete colour contrast from the greens and browns of the glens to the snowy summits.

Diet

The abnormal duration of the expedition coupled with the continual exposure to the cold made our diet of the prime concern. A high daily calorific intake was an obvious prerequisite but a properly balanced intake of all vitamins and minerals is equally essential to sustain an effort through 90 days. Neither a short-term depletion of immediate energy, nor a long-term physical run-down due to a lack of nutrients could be entertained. One dose of exhaustion in severe conditions might have spelt the end of the venture, to say nothing of *me*, especially given the tenuous thread of our lightweight strategy.

The long-term problem seems to have affected several previous Scottish marathons. In 1967 the Ripley brothers abandoned the first attempt on the continuous Munros round just 50 peaks from the end, reportedly in an advanced state of bodily exhaustion and malnutrition; whilst in 1984 Rick Ansell was so plagued by hunger on his non-stop walk of the mainland Munros that he was driven to searching for discarded 'half-eaten butties' around the summit cairns. Coming off Beinn Sgulaird, Rick was convinced of suffering hallucinations from hunger when an apple, a cake and three Opal Fruits appeared on the side of the track with the sign 'Please Eat' attached, but amazingly this wayside offering proved genuine and was promptly devoured.

On a non-stop walk it is naturally difficult to ensure a continuous supply of wholesome groceries, especially when they have to be carried on the back, but it is my strong suspicion that far too many walkers rely on dried, processed and prepackaged food to the exclusion of all else, and hence accelerate their dietary downfall. Dried food especially is squeezed and drained of its goodness, and has the reputation of exercising little else apart from the bowels, which in itself depletes the body's reserves.

With the use of transport there was certainly no excuse for our failing to visit the Highland village stores regularly, and Joy made the most strenuous efforts to procure fresh food stocks at every stage of our journey. Fresh fruit, milk and vegetables even featured on the bothy menu on occasions, and never once was a packet of dried stew or curry opened for our main meal, for which I give thanks, as eating surely is an enjoyment as well as a necessity.

Neither of us eat meat, and so we relied on fish, nuts and pulses (especially lentils) for our protein supply. The content of the diet was deliberately biased away from glucose. On a prolonged test of endurance one requires a 'slow, steady and sustained' stream of energy rather than the short-lived boosts provided by pure sweets and sugar, which can leave the body feeling even more depleted in their aftermath. Basic fats and carbohydrates are far more appropriate sources of calories.

A typical menu for one of the tougher days of the trip (ie, greater than 15 miles, 6,000ft) is given below, with calories per meal, as the best means of summarizing our diet. On easier days the calorie intake might drop to 3,250 as a minimum. With no oven and only 2 gas rings and a grill at our disposal Joy found a pressure cooker indispensable to maintain invention and variety in our meals.

Breakfast (700 calories)
Stewed prunes
Muesli, banana, milk
Toast, margarine and honey (2 rounds)
Tea

Lunch/Hill Food (1,500 calories)
Cheese and wholemeal bread sandwich
Flask of hot soup or drinking chocolate
Slice of fruit cake, fresh apple
2 'Crunchy' Bars (oats/almonds/honey)
Bar of fudge and/or chocolate

Dinner (1,650 calories)
Grilled grapefruit
Lentil and nut cakes
Cheese and garlic potatoes
Fried cabbage
Steamed apple sponge, cream or yogurt

Bedtime (150 calories)
Cup of drinking chocolate
Piece of fresh fruit

TOTAL FOR DAY: 4,000 calories

On the bothy trips the usual menu comprised:

Breakfast (500 calories)
Muesli, hot milk, dried fruit, sugar
Wholemeal biscuits, margarine and
  honey
Tea

Lunch (1,700 calories)
As normal but with extra energy bars

TOTAL FOR DAY: 3,600 calories

Dinner (1,400 calories)
Soup and oatcakes
125gm spaghetti, margarine, tinned
  tuna, cheese, fresh fried onion and
  garlic
Custard and dried apples or apricots
Tea and powdered orange drink

Health

The success of this diet was clearly manifested in our maintaining a clean bill of health, except for Joy's head cold, throughout the trip. Happily not a single aspirin, sleeping tablet, vitamin pill, iron booster or any other supplement passed our lips during the 83 days. The outdoor existence certainly proved to be a healthy way, but perhaps our living in a glorified refrigerator and quite apart from the rest of humanity also explains this apparent immunity to infection.

Remarkably, I finished the Munros at exactly the same weight with which the journey was commenced, just under 10½ stone. This is perhaps the best testimony to the accuracy of Joy's provisioning. A rapid weight loss was something to be feared, for though invigorating in the short-term it would have left me with precious little fat or muscle reserves for an emergency. Therefore I was deliberately indulgent in my eating even on the very rare occasions when an appetite was lacking. However, within my constant total weight something like a stone must have been transferred from my top half down to the legs, as was evident when I found myself hanging by the arms trying to rock climb again in the Spring!

The serious doubts over the fortitude of my much abused knees and ankles on commencing the trip proved needless. By taking due care to avoid excessive jarring on the joints especially early in the day when not warmed up, and on the long steep descents, no problems were encountered, and a build-up of muscles in the appropriate places compensated for my torn and strained ligaments. In fact the continuous activity seemed to do these ailments a power of good. Stiffness and fluid accumulation, usually so noticeable when at my sedentary accountancy job, magically disappeared.

A careful routine prevented other potentially disabling maladies. Nightly washing, a coat of talcum powder and clean socks kept the feet warm, healthy and blister-free. The only recurrently painful nuisance was the finger chilblains which seem to germinate excellently in the alternating hot and cold environments.

A good level of general fitness was attained after the expected struggles of the first ten days, and well sustained thereafter. However, the occasional rest days gave a tremendous boost to my energies, especially when I was flagging after a string of hard outings. The varying of daily mileage and ascent was found to be not only a wise concession to the fluxes of weather, but also an ideal regime for maintaining physical freshness, an adaptability between speed and endurance, and most vitally a keen mental interest throughout the expedition.

IV: WINTER MOUNTAIN WEATHER AND SNOW CONDITIONS

Not surprisingly, we maintained a vested interest in the weather throughout the winter, for the final fate of the Munros attempt lay firmly in the lap of the Gods, however great my endeavour or skilled our tactics. This element of chance was indeed one of the most appealing aspects of the expedition. We set off without an inkling of what was coming. Three months of snow and frost, or rain and gale – either possibility had to be faced with equanimity, for unpredictability and turbulence make Highland winter weather an impossible beast to tame.

Each day's forecast was therefore awaited with bated breath, and like a pair of hawks we scanned the skies for the slightest portent of a change in conditions. As part of this interest I kept regular daily records of the mountain weather features, mainly based on visual observations, for here was a unique chance to obtain a complete picture of a winter on the hills, there being few climbers who are out on the tops on *every* day of the season.

By publishing my observations, together with supplementary data from the Meteorological Office stations, and the Cairn Gorm summit Automatic Weather Station (AWS) both from 1984/85, and for previous years, it is hoped to contribute to three important aims.

(i)   The accumulation of a *pool of weather data* for the mountain summits in winter as a source of information to all hillgoers.
(ii) To assist the understanding of *synoptic weather maps* and forecasts, and especially their interpretation into the likely conditions that will be encountered on the mountains given the prevailing pattern of pressure, and airmass movements.
(iii) To show the link between the patterns of weather and the changes in snow type, depth and quality on the hills, especially in the prediction of good climbing conditions and of *avalanche risk*.

Undoubtedly there is a paramount need for an increased knowledge among climbers of all three aspects, particularly in winter and especially for the leaders of young or inexperienced parties.

The intending hillgoer is currently supplied with a plethora of weather information, much of which is irrelevant, or else requires a certain technical knowledge to interpret correctly. General weather forecasts are especially dangerous if digested without modification, for they try to reproduce the likely conditions at low-level altitudes and give little indication of the greater severity of climate higher up. Also they tend to be definitive, giving little idea of the possible *range* of conditions that could be faced, and this is where the weather chart offers a much broader picture, *if* it can be understood.

So the climber has to make a rather tricky translation of all this data to predict the happenings in the high corries or on the Munro summits. In summer if his prejudgement is widely amiss, a minor epic, a retreat or an unwanted wetting may ensue, the sort of experience that is part of the fun of the sport! In winter, when conditions can quickly pass beyond the threshold of physical tolerance, the same error may plunge him into a battle for survival. And also in winter the 'translation' problem is manifestly more complex, for it must take account of freezing levels, and the type of snow that might fall, or has fallen – witness our own failure to anticipate the white blanket on the Cuillin Ridge.

Awareness of these imperatives has increased in recent years, though it required several tragedies to arouse a proper concern. Since the closure of the Ben Nevis summit Observatory in 1904, mountain weather recording was highly fragmentary until in 1977 the Cairn Gorm AWS commenced operation. Partly utilising the data flow from Cairn Gorm, there are now several forecasts available for mountaineers and skiers either on radio (eg, BBC Radio Scotland), from the recorded 'Mountainline' forecast on British Telecom (041-248 5757) or on enquiry to the major met offices. Yet we still found these specialist predictions to be widely awry on certain occasions, most notably during the February windstorm on Cairn Gorm.

At the outset it must be stressed that apart from temperature readings, my own observations were wholly subjective, and were also of course highly 'mobile' – my experience on Ben Hope would hardly provide an accurate indicator of events on Ben Lomond 200 miles to the south; but wherever possible other data has been used to consolidate an average picture across the country, and better a rough sketch than none at all!

The climate of the 1984/1985 winter confounded my gloomiest anticipations. Stable continental and polar airmasses were predominant, and denied the westerly airstream its usual influence. This makes the supplement of average comparatives for previous periods especially vital. Never should our lucky experience be taken as a model for future years!

Temperature

The prevalence of Arctic and land-cooled continental airstreams produced a colder than average winter in 1984/85. There is still the misconception among many that the colder the weather the more severe and dangerous it is, but in fact the opposite holds more truth. Especially given the excellent insulation of modern boots and clothing, pure cold is not to be feared to the same degree as the wind, and especially a gale combined with a wet snowfall and a temperature hovering on zero, which produces a more immediate wetting, loss of insulation and consequent chilling of the body.

Table 1 shows that the depression of temperature was experienced both on the east and west sides of the country, especially in January when we recorded 21 successive nights with frost from 1st to 21st, and a winter minimum of −16°C at Newtonmore on the 24th–25th. Braemar's winter minimum of −22.7° came two nights later (when we were in the warmer west at Glencoe). The anticyclonic persistence throughout this period was highly unusual, for a stormy (and therefore warmer) early January is one of the major singularities of the seasonal weather cycles in the Highlands.

By comparison, our highest overnight minimum was +10°C at Inchnadamph on 22–23 February, when the great rainstorm commenced. Indeed, average temperature figures hide the marked variation between periods of westerly and easterly airstream dominance. Roughly ordering the daily situations between the two categories, 40 days of Atlantic low-pressure airflow were discerned with a mean minimum of +2.6°, and 43 days of Polar/continental high-pressure dominance with a mean of −3.6°.

The mountaineer must be especially vigilant for the rapid fluxes of temperature which accompany a switch in airstream and which can create great instability in the snow cover. A blizzard which begins cold and ends warm can lay down an undercoat of loose powder pellets beneath a topping of heavy wet flakes producing a snow profile in imminent danger of collapse. Conversely, a rapid thaw can cause an immediate risk of wet snowslide and cornice collapse. For instance, during 27 and 28 January, Braemar's temperature rocketed from $-17.9°$ to $+5.7°$.

Table 1 Minimum Daily Air Temperature (°C), Monthly Means

	Braemar (339 metres)	Onich (15 metres) (nr Ballachulish)	Own Readings (170 metres average)
Dec 1984	−0.1	2.6	2.1 (21st–31st)
1951 – 80 average	−0.9	1.9	−
Difference from average	+0.8	+0.7	−
Jan 1985	−4.8	−1.7	−2.8
1951 – 80 average	−2.5	0.9	−
Difference from average	−2.3	−2.6	−
Feb 1985	−3.7	−0.1	−1.6
1951 – 80 average	−3.1	0.5	−
Difference from average	−0.6	−0.6	−
Mar 1985	−1.7	1.2	3.9 (1st–13th)
1951 – 80 average	−0.9	2.0	−
Difference from average	−0.8	−0.8	−
4 month Means 1984/85	−2.6	0.5	−0.7
1951 – 80 average	−1.9	1.3	−
Difference from average	−0.7	−0.8	−

(*Source*: Meteorological Office, Edinburgh)

Conversion of valley temperatures to summit altitudes using the simple lapse rate of 0.64°C per 100 metres is inapplicable due to the prevalence of night-time inversions during anticyclones.

Table 2 Cairn Gorm Summit Temperatures (°C)

	1979–82 (averages)				1985			
	Jan	Feb	Mar	3 month Mean	Jan	Feb	Mar	3 month Mean
Average daily min	−4.8	−6.0	−5.5	−5.4	−6.5	−5.4	−5.7	−5.9
Mean	−2.7	−4.5	−3.8	−3.7	−5.1	−3.1	−3.9	−4.0
Average daily max	−0.3	−2.5	−1.5	−1.4	−3.6	−1.0	−2.1	−2.2

(*Sources*: Heriot-Watt University, Dept of Physics and Meteorological Office, Edinburgh)

Table 2 gives some key comparative statistics from the Cairn Gorm AWS at 1,245 metres. Mean and *average* daily minimum temperatures are considerably lower than those at sea level, but the *absolute* range of temperatures is greater in the glen bottoms due to the inversion phenomenon. Comparing the 1985 data to that for the 1979–82 period, whilst January was significantly colder than usual, it is notable that February was in fact warmer than average in reversal of the sea-level pattern, for which difference inversions are again responsible.

Precipitation

Within the general paucity of snow and rainfall during the winter season there were significant regional variations, which directly impinged on the route and progress of the expedition, and are well shown by the Braemar-Onich data in Table 3. Most notably, January's 'drought' was confined to the western half of the country whilst the Cairngorms and Grampians experienced above-average precipitation (almost entirely as snow) under the continual attention of weak fronts advancing from the North Sea. Reversing the normal pattern, the west side was effectively in the 'rain shadow' of the eastern hills which soaked up most of the month's limited available moisture.

Table 3 Rainfall Totals (mm)

		Braemar	Onich
Dec	1984	77	322
	1951 – 80 average	96	238
	% of average	80%	135%
Jan	1985	117	72
	1951 – 80 average	93	200
	% of average	126%	36%
Feb	1985	19	99
	1951 – 80 average	59	132
	% of average	32%	75%
Mar	1985	60	107
	1951 – 80 average	59	152
	% of average	102%	70%
4 month totals	1984/85	273	600
	1951 – 80 average	307	722
	% of average	89%	83%

(*Source*: Meteorological Office, Edinburgh)

In February, the persistence of dry anticyclonic conditions produced exceptionally low precipitation in the east, whereas the only rain-bearing air was borne during the brief periods of Atlantic influence and so affected only the west coast.

In close contact with these variations, and applying our chosen flexibility of movement, we therefore stayed in the west for most of January, then captured the eastern hills during their own drought in February. Here our mobile tactics were applied to the greatest effect, and one can envisage the problems of a continuous winter Munros journey on a predetermined route when such sly manoeuvres would be unavailable.

The 1984–85 experience shows how judicious the winter walker and climber needs to be in his selection of venue. The West Highlands provided superb hard walking conditions for most of January, while the Cairngorms were repeatedly being sprinkled with difficult fresh snow. The ice climber however has different requirements. Due to the absence of drainage on the cliffs, there were poor pickings in the west in January, and he would have fared better in the east where at least there was plenty of powder snow on the faces.

The regional detail should not colour the basic fact that this was one of the most snowless winters on record. Much of the precipitation that did fall came as rain at all levels, eg late December, 8–9 March, and 23 February when Onich had its highest day's total in the season, of 37.2mm.

The *type* of precipitation on the mountain tops is a particular determinant of the climbing conditions, and almost infinite gradations can be observed when temperatures are around zero. Table 4 shows an attempted classification of the types I witnessed at the 3,000 foot level.

Table 4 Types of Precipitation during Winter 1984/85

Dominant Form at 3,000ft	Days	
Drizzle	5	
Rain	8	
Sleet	5	
Hail	3	+2 to −2°C
Contact freezing (rime ice)	3	air temperature
Freezing rain	2	
Wet snow	7	
Wind-driven snow (ie, pulverised)	5	
Light dry snow	12	
Total numbers of days with precipitation	50	

Freezing rain creates a special hazard to the mountaineer. It occurs when supercooled water droplets freeze on impact with the ground surface, producing sheet ice. By comparison, rime ice commonly forms on an influx of warm moist air after a prolonged period of frost.

Cloud Cover

Anticyclonic conditions are not always clear, and can produce either valley fogs associated with inversions or a high level 'stratocumulus' type of cloud which rarely drops below the summits and gives those raw leaden days of which we had several in January; but the thick low cloud associated with the moist Atlantic depressions was much less conspicuous than usual in the 1984/85 season.

Cloud cover is of course one of the most crucial factors to the safety and especially the enjoyment of mountaineers, and whilst the cloud-base is predicted in the specialist forecasts, there are no records of visibility levels on the summits. Table 5 provides a summary of my own observations during the 83 days (with estimates for the rest days!).

Table 5 Cloud Cover and Visibility during the 1984/85 Winter

Avge Daytime Cloudbase (Height in metres)	Days	Min Visibility at 3,000ft (Distance in metres)	Days
0– 300	2	Less than 25	10*
300– 600	21	25– 50	10
600– 900	25	50–100	20
900–1200	11	100–200	14
Cloud above 1200	8	Clear	29
Sky clear	16		

(*Including 7 'white outs' with nil visibility)
NB Total no of Munros which gave me a view – 172 (62%)

Wind

The climber must be aware of the impact on human movement of different windspeeds before any proper perspective can be gained of this crucial factor. Any wind in excess of 30mph (26 knots or Force 6) can exert a chilling effect of around 20°C on a moving walker and will palpably slow his progress. At Gale Force 8 (39–46mph) progress is severely impeded (energy output probably at least trebled); at Force 10 (55–63mph) walking becomes difficult in itself; and at Force 12 (over 73mph) balance and breathing are affected, and crawling is the most efficient mode of travel. However, a clear distinction must be made between the velocity of the maximum *gusts*, and the *average* windspeed encountered on the summits. Generally gusts are around 25% greater than the mean speed, but occasionally can be double the average velocity. Our experience on the Feshie Hills on 9–10 February typifies the scenario when a Force 10 *average* gale is in flow – struggling gamely in the 'lulls', then crawling and clinging to axes in the gusts of 80mph. Gustiness can never be adequately forecast in official bulletins, being largely determined by local terrain, but should always be added to the climber's calculations to derive the likely windspeeds that will be met on the hill tops.

Autumn and winter are by far the windiest seasons on the Scottish mountains. Taking the 1979–82 Cairn Gorm AWS data, the *percentage* of hours in which at least one 2½ minute period of gale-force winds was recorded was 30.8 in both autumn and winter, but only 13.2 and 9.5 in spring and summer respectively. It is also noticeable that the *relative* windiness at high compared to low altitudes is much greater in winter. The Cairn Gorm winter mean of 34.3mph is nearly three times greater than that for Kinloss on the Moray Firth, whereas the summer average is only double that at the sea-level station.

The ambient gradient of air pressure is the main determinant of mean windspeed, although the vertical boundaries between airmasses of significantly different temperature and moisture are major additional sources of atmospheric turbulence over and around hills. Thus, due to the dominance of stable high-pressure systems, the 1984/85 season was relatively windless. The steep pressure drops and airmass mixing associated with the Atlantic depressions were generally absent, except at the beginning and end of the season, and for brief periods in late January and mid-February. At Kinloss the mean windspeed for the four winter months was only 80% of its average over the previous 22 years. Tiree on the West coast showed an even more striking lack of wind with only 4 days with gales in January and February compared to an average of 13 over the previous 10 years, which especially illustrates the absence of Atlantic storms. And whilst these sea-level stations do not in any way replicate the mountain-top conditions, my own observations as shown on Table 6 clearly confirm the conclusion.

Table 6 Distribution of Maximum Windspeeds Experienced at 3,000ft during 1984/85 winter

Maximum Daytime Windspeed*	Days
Gale, greater than 39mph	26
Strong, 29–38mph	11
Fresh, 19–28mph	17
Moderate, 9–18mph	11
Nil/light, 0–8mph	18

(*Max estimated speed sustained over a period of more than 10 minutes)
(NB The *expected* no of days with significant gales was 42, see Ch 1)

The highest 2½ minute mean on Cairn Gorm summit in 1984/85 was 106mph on 8 February when we turned back from the White Lady Shieling. This compares to an all-time maximum 2½ minute mean of 124mph in January 1983, and a single-gust maximum of 148mph in December 1978. Unfortunately the instruments mal-functioned during the great blizzard of 21 January 1984 and so no reliable data was obtained.

Fig 1 Directional distribution (in percentages) of Scotland's winter winds (*source: Meteorological Office, Edinburgh*)

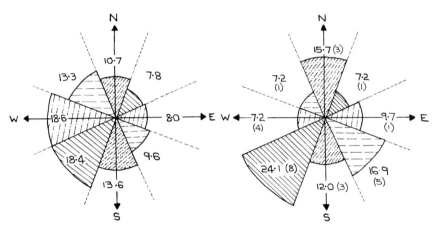

Stornoway: average free air wind directions; December–March 1961–70

Observed wind directions on Munro summits; 1984/85 winter (83 days). Days with gales in brackets

The analysis of the *directional distribution* of each day's wind in Fig 1 provides a good basis for assessing the prevalent climatic influences on Scotland's winter conditions. Whilst the most likely air stream is from the south-west quarter, the average data for Stornoway on the Outer Hebrides shows that the winds (and gales) can blow from any direction with appreciable frequency, and indeed these readings are obviously biased towards the Westerlies compared to the norms experienced in the Central or Eastern Highlands. However the east and south-east winds are only significantly influential in January and February when continental airmasses commonly take command of the weather.

The comparison of my own summit observations illustrates the abnormal switch away from the westerly airflow during the 1984/85 season. The climber might also note that my 26 'days with gales' were spread around all points of the compass, but with 8 Sou'Westers and 5 Sou'Easters as the greatest individual scores.

Weather Maps and Mountain Climate

It is the synoptic weather chart which gives the climber the greatest scope for predicting the *range* of possibilities in hill conditions, provided the necessary degree of basic meteorological knowledge is possessed.

A comparison of four of the widely differing weather situations we encountered during the 1984–5 season with the forecast weather charts for those days might help to illustrate some of the rules and guidelines which can be applied in their interpretation.

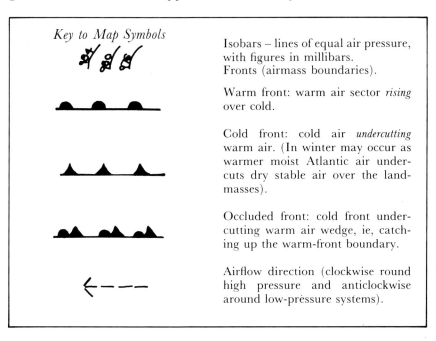

Key to Map Symbols

Isobars – lines of equal air pressure, with figures in millibars.
Fronts (airmass boundaries).

Warm front: warm air sector *rising* over cold.

Cold front: cold air *undercutting* warm air. (In winter may occur as warmer moist Atlantic air undercuts dry stable air over the landmasses).

Occluded front: cold front undercutting warm air wedge, ie, catching up the warm-front boundary.

Airflow direction (clockwise round high pressure and anticlockwise around low-pressure systems).

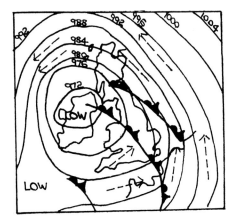

Noon, 21 Jan, 1985 – The Start of the Big Blizzard
Deep depression crossing from SW to NE of Scotland; advancing fronts drawing moist Atlantic air over colder continental airmasses and winding round the depression centre to form a strong easterly airstream over Scotland.
Mountain Weather Strong E Wind, temperature rising, thick cloud above 300 metres, heavy snowfall from mid-morning onwards, freezing level 400 metres, visibility less than 25 metres in blizzard.

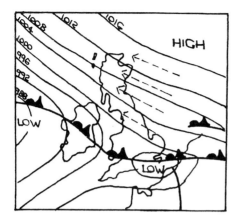

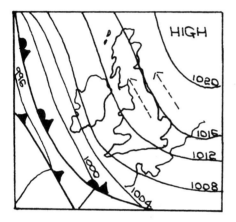

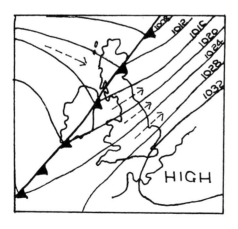

Noon, 9 Feb, 1985 – The Cairngorm Windstorm

Trough of low pressure across SW Britain blocked against Scandinavian anticyclone; steep pressure gradient producing strong continental airstream across Scotland; heavy snowfall confined to airmass boundary over south of country.

Mountain Weather Gale from SE up to Force 12 on summits; upper sky clear but storm shroud on tops fuelled by spindrift and scattered shower clouds blown in off North Sea; freezing all levels; 'white-out' conditions; moderate drifting and windslabbing on W slopes.

Noon, 12 Feb, 1985 – Mid-Month Freeze-up

Atlantic trough repelled by strengthening continental high, its associated depression forced northwards in mid-Atlantic and pressure gradient released. Very cold, dry but gentle SE airflow established.

Mountain Weather Light to moderate SE breeze, bitterly cold, summit temperatures about −5°C. Clear and dry; some high-level strato cloud; snow loose and unaltered on tops, windslab on drifted lee slopes.

Noon, 19 Feb, 1985 – The Storm that Faltered

Cold front of moist Atlantic air undercutting the stable anticyclone from the NW; heavy cloud formation as moist air condenses on contact with colder dry air mass; *but* front pinned back by dominant 'high' – significant rain only on W side of country.

Mountain Weather (in Cairngorms) Gale from S and SW on tops, dense cloud above 500 metres; 'white-out' on summits, light snow-fall with moderate drifting; freezing level rising to 600 metres briefly; clearing and calmer in evening as 'high' regains command and pressure gradient drops.

Snow Conditions and Avalanche Risk

The *freezing level* bears the greatest influence on the snow conditions on the mountains, and Fig 2 gives the trace of the estimated shade daytime levels observed throughout the Munros expedition. However the plot does not show the variation in the freezing heights between night and day which crucially determines the range of altitudes at which good climbing conditions might develop. For instance, a diurnal range of 600–900 metres will ensure consolidation of snow and build up of ice at intermediate altitudes, but above 900 metres where there is no thawing at any time, the snow will remain loose, unaltered and unsatisfactory.

The recent history of the freezing levels also counts significantly in the evolution of conditions. The widespread freeze which followed the 21–22 January blizzard prevented any consolidation of the new snow. Deep drifts hindered travel, and the lee slope windslabs lay unaltered, forming a suspended avalanche risk for several days. Conversely, the freeze-up of early January in the west succeeded a warm and wet late December so producing hard ice, frozen ground, and dependable snow.

In general, the 1984/85 winter gave long stable periods of frost in which snow and avalanche prediction was fairly simple. The greater problem comes when the freezing level yo-yos up and down and is accompanied by an assortment of precipitation under the attention of successive frontal passages. As Fig 2 shows, this only occurred in late December, at which time there was insufficient build up of snow to create any complexity of conditions or avalanche risk. Indeed, avalanche danger remained minimal for a large proportion of the season, and yet, for brief but crucial periods, the required pre-disposing factors combined to create a severe risk (as we discovered!). In fact, for 61 out of our 83 days on the Munros, I perceived that the

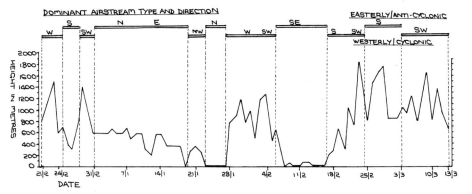

Fig 2 1984/85 winter: observed daytime freezing levels (shade)

225

avalanche risk in the high corries would have been minimal or weak, but there were four spells when the danger rose sharply, as shown below.

22–27 January

Heavy initial snowfall (at least 30cm at all levels).

Strong winds from E, N, and NW causing severe drifting on several slope aspects.

Persistent sub-zero temperatures preventing any breakdown or bonding of the lee-slope windslabs.

Danger An acute windslab danger thus persisted for 5 days requiring an external trigger. During the blizzard, accumulations were sufficiently heavy to cause natural avalanches of new snow, but on a modest scale.

8–12 February

Continuous SE gales packing all loose snow onto NW slopes.

Rapid freeze up after mild spell at start of month – all old snow frozen hard, providing a perfect sliding surface for the new windslabs.

Sub-zero temperatures sustained throughout the period. ($-10.5°$C on Cairngorm summit 8 Feb.)

Danger Windslab risk but limited due to the absence of recent snowfall; depths of slabs never greater than 1 metre except on the most sheltered corrie slopes.

28–29 January/23–24 February

Extremely rapid thaw (overnight rise in freezing level from 0 to 900 metres).

Deep unconsolidated existing snow cover in the case of 28–29 Jan.

Very heavy rainfall in the case of 23–24 Feb.

Danger Wet Snow avalanche danger during melt and particularly a risk of cornice collapse; possible slides under the lubrication of running water at the base of the snow cover especially in the case of 23–24 Feb.

NB see Bibliography for other books on mountain weather and avalanches.

V: RECENT SCOTTISH MOUNTAIN MARATHON RUNS AND WALKS

Whilst the pursuit of long-distance wildland runs and walks has proliferated in the last 15 years, the very considerable feats which have been achieved in Scotland have remained little known, with the exception of course of Hamish Brown's first continuous Munros round in 1974. Yet the scope of Scotland's future challenge for ambitious marathon exploits is quite without parallel in Britain.

This history has a twofold purpose; firstly to provide a summary of the most notable achievements in recent times in as complete and objective a manner as possible, drawing together the widely scattered records of these deeds. It is likely that my list, despite being based on extensive enquiries of a wide range of the participants, will miss out a few creditworthy endeavours for which I apologise in advance. The second aim is to set down a basis by which future efforts may be stimulated and compared, especially record breaking or creating attempts.

This leads me straight onto the charge, which understandably troubles many people, that such a codification of specific route and time challenges reduces the mountains to a series of racetracks devoid of natural freedom and adventure, and pursued by fanatics who merely *use* the hills for personal ends. My only concern in this respect is that the overuse of certain mountain routes may accelerate the growth and erosion of paths, but the danger posed by a handful of seasoned walkers or lightly shod runners is surely minimal compared to that consequent on the intensive usage of popular routes by the broad mass of walkers, especially the 'official' long-distance paths like the West Highland Way. And unless there is a visible impact people are quite free to acknowledge or ignore such feats and records.

It should never be thought that the protagonists of these marathon runs are soul-less and lacking in appreciation of the mountains. My personal experience is quite the opposite, and this *must* be true in nearly all cases, for to endure the prolonged exertion and gruelling pain of an effort up to and sometimes beyond 24 hours requires the utmost enthusiasm and passion for one's surroundings. The ever-changing terrain, views and weather are vital to sustain one's deter-mination.

Adventure and uncertainty are never lacking on such escapades. Adverse weather and route finding problems, when posed within pre-set targets of time or distance give the most exciting mountain encounters, with which the memory will reverberate for long after. Failures can be narrow and terribly cruel. Just in 1985 I hear of an attempt on the eight 4,000ft peaks by Steve Parr which was aban-doned due to atrocious weather and a risk of hypothermia with just 8 miles to go over Macdui and Cairn Gorm, after 18½ hours of effort, and with the current record of 22½ hours comfortably in hand. What unimaginable anguish!

Long-distance mountain tours should not however be regarded as a phenomenon of the present generation. The stalwart early moun-taineers obviously enjoyed such challenges and achieved some fairly prodigious rounds. In 1909, for instance, D. H. Menzies and W. M. Wilson circuited 12 tops on the upper Tilt and Shee hills from Blair

Atholl in 29½ hours, a walk of 56 miles with 11,000ft of ascent. Munro himself was a noted enthusiast of extended excursions in the hills.

The current field of activities conveniently divides between Munro marathon walks of several months, and mountain runs generally of less than 24 hours duration. In this latter category I have included only mountain-top runs of over 4 hours in length. Details of a few notable long-distance ski-tours are also added, to broaden the picture.

The Munros: Complete and Continuous Journeys
1967 The Ripleys' Attempt
Brian and Alan Ripley; 13 August–10 November; abandoned on Beinn Dorain after 230 Munros, 1,325 miles and 337,850ft of ascent. A bold effort at a hitherto unspoken challenge by a team from outside the mainstream of Scottish climbing circles; progressive exhaustion and appalling weather finally defeated an attempt which had been variously plagued from its outset by midges, access problems in the stalking season, wet Autumn weather, and supply difficulties. Though begun with the idea of a self-propelled journey, some motor lifts were taken en-route.

1974 'Hamish's Mountain Walk'
Hamish M. Brown; 4 April–24 July, 112 days; the *first* continuous self-propelled round (save for the Skye and Mull ferries); 1,639 miles (of which c150 were on bicycle) and 449,000ft of ascent. Fully documented in his excellent book of the above name; intricately planned and executed by the man who even before this walk was the most prolific Munroist of all time with 3 previous rounds. Apart from 12 days, a wholly solo journey but with regular support rendezvous and food parcels/dumps. Canny tactics, and an intimate knowledge of the hills underpinned his success.

1982 The First Lady
Kathy Murgatroyd aged 34 from the New Forest; 1 May–11 September, 134 days; 2,250 miles (including 1,000 by bicycle) and 460,000ft of ascent. The second continuous round with tactics comparable to Hamish, but executed in a more modular style (ie, cycling to a base and climbing all surrounding Munros lightly laden from a fixed camp). Started Ben More, Mull and finished on Sgurr Mhic Choinnich, Skye – planned route altered to avoid stalking problems in August. 154 Munros previously climbed before the trip; 196 done solo on the walk. Regular weekend support from boyfriend; heatwave and nutritional deficit in June caused the main difficulties. Resigned from job in outdoor education to undertake the walk.

228

1984 Britain's Three Thousanders

George Keeping of Preston; 14 April–27 August, 136 days; the third continuous round (and the first without using a bicycle); 1,784 miles, and 464,000ft of ascent. Walk extended for a further 29 days to include the English and Welsh 3,000ft summits. Started Ben Klibreck, finished Ben Chonzie. 89 nights camping, rest in bothies, hostels, B&B; only 2 complete rest days taken; accompanied for approximately half of the walk; supported by a series of food parcels posted by his girlfriend to PO's en-route; diet carefully planned and balanced throughout. George's previous Scottish experience was confined to 'the Cairngorms and a few forays further West'; however, the abnormally dry spring and summer must have greatly helped his routefinding.

1984 The Mainland Munros

Rick Ansell of Hertfordshire; 3 May–10 August, 100 days. In his own words, 'the mainland Munros in one bash, using no support, no bicycles, canoes or food parcels'; but as to why he left out the islands, his reasons were confessedly ambiguous, 'the ferries would have spoilt the purity of the walk, which is a good excuse for not feeling competent to solo the Skye ridge!' Rest days used for shopping trips to towns; as with the other big walks most nights were spent camping with occasional stays in bothies and hostels. Started Ben Lomond, finished Ben Hope; Rick claims the *driest* ever Munros round – only 4 dowsings. In physical and ethical terms the best performance so far, but flawed by its incompleteness and badly hampered by food shortage in the early weeks (see Appendix III).

NB In 1982, two other separate continuous attempts were mounted, but neither was successful. Records of failures are not always forthcoming. Few contenders have publicised their intentions before commencing, but no other continuous attempts are known, except for Craig Caldwell's campaign on the Munros and Corbetts currently in progress.

Scottish Mountain Runs

These are grouped for convenience in ascending order of duration. In all details an attempt is made to specify the obligatory checkpoints which define the complete route followed. The quoting of a time should not in all cases be taken to imply a hell-bent record-setting effort; some of these runs were undertaken in a recreational spirit, albeit an energetic one. Style, support and tactics are given where known, and are crucial in assessing the merit of particular endeavours.

The Black Cuillin Ridge of Skye

Gars-bheinn to Sgurr nan Gillean; first achieved by Leslie Shadbolt and A. McLaren in 1911 in 12 hours 20 minutes, and progressively reduced to a time of 6.45 by D. Stewart, though apparently without specific record-breaking intent.

1966 Eric Beard created an astounding record with his time of 4.09 which appeared truly invincible. Details remain scant, but it is known that the Inaccessible Pinnacle was by-passed and the Thearlaich-Dubh gap roped. However, to compensate for these blemishes it is also known that Eric failed to meet up with his *sole* supporter! Beard was the first man to harness a competence in difficult rock climbing with brilliance in running, and 16 years after his death is still the most noted exponent of the art.

1984 Andy Hyslop, aged 25 of Ambleside; 7 May; time 4.04.19. A more complete and definitive route taking in all Munro summits, and the four main climbing sections (T-D Gap, Sgurr Mhic Choinnich, the In Pinn, and the Bhasteir Tooth); two support points en-route; all climbing sections soloed without a rope; route reconnoitred previously in detail. This was the first reported attempt on Beardie's record, though several others are rumoured. However, because of the differences in route, Andy did not wish a direct comparison to be made.

The Arrochar Munros

Bens Narnain, Ime, Vane, Vorlich; starting and finishing on main road (presumably by Arrochar village). Time 4.29 in April 1985 by Brian Finlayson of Edinburgh. No further details are available, but at around 13 miles and 7,500ft of very rough climbing this appears a worthy round.

The Cairngorm Four Thousanders

Braeriach, Cairn Toul, Ben Macdui, Cairn Gorm; start and finish at Glenmore Lodge, 25 miles and 8,000ft of ascent.

1967 With a time of 4.41 Eric Beard set another stiff record for one of the most popular high-level walks (and winter ski tours) in the Highlands.

1979 Mel Edwards of Aberdeen broke Beardie's mark with an anti-clockwise round of 4.34.08; one wonders whether another 12 years will elapse before this new time is lowered.

Ben Cruachan Range

Beinn Eunaich, Beinn a'Chochuill, all Munros and Tops of Cruachan, Beinn a'Bhuiridh; round trip from bridge by Castles farm roadend; 14 miles, 9,000ft of ascent. Time 5.22, 23 May, 1982 by Colin Donnelly as an unsupported solo run.

Colin, once a ghillie on the Attadale Estate by Lochcarron, but now with the RAF on Anglesey, has probably been the most active hill runner on the Scottish peaks, having made dozens of 7–12 hour, 20–30 mile rounds of the major Munro groups, often based on remote bothies and camps, but without searching for or even wishing to make 'record' times.

Torridon Hills

Beinn Eighe, Liathach, Beinn Alligin (all Munros and Tops, except for Am Fasarinen and the Northern Pinnacles on Liathach), plus the three Horns of Alligin. Start Cairn Shiel cottage (Kinlochewe), finish Alligin car park; 20 miles, 12,450ft of ascent. Time 6.55, 27 October, 1985 by Martin Moran solo with two support points. An arduous but magnificent mountain day with all types of terrain from exposed scrambling and open-ridge running to knee-deep heather moor. The finest highlight must be the hair raising dash along the exposed trod under Liathach's pinnacles which is decidedly not for the faint of heart or clumsy of foot!

Tour of the Mamores

All 11 Munros and 6 Tops in a round trip from Achriabhach Cottage in Glen Nevis; 21 miles with 10,000ft of ascent. Time 7.02, 1 July, 1980 by Colin Donnelly solo and unsupported. With a delightful inconsistency that perfectly demonstrates the dilemma often facing the mountain runner, the 7 hour barrier was missed by a hair's breadth thanks to an extended stop on Na Gruagaichean where Colin was 'held spellbound by the view down Loch Leven, a jagged shaft of water penetrating far inland . . .' Despite a maniacal descent from Binnein Beag to the finish in 56 minutes, the time was not recaptured. This sacrifice of an attainable prize shows that the runner's enjoyment of the mountains is not subjugated to the demands of the clock; previous times for this route had never been lower than 8 hours.

Glencoe

The circuit of all 5 Munros flanking the glen from a base at the Clachaig Inn; 19 miles with 12,750ft of ascent, beginning with Bidean nam Bian and finishing along the Aonach Eagach ridge. Time 7.05, 31 May, 1980 by Bobby Shields of Lochaber Athletic Club.

A similar run was done by Ros Coats (now Evans) on 19 September, 1981 in the opposite direction, and climbing Buachaille Etive Mor by Curved Ridge; despite bad weather her time was 10.54.

The Six Cairngorm Tops

The four thousanders plus Beinn a'Bhuird and Ben Avon; traditionally done east-west starting from Loch Builg. First recorded by a party of five from Aberdeen on 21 June, 1908 in a time of 19 hours, and progressively reduced until Prof V. C. Wynne-Edwards (then in his sixties) recorded this route of 28 miles and 9,000ft of ascent in 9.34 on 1 September, 1968 – a notable feat for a 'super-veteran'!

1967 12 June; Eric Beard did the round trip from Glenmore Lodge (excluding Ben Avon) in 9 hours, finishing at midnight, this timing suggesting that the run was done on impulse.

1985 The circuit of all 6 Tops, starting and finishing at Glenmore Lodge was formalised by Dave Armitage, Phil Kammer and Mel Edwards in a time of 11.39; starting with Ben Avon, a distance of 39 miles with around 12,500ft of climbing.

'Tranter's Round'

The complete circuit of Glen Nevis taking in all the 19 Munro summits of the Ben Nevis–Grey Corries and Mamores ranges; 40 miles and 20,600ft of ascent. Originated and achieved as a 24 hour challenge in 1964 by the late Philip Tranter, who was a double Munroist and one of the best and keenest Scottish mountaineers of his era. Not surprisingly, given the superb quality of his route, the round was repeated several times, notably by a team of seven from Lochaber AC in 19.15 in 1978.

1983 3 June; Martin Hudson of Keswick AC made a solo and unsupported run of the round in 13.54 with a starting point close to Glen Nevis Youth Hostel, a formidable record. A notable feature of Martin's run was that he met nobody on the hills until reaching Ben Nevis after 13 hours; conditions were moist and misty.

Scotland's 4,000ft Summits

Established as a long-distance walk by the Rucksack Club in 1954, linking the ascents of the 4,000ft Cairngorm and Ben Nevis summits by a classic overland trek from Glen Feshie through the Ben Alder Forest to Glen Nevis in a total distance of 85 miles and 17,000ft of ascent for the 8 peaks with full Munro status (in which Aonach Mor at 3,999ft is included for safety's sake!). As a walk, repeated by Stan Bradshaw (senior) and Alan Heaton during the 1960's, and then considered as a feasible 24 hour run.

1979–80 Attempted as 24 hour run twice by Alan Heaton (a former holder of the 24 hour Lakeland peaks record). Not finished in 1979, and then on 14 June, 1980 thwarted by gale-force winds although the course was completed in 26.05.

1980 19–20 July; Chris Dodd (of Dark Peak Fell Runners) and

Howard Artiss (of Verlea AC) broke the one-day barrier, Chris finishing in 23.14 after his companion had dropped out with an ankle injury before the Ben Nevis climbs. The time is inclusive from the start at Glenmore Youth Hostel to the finish at Glen Nevis YH; a three man pacing and support team was used. Angel's Peak (Cairn Toul) was added to the 8 main summits. The night section through the Bealach Dubh from Culra to Ossian provided the most exciting moments with several involuntary swims being taken in the burns adjoining the route!

1982 30 May; Stan Bradshaw (junior) completed the route in 22.33 in a comparable supported effort, and to date this remains the record.

'Ramsay's Round'

The extension of Tranter's route to incorporate the 5 Loch Treig Munros (Beinn na Lap, Chno Dearg, Stob Coire Sgriodain, Stob a'Choire Mheadhoin, Stob Coire Easain) to give a total of 58 miles and 28,000ft of ascent, and provide Scotland's definitive 24 hour hill challenge. Comparable to the Bob Graham Round in the Lake District, but though shorter lies over much rougher and steeper terrain and in more remote surroundings. The route has the added appeal of climbing 24 Munros in a day, the maximum yet achieved in a continuous circular tour, and which could only possibly be surpassed by extending the route into Ben Alder Forest, or devising a comparable round in the Shiel-Affric hills.

1978 8–9 July; Charlie Ramsay of Edinburgh who devised the route, and did 1,600 miles and 270,000ft of preparatory training in the 6 months before the attempt, just pipped the one-day goal with a time of 23.58. Bobby Shields, his companion, was forced to retire at the two thirds stage. Supported and paced throughout; route done anticlockwise, ie, with the Mamores Ridge first. This must have been one of the most exciting finishes imaginable, for after losing his route twice in mist, once on the Grey Corries and more seriously coming off Aonach Beag, he stampeded the last section from Aonach Mor to the end in 2.13, the final descent of Ben Nevis taking just 33 minutes; none of his pacers were able to keep up with him on this final dash.

1980 9 July; Eddie Campbell of Fort William; running clockwise repeated the Round in 24.40 (no other details available).

1981 23–24 July; Pete Simpson of Dark Peak Fell Runners also recorded 24.40 in a solo round with only one point of support at Loch Treig dam, and without a detailed prior reconnoitre. Rain and cloud throughout the Nevis-Grey Corries section but at the half-way point he was 45 minutes ahead of Charlie's schedule. The loneliness of the night section gradually sapped Pete's resilience but he grimly kept going over the Mamores and was left with 55 minutes for the last descent to Glen Nevis YH. However, not having previously inspected this section, he seriously lost his way, became badly enmeshed in forest plantations and the deadline passed with just 2 miles of valley road left. Such a pure and self-willed effort surely deserved a better fate.

No other attempts on the Round are known at present.

Scotland Coast to Coast

A mountain traverse from the west to the east coast of the country has for many years been the object of the 'Ultimate Challenge', a non-competitive event with the choice of route entirely left to the partici-pants, and a worthwhile stimulus for long distance walkers to explore the Highlands in greater depth.

1983 Summer; the 'coast to coast' concept was expanded into an incredible high-level running voyage by Ian Leighton and Robin Price, who without support or equipment ran from Inverie in Knoydart to Montrose in 5 days, taking in 18 Munros, including the 8 four-thousanders, in a distance of 230 miles with 35,000ft of climbing. Living truly as vagabonds of the hills they survived open bivouacs and a diet of Complan and glucose mixed with stream water taken in 6oz doses at 5 hourly intervals. Their route was very loosely defined and often varied on impulse; for instance, crossing the Lochnagar plateau in the early evening and pining for more substantial sustenance, they took a 12 mile detour for fish suppers at the Ballater chippie before running the last 40 miles through the night!

For unfettered and non-competitive freedom, the style and enormity of their effort surely captures the true spirit of mountain travel to which we all aspire, and I am sure that Tilman and Shipton would have approved.

The Southern Uplands 2,000ft Tops

Though not in the Highlands, Colin Donnelly's run over all 138 2,000ft tops (as listed in Donald's Tables) in the summer of 1981 is perhaps the greatest single peak-bagging run on record in Britain (only Chris Bland's 7 day attempt on all of Wainwrights' Lake District hills stands in reasonable comparison). In his 11 day com-pletion, 380 miles and 82,000ft of ascent were achieved, and included one complete rest day enforced through exhaustion. This achievement is a good pointer to the sort of extended adventures which are waiting aplenty on the Highland mountains.

Long-distance Ski Tours

The Six Cairngorm Tops

1962 April; Adam Watson solo; starting from Invercauld by Braemar and finishing at Derry Lodge in a time of 16 hours; 38 miles, of which 34 were on ski, and 8,700ft of climbing. Light wooden skis from Lapland were used, and 6 tins of fruit sustained the effort! This great day was done on impulse, with no preparatory training, and carrying a heavy sack with overnight gear. It stands as a remarkable effort, surely one of those occasions when the glory of the weather and hills buoyed the spirit to unexpected deeds.

1980 Spring; Graham Boyd and Norman Keir completed a similar route taking 2 hours longer. Adam Watson writing in the 1983 SMC Journal cautioned against placing great significance on the timing difference since the perfection of snow conditions and an invigorating breeze had greatly assisted his own 1962 traverse, and nor was his 'primitive' equipment to be in any way considered a relative disadvantage, the wooden Langlauf skis being well suited to long solo tours.

1983 Easter Sunday; Raymond Simpson and Rob Ferguson did 'the six' in a round trip from Derry Gate of 19 hours plus a 5 hour sleep at Corrour Bothy. Nordic-style skis were used.

Coast to Coast

1982 13 January; Sam Crymble, Keith Geddes, Tim Walker and Blyth Wright, all instructors at Glenmore Lodge, traversed Scotland from Loch Duich on the West coast to the Beauly Firth, a distance of over 60 miles in 17 hours. The Glen Affric through-route was taken and no major mountain tops were crossed. The Affric lochs were thickly iced and coated with snow, and were skied over. Nordic equipment was used.

The Scottish 'Haute Route'

The Aberdonian answer to the famous tour from Chamonix to Zermatt, a 100 mile crossing from Crathie on Deeside to Fort William taking in nine major summits including Macdui and Nevis. Completed in 7 days, 26 February–5 March, 1978, by David Grieve and Mike Taylor with part-company and support from Sandy Cousins and Derek Pyper. Alpine 'compact' skis with heel-lift bindings were used, this heavier gear being justified to improve the enjoyment of long downhill sections, and gives the easier portability of shorter skis.

BIBLIOGRAPHY

For complete and detailed guidance to the ascent of not only the Munros but also all of Scotland's mountains, one need look no further than the Scottish Mountaineering Club's own publications:

Munro's Tables (1984), the Munro collector's 'bible', with an excellent historical section and a Gaelic guide.

The Munros (1985), a peak by peak guide, with recommended routes, maps and excellent illustrations – hardly fostering the spirit of adventure, but designed to get the walker onto the tops and down again safely.

District Guides (various), more comprehensive guides to each mountain area with sections on geology, fauna, flora, social history and rock and ice climbing.

Additionally, the SMC's annual *Journal* offers excellent articles and an informative and entertaining update of all notable activities on the mountains. It is available from some retail shops, or can be obtained direct from the SMC.

These apart, *Hamish's Mountain Walk*, H. M. Brown (Gollancz, hardback), (Granada, paperback) gives the story of the first non-stop Munros walk, and a full Munros history up to 1974. It is also a delightful anecdotal companion to the mountains, in all their aspects – natural, historical and social.

Mountain Weather and Avalanches: Suggested reading
Mountain Weather David Pedgley (Cicerone Press, 1980), a good introductory text.

Mountaincraft and Leadership Eric Langmuir (the Scottish Sports Council/ MLTB, 1984), which has a useful and relevant chapter.

A Chance in a Million? Bob Barton and Blyth Wright (Scottish Mountaineering Trust 1985), a cheap and very readable avalanche handbook, written specifically for Scottish conditions.

Intermediate Technology
Readers who are interested to learn more of the organisation, work, and goals of the charity may obtain much fuller details than could ever be given here by writing to: Intermediate Technology, FREEPOST (SM), 9 King Street, London, WC2E 8BR.

INDEX

Munros are in capitals, references to maps are in italic. Names beginning A', Am, An, Allt, Bealach, Beinn, Ben, Carn, Coire, Creag, Gleann, Loch, Lochan, Meall, Sgorr, Sgurr, Stob, etc, are not indexed under those words – look under the next part of the name.